RICHARD BURTON
My Brother

RICHARD BURTON
My
Brother

Graham Jenkins

with Barry Turner

First published in Great Britain 1988 by
Michael Joseph Ltd.

Published in Large Print 1988 by Clio Press,
55 St Thomas' Street, Oxford OX1 1JG,
by arrangement with Michael Joseph Ltd and Harper & Row

British Library Cataloguing in Publication Data

Jenkins, Graham, *1927–*
    Richard Burton, my brother.
    1. Cinema films. Acting. Burton, Richard,
    1925–1984. Biographies
    I. Title
    791.43′028′0924

ISBN 1-85089-271-7

Printed and bound by
Hartnolls Ltd., Bodmin, Cornwall

Cover designed by CGS Studios, Cheltenham

Contents

Acknowledgements

This book could not have been written without the assistance of a large number of people who gave freely and generously of their time and knowledge. So first of all I should like to thank: Ron Berkeley, Elizabeth Bush, Alexander Cohen, Dai Dwsh Davies, John Dexter, John Dolan, Daniel Dillon Evans, Leslie Evans, the late Trevor George, Robert Hardy, Richard Harris, Kitty Carlisle Hart, Frank Hauser, Marjorie Lee, Richard Leech, Andrew Leigh, Carol Martin, John Parry, Sir Anthony Quayle, Chen Sam, Peter Shaffer, William Squire and the Reverend Eric Williams.

I owe a very special vote of thanks to all my family and particularly to my sisters Cis and Hilda. Elizabeth Taylor and her agent Robert Lantz have been an inspiration to me throughout the preparation of this book.

Dr Sonia Robertson and Mary Fulton were a constant source of cheerful encouragement and hospitality, and my good friend Ian Robertson played a vital part in the early stages of researching the story of my brother's life and career. Without Ian's assistance from the very beginning and his continued support throughout, this story would not have been told.

My warm thanks, too, to Barry Turner for making the manuscript a reality and to my editor, Roger Houghton, for guiding the book through to publication.

Above all I would like to thank my wife Hilary for her patience and understanding during the three years that I have been working on this book.

Ti wyddost beth ddywed fy nghalon.

Graham Jenkins
Porthcawl, Wales January 1988

Introduction

I cannot, nor will I try to, explain here what Richard was and still is to my life, it would take an entire book to say what I feel. One day I may write that book, but not now, it's still too soon for me.

I am delighted that his family, with Graham as their representative, have put together this book to share with you some of the aspects of what made Richard the most remarkable man I have ever known.

The love he and his family shared was beautiful, rare, volatile, tender and as strong and wild as the Welsh valleys he loved so well.

He lives on in the memory of everyone he touched — his family are his history and his living heritage, and only they can understand what made this man the son and soul of Wales (which is a state of being, not just a nationality). Maybe their reminiscences will bring you closer to understanding this magnificent enigma.

I hope that this book makes you smile and feel happy he was here, even if it was only for a short while.

Elizabeth Taylor
New York January 1988

To my brother Tom and
my adopted mother Cassie

CHAPTER
ONE

Stumbling on the extraordinary, we lose faith in our senses.

Can this really be happening to me?

For most, this feeling of amazement, of being of the world while somehow rising above the world, comes rarely. For Richard Burton it was an experience so frequent and so intense that in the end it parted him from reality.

He demanded to be extraordinary but never came to terms with his talent or his luck.

He was forever saying, "Is this really happening to me?"

We were met at Geneva airport by two black limousines. We saw them immediately we came out of customs, parked close up to the central doors where there were signs for taxis and buses.

In charge of transport was Brook Williams, long time companion and chief gofer in the Burton household. As we approached, he started apologising. "It was such a shock . . . Bound to be a muddle . . . So many wanted to come . . . Hotels are overbooked in the season."

"I can imagine," I said, and left it at that.

Outside were photographers and a television crew. We paused for them to take pictures.

I went to the front car with two sisters, the eldest, Cis, then in her eightieth year, and Hilda. Brother

Verdun, his wife, Betty and sister Cassie followed in the second car.

Barely a word was spoken on the twenty minute drive to Pays de Galles. It was a time for memories. Now Rich was dead, none of us could expect to pass this way again.

My own feelings were a confusing mix of sadness, shock and anger.

Sadness for a brother gone and sadness for what might have been. Somewhere in my luggage was a copy of that morning's *Times*. The headline read, "Career Madly Thrown Away". Many others had made the same point, if perhaps less callously. But it was not the whole story. In the last few years Richard had exorcised a devil. He was off the booze and his work, once so fickle, was again attracting serious interest.

Maybe it was all too late. I know now that his memory was leaving him faster than water out a leaky bucket. But in the last weeks he had looked fit and well. He was more confident than for a decade past. And he talked a lot about the future.

This is where sadness overlapped with shock. Why *now*?

And where shock overlapped with anger. We were told so little of the circumstances of Rich's death. When the news came through it was no more than the bare details. Verdun was the first to know. He was telephoned at his home in Cwmafan from Los Angeles of all places by Valerie Douglas, Rich's personal secretary.

She told him Rich had become ill at home, had been rushed to a hospital in Geneva, but had died before the doctors could help him. Verdun's first thought was how to tell the rest of the family. Hilda and Cassie lived nearby but on a Sunday morning he knew they would be at chapel. He went to find them.

An hour or so later Hilda rang me in Hampshire.

"Have you heard?" she asked tentatively.

"Heard what?"

"Richard is dead."

We both had to struggle to talk and there were long silences as we fought back tears.

"Does Cis know?"

Cis or Cecilia was closer to Rich than any of us. After our mother's death when Rich was only two, she brought him up as her own child. In her later years Cis gives every appearance of frailty. Small and slight with white wispy hair and a voice as gentle as a breeze, she is every child's idea of a perfect grandmother. But her authority is undiminished. The family love and revere her and would do anything to stop her being hurt.

But on that fifth day of August 1984, there was no way of shielding her. Hilda, the strongest of our breed, rang Cis at her home in Hadley Wood where she lives near her two daughters and their families.

Her response was so much in character I might have guessed it before the words were spoken.

"Why couldn't it have been me?"

After the call from Hilda I sat quietly with my wife, Hilary, talking at random about the past and then, as the shock subsided, a little about the future.

Richard had made known his wish to be buried at Pontrhydyfen, his birthplace, and, for him, the heart of his beloved Wales. But I guessed there might be difficulties. There were too many vested interests at stake.

"Shouldn't you ring Sally?" Hilary suggested.

"No, I don't think so. At least, not yet."

But should I have rung Sally? She was, after all, Rich's wife. Any plans we had for the next few days had to start with her.

The fact was, I wanted time to reflect. Sally was young, tough and reasonably resourceful and, in those characteristics at least, everything Richard had needed in his fight to regain his self respect. But Sally was also a woman made jealous by her late arrival on the Burton marital scene. After just two years of living with Rich she resented any assumptions of intimacy from family or friends which excluded her. Most particularly, she resented the enduring love of the woman who gave Rich his happiest years — Elizabeth Taylor.

A battle of wills seemed inevitable.

To step into that contest uninvited was to ask for trouble. Instead, I drove north to Hadley Wood to be with Cis. But no sooner had I walked in the door and into her arms than the phone rang. It was Sally and she wanted to talk to me.

I took a deep breath, not quite knowing what to expect. Her voice was steady and clinically precise. She skipped over the clichés. Then, "I want to make it clear. I don't want Cis to be at the funeral. She'll only trigger me off."

"Look," I said, "I know you're upset. It's a terrible time for all of us. Can't we leave ourselves a few hours to think? I need to talk with the family."

"I've done my thinking. You know what I want."

We talked for another five minutes but I was feeling numb. How was I to tell Cis?

I slept on it and the following morning I passed on

the gist of the conversation. Cis said quietly, "So the funeral is to be in Celigny, not in Pontrhydyfen."

Curiously, the assumption built in to Sally's opening words had not occurred to me. Of course, she had already made up her mind. There was to be no discussion.

"Well, you tell her," declared Cis, "I will be in Celigny for the funeral. I will be at the service and I will be at the graveside to say goodbye to Richard. It is what Richard would have wanted and it is what I am going to do."

"And that makes two of us," I said.

It was for the rest of the family to make up their own minds.

But what of Elizabeth? That she too had been warned off was a near certainty. Her reaction was more difficult to surmise.

In fact, like the rest of us, she was thinking it over. I discovered this later in the day when she rang from Los Angeles.

"What do you suggest I should do?" she asked.

By now, my brain was working and I was ready with an answer.

"I might quarrel with Sally's motives, but I can understand the problem. The funeral will be front page news all over the world. If you put in an appearance, the press will really have a field day. We could end up with a riot on our hands. And none of us wants that. Why not leave it a few days until the fuss has died down and then come to the memorial service at Pontrhydy-fen?"

"Sally is ahead of you," said Elizabeth. "She's already thought of the memorial service. She doesn't want me in Wales either."

For the rest of the day and half the night, the phone rang incessantly. One journalist after another asked the same questions and got the same answers. "Just a few words, Mr Jenkins; just a few words."

The following morning there was another call from Celigny, not Sally this time but Valerie Douglas who had flown in from Los Angeles to take charge of the funeral arrangements. I have a respect for Valerie which stops short of affection though it's fair to say that she was very good at her job and Rich thought the world of her. A secretary cum manager of the crabapple school, she had been with Richard since his early days in Hollywood. But her proprietorial view of her duties did not endear her to Elizabeth. When Rich and Elizabeth married her star faded though it did not disappear completely. Now, in her late sixties, she was enjoying her comeback — every minute of it.

I had tangled with Valerie three years earlier. Richard had asked me to host a dinner for Elizabeth who was in London starring in *The Little Foxes*. The bill — a hefty Dorchester one — was duly sent on to Valerie as Richard had instructed. Back came a blistering reprimand for my extravagance. (Where was I supposed to take Elizabeth Taylor? McDonalds?) At the Pontrhydyfen memorial service Valerie told me, "I know you won't believe me, but it was your brother who told me to write about overdoing the entertainment."

She was right. I did not believe her.

When Valerie rang the day after Rich's death, it was to demand that we should all stay away from the funeral.

"It would be best for all of us," she explained sweetly, "if the whole affair was kept low key. Surely you can see that."

The logic of the argument was lost on me.

"What are you frightened of?" I asked. "Surely you can't object to close family. If we're not eligible to attend, who is?"

There was a long pause.

"Well, if you must, you must," she said finally.

"Thank you," I said, and put down the phone.

They had one more try. Next in line for the role of dissuader was Brook Williams. Brook is the son of Emlyn Williams. Mostly, Rich valued him as an amiable and amusing companion.

After a few drinks, Brook can be outrageously camp.

"Graham, love," he began. "You know what it's like at this time of year. I've been trying to book rooms for you and your family but all the hotels are packed out. It's the tourists; they're everywhere."

Suddenly, I was on firm ground.

"Forget it, Brook. I'm sure you have other things to worry about. Perhaps you don't know but I am chairman of a travel firm. I can fix everything from this end."

He interrupted. "No, no. There's no need for that. We'll arrange something. It's just that, well, it's all very difficult."

I wished him the best of luck.

So here we were, two days later, in a plush Mercedes travelling the Lausanne road along Lake Geneva with a small procession of press cars closely in tow.

We came into the village of Celigny, past the station with its Café de la Gare where Rich could always be found if he was not at home, and down the road toward Pays de Galles, or "Land of the Welsh".

"If I should die think only this of me — there is some corner of a foreign field that is, for ever — Wales."

The gates were shut and bolted.

Standing outside were a pack of security guards distinguished by their navy blue denims and dark glasses. They carried pistols and truncheons. We showed the identity cards (like calling-cards) which Brook Williams had given us at the airport. The gates opened and the limousines edged through, leaving the rest of the procession to park on the roadside.

I had seen Pays de Galles many times before but I never ceased to wonder at its ordinariness. It is a provincial villa of the sort to be found in any suburb of any European city. Pale cement, on box style architecture. Where is the splendid luxury of the Hollywood superstar? Not here. But this is what Rich called home — the antidote perhaps to the lavish fantasy of acting out his life on screen.

Brook led us into the living room — all cosy chintz and thick carpet. Sally's mother was there with Doris, Yul Brynner's former wife. We were introduced and sat down. Valerie Douglas appeared.

"You'll be wondering about Sally," she said. "She's resting at the moment and is not to be disturbed. She'll join you shortly."

We made safe, courteous conversation. I let my thoughts drift.

Do you remember, Rich, when you and I were boys?

There was a singing competition at a county Eisteddfod. Rich and I were entered for the junior section where I was expected to take first prize. I shared the confidence of my elders. Was I not known as the Wonder Boy Soprano? No one else came within miles of my natural talent now perfected, or so I thought, by the training of a retired tin miner, Johnny Jenkins, himself the champion of many an Eisteddfod.

Came the day, I marched on to the stage, took one look at the ranks of important faces, and felt my throat go dry.

My performance was no more than adequate. Next on was Rich. All of ten years old, he faced the audience like a champion gladiator. A moment or two of silence until the paper rustlers and apple eaters settled down and then he was off. His voice lacked a certain finesse, but he sang and acted with pure rapture. The applause followed him all the way to the winner's rostrum, leaving me to collect the prize for runner-up.

It was Rich all over. Talented, yes, but he had something more — the knowledge that winning has most to do with wanting. And he wanted to succeed very much indeed.

There was another side to his character revealed that day. When the audience had dispersed and we were getting ready to go home, he came up to me, put his hand in mine and left me holding — the winner's medal. "You take it," he said, "I thought you were the best."

The unpredictable act of great generosity was to be a recurring feature of his life.

Sally came in. She was wearing a bedrobe done up to the neck. Her hair was neatly arranged but her face was stone white. Her eyes stared as if she was in a trance. She did not say a word.

The dozen or so people in the room who had been speaking in whispers were now silent. Cis made the first move. She went over to Sally and gave her a hug. She did not respond.

Then we all started talking again — a forced, embarrassed conversation half directed at Sally. "Have you been able to rest, dear?" — "She does look tired doesn't she?" — "Come over here and sit down" — "Now is there anything we can do?"

Sally found her voice.

"I suppose you want to know what happened?" We all nodded, as if one.

"I woke up at about seven. Richard was still in bed which was unusual for him. He liked getting up early. I went back to sleep. When I woke up again, Richard was making funny gurgling noises. I couldn't wake him. I rang Valerie."

"You did what?" I could not hide my amazement.

"I rang Valerie."

"Seven thousand miles away? In Los Angeles?"

"I told you. I was frightened."

"And what did Valerie say?"

"She said to get a doctor."

I murmured something but Cis and Hilda signalled me to be quiet. Valerie Douglas chimed in.

"Isn't it time you checked in at the hotel? We're eating early this evening. Sally has arranged Richard's favourite meal. I'm sure you'll want to brush up."

The cars were waiting to take us the mile down the road. I would have preferred to walk but to do so would have been to risk being hijacked by the reporters massing outside the gates.

The Hotel Port d'Elleves is a cosy Swiss chalet affair overlooking the lake. Contrary to Brook Williams' predictions, there seemed to be rooms to spare. A few puzzled tourists mingled uneasily with the press corps who knew enough about the district not to book in to the smart hotels in Geneva.

When I emptied my case, I went down to the bar. I needed a drink.

The conflict of emotions left me with a sense of painful bewilderment. To feel like a stranger at my own brother's funeral was bad enough, but there was more — the overwhelming sensation that everyone in the Burton entourage was determined to put on a great performance. This was to be the last Burton extravaganza. All that was missing was the star.

There were some journalists sitting at a table. One of them recognised me and invited me over. The last thing I wanted was to launch into an introspection on the Burton tragedy. But the talk was of the early days. The promise of greatness to come.

I was asked, "Have you seen the grave?"

"No," I said, "I'm not even sure where it is."

"We'll show you if you like. But you won't be very impressed."

"What's wrong with it?"

"It's so overgrown. The cemetery looks like a wilderness. Do you want to see it?"

I caught sight of Cis and the others coming down the stairs.

"Tomorrow," I said. "We'll go tomorrow morning."

Dinner at Pays de Galles was less fraught than I had anticipated. Sally did not say very much but she warmed to Verdun who told her stories about Rich which made her smile. The rest of us had heard them a hundred times before, but we caught the mood of the occasion and kept the conversation to neutral topics. The only harsh note came from Valerie Douglas who, feeling out of it, brought us back to the business in hand with a sharp reminder — "Don't forget I want to talk to you guys tomorrow. I have some news for you."

We presumed she was talking about the will.

Later, I tried to have a private word with Valerie. She had set up office in the library, Rich's hideaway, a part conversion of the old stables which were some way back from the house. It was a long room with one side lined with overlapping shelves. The opposite wall and the beams were decorated with acting awards, hung up like hunting trophies.

Valerie sat at the far end from the door. She was behind a table swamped with papers. Beside her was a small desk similarly laden. Telephones were placed strategically. I walked the full length of the room.

"I'm still trying to understand," I said.

"Understand what?"

"How, why, Rich died."

"It was a colossal haemorrhage. There was nothing anyone could do."

I thought, that was what they said about Dadi Ni. He had died the same way, but at eighty-one. Rich had not reached fifty-nine.

"It was just that when I last saw him, he was on top form."

"He may have looked that way to you, but he'd taken a lot of punishment."

I could hardly disagree. Anyway, she was not keen to continue the conversation.

"Let's go down," she suggested. "The others will be waiting."

12

She let me go ahead. Turning back I saw her locking the door behind her.

The day before the funeral, more family and friends arrived. Staying at the hotel were brother Dai and Gareth, Hilda's eldest son, who cut short his holiday to be with us. Ron Berkeley with his wife and son flew in from Paris. Ron had worked with Rich as his hairdresser and make-up man on nearly all his big films. Like every survivor in the movie jungle, he developed a shrewd business sense which he now puts to good use as head of a multi-million dollar fashion business. I was delighted to see Ron, who always manages to impart a sense of confidence and well being however desperate the circumstances. I was not altogether surprised to hear that he had come of his own volition when the expected invitation failed to materialise. Ron had assumed what we had been told, that accommodation would be tight. But we noted that evening that despite the growing accumulation of mourners and reporters, our hotel still had vacancies.

The children of Richard's extended family stayed at Pays de Galles. There was Kate, his daughter by his first wife, and her future husband Christopher, Sybil, who was not invited or, at any rate, did not appear; Richard's stepchild from his marriage to Elizabeth Taylor, Liza Todd with her husband Hap (short for Happy); and then Maria Burton, the adopted daughter of Richard and Elizabeth, and her husband Steve Carson. Neither Christopher nor Michael Wilding put in an appearance, which surprised me.

All of us were to meet together for the first time that evening.

After lunch, I and my two brothers with Gareth went

to the church to rehearse our part in the funeral service. We were followed by a swarm of reporters who occupied a nearby café while we tested our voices against the acoustics of domed arches and heavy stonework. We put a lot of emotion into our singing and it did us the world of good.

"What next?" Gareth asked as we came out of the church.

"Shouldn't we go to the cemetery?" I suggested.

"What for? To see the grave? Even if it is in a bit of a mess, there's nothing much we can do."

"Anyway," said Verdun, "we don't know where it is."

I pointed to the reporters who were gathering outside the café. "They'll show us."

So, for the first and last time that week, instead of the press following us, we followed the press.

That Catholicism is the dominant faith in this part of Switzerland is evident by the location of the Protestant cemetery, well away from the public gaze. We got there through a field on a long muddy track to what looked like a small copse. In amongst the trees were four or five headstones and an open grave.

"It doesn't look too bad," said Verdun. "A bit remote, but what can you expect?"

It was true, the scene was much neater than I had expected. From the smell of freshly-cut grass, I assumed the gardeners had been hard at work all morning.

The spot where Rich was to be buried held our gaze. We were quiet for a moment as we thought forward twenty-four hours. Verdun broke the spell. "Come on," he said. "Let's get back to the hotel."

When the cars delivered us at Pays de Galles later in

the afternoon, I made a beeline for the garden. I was not keen on more intense family heart searching. But before I could get out of the house I was cornered by Valerie Douglas.

"I suppose you've heard, Elizabeth wants to come to the funeral."

I said I had not heard, but I was hardly surprised.

"Her appearance here would be inappropriate," Valerie went on. "It might be different if the funeral was in Wales. But here! What does she think she's up to?"

"I don't see how you can blame Elizabeth for the funeral arrangements."

"I've already told you," said Valerie, "the funeral has to be in Switzerland. For tax reasons."

Cis was standing close by. I had not realised she was listening until she cut across the conversation. She spoke quietly but with great emphasis.

"For why do you say Rich is to be buried here? For reasons of tax? But Rich is not worried about tax. And we, his family, are not worried about tax."

"That's not the point," said Valerie, knowing full well she had made a tactical error. "The point is, the funeral will be here and Elizabeth Taylor must be told not to come."

I felt my temper stretch.

"It's not up to you or us to tell Elizabeth what to do. She'll make up her own mind."

"Well, Sally's not going to like it," retorted Valerie and stalked off.

It occurred to me that if Elizabeth did plan on coming — and judging by Valerie's outburst the odds looked in favour — there was precious little any of us could do

15

because she would be on the plane. Unless, of course, she intended arriving after the service. That way she might fulfil her wish to be with us but avoid disrupting the ceremony.

I went into the living room where Sally was receiving her guests. Liza Todd was on the telephone, concentrating hard. But as I entered she looked up and said into the receiver, "Uncle Graham's just come in, do you want a word with him?"

From this I gathered she was talking to her mother.

As I took over from Liza I kept my eye on Sally who was glaring at me with obvious disapproval.

Elizabeth said, "I won't be at the funeral tomorrow, Graham. I'm sure that's best for everyone. But I haven't made up my mind about Wales. Does the family want me at the memorial service?"

"Of course," I said. "But it's just, just a bit difficult to go into right now."

"Oh, I see. You're overheard?"

"You could say so."

"OK, let's talk later."

I put down the receiver.

Sally got up. "Why did you do that?"

"What?" I could not think what she was talking about.

"Why did you ring off? I wanted to talk to Elizabeth."

"I'm sorry. I've only just come in. I assumed you'd already spoken to her."

"Well, I hadn't."

Her sharp tone told me I was in for a row I did not want. I made another apology and retreated, but she followed me out into the hall. She spoke now in a clenched whisper.

"Can't you get it straight? I don't want Elizabeth Taylor here or at the service in Wales."

"And can't you understand, you have no right to make demands of the family or of Elizabeth. We will do what we think best."

She had a lot more to say, but fortunately we were interrupted by one of the girls telling us that dinner was ready. The conversation over the table was subdued. The hotel party did not stay long.

Afterwards, in the car, Cis wanted to know. "What was that between you and Sally?"

"It was about Elizabeth. She wants to come to the service in Pontrhydyfen. And I think she should."

Cis nodded. "And so do I."

The third day was the day of the funeral.

We went to Pays de Galles to be allocated places in the convoy of luminaries. I sat alongside Cis with Gareth in the front passenger seat. At six foot and seventeen stone, I reckoned that Gareth was our best protection against over-attentive photographers. How right I was.

The crowd filled the road and stopped our car some fifty yards short of the church. After that we were on our own with me holding on to Cis while Gareth forced a way ahead. No doubt there were a few genuine mourners in attendance, but they were vastly outnumbered by the press. The cameras were pushed close in on our faces. Up ahead I could see a television crew on top of their van recording a panoramic view of the melée.

During our slow shoulder-to-shoulder progression, Cis remained tight-lipped. But when we reached the sanctuary of the church, and the noise subsided behind us, she allowed herself a little smile. "Who would have thought that Rich would become so popular."

Occupying two front rows of seats, the Jenkins family was to lead the singing, or rather to take over the singing because all the hymns were in Welsh. I am pleased to say that when it came to it we put on a performance of which our brother would have been proud. Those listening outside said later that it sounded as if we had smuggled in all of South Wales to swell the volume.

But it was a long wait before we got started. As the minutes ticked by, my worries intensified. Where was Sally? It was some comfort to know that Verdun was with her in the car immediately following the hearse. Even so . . .

In fact, what had happened was that the crush beyond the church was so great, the undertakers had been unable to unload the coffin. Instead, the hearse had set off on another circle of the village, ending up outside the vicarage. There, the coffin was carried through the garden, over the back wall and into the church by a side entrance. Sally, Verdun and the others who filed in behind the coffin looked nervous and confused.

Then we had to stand for five minutes' silence. This was Sally's contribution to the proceedings which she insisted upon against all advice. The tension was barely tolerable. It was like being in a library with notices everywhere saying Quiet. I wanted to scream just to break the trance. When, mercifully, the service proper began, for at least half an hour everything went according to plan. The prayers and the short address by Pastor Arnold Mobbs, who had known Rich since he moved to Switzerland, were given in English and French. Richard's beloved Kate, in her soft American accent, read Dylan Thomas's "Do Not Go Gentle Into That Good Night".

> ". . . old age should burn and rave at close of day
> Rage, rage, against the dying of the light.
> And you, my father, there on the sad height,
> Curse, bless me now with your fierce tears I pray.
> Do not go gentle into that good night.
> Rage, rage against the dying of the light."

My part was to read the lesson, Chapter 13 of the First Epistle to the Corinthians, in English and Welsh: "Though I speak with the tongues of men and angels, I am become as sounding brass, or a tinkling cymbal." It was a favourite, learnt by heart, in Welsh, when Rich was knee-high.

When I left my seat in the congregation to go to the lectern, I stood for the first time above the level of the coffin. The mass of red flowers on top now took on a discernable pattern. It made me stop and catch my breath. I was looking down at the fiery red dragon of Wales.

As we filed out of the church into bright sunlight it took a moment or two to find our bearings. The cars were parked close by but we could not see them for the crowd of onlookers. There was nothing for it but to push forward and hope for the best.

As it happened, it was easier getting out of the church than getting in. It was only when we reached the cemetery that I realised why. The press had moved ahead of us to take up positions around the grave. Perched on ladders up against trees and the dry stone wall which edged the cemetery, the photographers peered down at us. I guessed they sought a high position to snap the best overall view of the ceremony but afterwards I found out that they were all looking beyond the tiny group of mourners. There was a rumour that Elizabeth Taylor would turn up at the last minute and they wanted to be in the best position to record her arrival. One particularly keen member of the paparazzi was lodged in the highest branches of a tree, almost directly above our heads. The irreverent thought occurred to me, how would it be if we shook him out of his perch? With luck, he might plummet into the grave. Now that would be a story worth reporting.

The service was a gentle murmur from Pastor Arnold Mobbs who had known Rich since he first came to Celigny in 1955. The Presbyterian minister had christened Kate and her sister Jessica, a sad child who was autistic and lived in a special home. When the formalities were completed the Welsh contingent prepared to launch into ''Sospan Fach'', the rugby anthem much loved by Rich. The tune is from the old Welsh hymnal but the words are sheer nonsense. Cis thought the song inappropriate but Rich had often said that he wanted it sung at his funeral and Sally strenuously approved.

I was grateful to her; grateful too when, as our voices lifted, she permitted herself a little smile. Only once did she come close to breaking down. This was when she moved forward to place a letter on top of the coffin.

When we dispersed, I said to the reporters, "It was Welsh enough, wasn't it? There were only six of us singing ''Sospan Fach'' but we made it sound like the national male voice choir."

Someone asked, "What was in the letter?"

I said I did not know, which was true.

"And what about the rose?"

20

"The rose?"

"Didn't you see? There was a single red rose among the tributes. Do you know who sent it?"

I said I did not know, which was true. But I could guess.

After the funeral there was a gathering of local people at the Café de la Gare. Sally backed off at the last minute and returned directly to the house. But the rest of us went along to make polite conversation. In fact, the occasion was not as heavy going as I expected. With so many happy memories of Rich who was a generous friend to the village, the conversation flowed. Just a few weeks earlier, I discovered, Rich had been due to preside at the celebrations for the Swiss national day. It was a function he had performed most years when he was in Celigny in August. As the party broke up I had a word with the owner of the Café de la Gare who prepared all the meals at the Pays de Galles throughout our stay.

"Don't take this wrongly," I said, "but do you mind telling me what we are eating tonight?"

"Fish," he said.

"Fish? Again?"

And it was the same fish — a sprat-sized creature fried, with chips. It did not figure in my list of great meals of our time.

"Look," I said, "do me a favour, make me something simple. What about a steak, medium rare?"

Paul said he would be happy to oblige.

Back at the house, we gathered for an early dinner. Sally was quick to spot the change in the menu. It was almost as if she was spoiling for a fight.

"What the hell do you think you're up to? Don't you like fish? It was your brother's favourite meal."

"Yes," I said, "I like fish, but not every night."

There was an embarrassed silence. We ate quickly and made ready to return to the hotel. The cars were waiting. The idea was for everyone to gather back at the house an hour or two later for a farewell drink. I cannot say I was very keen. I would have been happier with a short leave-taking there and then. But the rest of the family was properly wary of upsetting the prescribed timetable.

In the hotel lobby I met up with John Parry, BBC arts correspondent whom I knew well from my days at Broadcasting House. We chatted about this and that while I waited for our drivers to appear. Eventually, just one turned up. He did not know where his colleague was; maybe he had misunderstood his instructions. John Parry broke in. "Don't worry. I'll give you a lift. I was going up that way."

John followed the official car through the gates of Pays de Galles to the top of the drive. As we all got out Sally, who was waiting for us, shouted from the steps. I went over to her.

"Who's that with you?"

I told her.

"Are you mad?" she shouted. "Do you think I want the BBC here? I hate the lot of them. Get him out! Get him out!"

At her volume, it was unnecessary to relay the message to John Parry. At thirty paces he heard enough to know he was most definitely not welcome. I shrugged my shoulders in his direction, we gave each other a wave and he drove off. As we went into the house, Cis took hold of Sally's arm.

"What is the matter, now. What has Graham done?"

Sally shook herself free, while saying to me, "What did I tell you? I warned you not to bring Cis. I told you she'd get uptight."

Then she stormed off.

Sally was not alone in her anger. It was as much as I could do to stay in the house long enough for the briefest formalities. As soon as I could get away I walked to the hotel, trying to shake off an ill temper. It was not difficult to understand why Sally was as she was. She had known Richard for little more than two years; they had been married for half that time. From Rich's side it was a relationship founded on uncertainty, about his career and where it was taking him, but more importantly about what he needed for peace of mind. Part of him was always with Elizabeth Taylor. If Sally had any single purpose it was to shake off the other woman. But she was not quite given long enough to achieve her ambition. She had never possessed Rich in the way she wanted. Now she was doubly sad; for a lost love and for what might have been. Did she not then deserve sympathy? Of course, without question. But what I could not take was her assumption that, somehow, we were all locked in a conspiracy against her; that by claiming some part of the memory of Rich we were trying to steal what was rightfully hers.

I was sitting on the hotel verandah looking out over the water, when Ron Berkeley nudged my elbow.

"It doesn't look as if you're out of the wood yet," he said. "Sally's just come in."

I glanced back towards the lobby where Sally was talking earnestly with Ron's wife. I thought it best to let events take their course.

"You know what she's worried about," said Ron. "She thinks you're trying to get Elizabeth Taylor to the memorial service in Wales."

"But that's not true," I said. "I'm fed up with telling everybody. What Elizabeth decides to do is her own affair."

"It looks as if you'll have to be more persuasive," suggested Ron.

Sally came up to me. She was tight-lipped and clearly very angry.

"I want you to tell Elizabeth you've changed your mind; that you don't want her to come to Wales."

I got out of my chair. "Look, I'll say it one more time. If Elizabeth wants to come, she'll be welcome. But she has to make up her own mind."

"You're doing this deliberately," Sally shouted. "You could help if you wanted to. Unless you ring the woman, I'll do something desperate."

Suddenly I was very tired.

An hour or so later Elizabeth rang me at the hotel. I told her all that had happened in the day including my rows with Sally.

"I don't know what to do," said Elizabeth. "I want to be at the memorial service but I don't want a fight with Sally. Do you think she will do something stupid?"

"I wouldn't be surprised," I admitted.

"Well, I can't wait much longer. If I'm coming I must get a flight tomorrow morning. But I don't want to cause a great upset."

The following morning as we were about to leave for the airport, I talked with Kate.

"Will she come?" she wanted to know.

"Maybe," I said, "but I think it's less likely by the minute."

"Did you invite her?"

"No, because it's not up to me to issue invitations."

There was a peep from a car horn.

"You'd better go," said Kate. "You don't want to miss the plane. You have a lot to do back in Wales."

I picked up my suitcase. "A memorial service I can handle," I said. "What I can do without is a civil war."

CHAPTER
TWO

The person that was Richard Burton — or Richard Walter Jenkins as he was for the first seventeen years — was shaped by a succession of accidents, not all of them happy ones.

The first and most tragic was the death of our mother. It happened soon after I was born in 1927 when she was forty-four. By all accounts she was a most extraordinary woman. That she gave birth to thirteen children was not of itself unusual for those days, but her pains to keep the family in good health and spirits, free from want were greater than any of us had a right to expect.

We were born in a terraced cottage in Pontrhydyfen, a hillside village just off the road from Cymmer to Port Talbot. Pontrhydyfen means bridge over the ford across two rivers, and indeed from our back garden we looked down into the valley, where the old ford used to be. It crossed the River Afan (Yr Afon Afan), which is Welsh for river — an example of the often ludicrous results of two languages co-existing.

In my day the traffic moved not below but above — on a viaduct which shadows the entire village with its lofty stilts. Long since converted to a ramblers' footpath, the view from the top is of the entire length of the Afan valley.

Pontrhydyfen made its living from coal mining and smelting — and, in the twenties, a poor living it was. When my father, known to us as Dadi Ni, first went into the mines, well before the turn of the century, every male teenager in the district worked with coal or copper. It was a measure of the decay of heavy industry that of Dadi Ni's own boys only Tom followed in his footsteps.

Dadi Ni took an enormous pride in honest labour. Slight and little more than five feet tall, his strength was a wiry agility and prodigious energy which he fuelled with large quantities of beer. It was a huge shock to him when, after the General Strike, his colliery shut down and left him on the dole. Later, he took on a succession of casual jobs, including night watchman at Port Talbot docks until, at seventy-one, he achieved his heart's desire — another chance to go down the pit. At the Wern Dolu colliery he worked underground for four years — until the retirement regulations at last caught up with him.

When father was young and in work, Edith his wife organised the family timetable around him. The big meals of the day were early in the morning and late in the evening. In the winter months when he was out of the house by 6.30 and not back before 7.00, he saw daylight only on Sunday.

After the General Strike and in the depths of recession, much of the burden for keeping us all fed and clothed fell to our mother. She took in washing, made sweets and non-alcoholic "small" beer which she sold to neighbours and even tried her hand at wallpapering and decorating.

When he was famous, Rich loved to tell stories of the terrible deprivations of his boyhood. But it was our parents who had the hard time, not us. We ate plentifully and with great gusto. The main diet was fresh fish but there was a joint once a week and on Saturday we had cockles and lava bread — a huge treat. Lava bread is the cream of boiled seaweed — not very appetising for the uninitiated particularly as, on the plate, it looks like a cow pat — but to those who are raised on lava bread, it is sheer delight, the "Welshman's caviar", as Richard called it.

I am still amazed to think of the culinary splendours created from such simple ingredients. One of my choice delicacies was sîencyn which utilised the leftovers from the bread bin. With grated cheese, a deep soaking in boiling hot tea and milk produced a delicious mush which compared favourably to the English bread and butter pudding.

But if the Jenkins family did better than most, this is not to say that additions to the family were welcomed unreservedly. An hour or so after Rich was born, he was carried downstairs for a general inspection. Ivor was preparing for work.

"What do you think of him?" asked Cis, who was cradling the baby in her arms.

Ivor gave his new brother a long look. "He's all right, I suppose," he conceded. "But he's another mouth to feed." And he walked out of the house.

Knowing that Mam would be worried about what Ivor thought, Cis went back to her to report that Ivor was delighted with the child.

Rich was accommodated in his parents' bedroom, in a cot beside the big double bed. In the room next door were two double beds, side by side. Cis, Hilda, Cassie and Edie slept in one; Dai, Will and Verdun in the other. Ivor had the tiny box room at the top of the house, having recently taken it over from Tom, the eldest, who had married and set up his own home. No wonder we were a close-knit family.

On the day of my birth, Mam was up bright and early to tackle a pile of washing. When the children left for school she was already on to the ironing. Before the morning was out, the midwife had called and by mid-afternoon the Jenkins family had increased to eleven.

It is said that Mam, usually so calm and untroubled, was visibly worried by this latest pregnancy. Well into her forties, she was at an age when so much could, and often did, go wrong.

In the days following there was much to'ing and fro'ing by the doctor and by neighbours who helped out with meals and other chores. Everyone kept saying it would be all right. But as time went on, the older ones knew it was not all right.

On the sixth day, Hilda, on her way home from school, overheard two women gossiping. One was asking the latest news on Mrs Jenkins. The other shook her head and slowly waved a hand in front of her face. Hilda immediately guessed what had happened but tried not to think of the obvious truth as she ran the short distance to the house. On the way she met Verdun who had been giving Rich a piggyback along the grass verge of the cemetery. He too had heard the neighbours talking. When they stepped in at the front door, the sound of weeping left them without doubt.

Mam died of septicemia, a common infection after childbirth — and when antibiotics were unavailable, often fatal.

In those days, grief was unrestrained. There was no attempt to stiffen the upper lip, to put on a brave face or any of that nonsense. To let loose the emotion was to create an antidote to suffering. Opportunities to express mourning were sought and encouraged. Even so, viewed from this distance, it seems a little hard on Verdun that less than a week after the funeral he should have to sing at a concert in the Jerusalem Chapel. His solo was "A Mother's Prayer".

> I never can forget the day,
> I heard my mother kindly say,
> "I'm leaving now your tender care,
> Remember, child, your mother's prayer."

Sixty years on, Verdun has no doubt that the day Mam died and the day of the concert were the unhappiest of his life.

Dadi Ni suffered most of all. Half his life had disappeared. In less than eighteen months he had lost his wife and his livelihood. He was never quite the same man again. No one could ever replace his Maud. As a teenager I asked my father, "What was Mam really like?" He answered, with tears in his eyes, "As good as gold, the best in the world." And with all the insensitivity of youth I felt embarrassed and left him alone to his memories.

Ivor took over as head of the house. He was barely twenty-one but he knew his own mind and was capable of bringing a sense of order to the family. His nearest contemporary, Cis, had married four months earlier leaving Hilda as the next girl in line. But Hilda was only nine, an age when, despite herself, she would be more of a hindrance than a help. Her attempts to bamboozle Ivor were to provide Rich the actor and raconteur with a prolific fund of stories. And what if they were exaggerated a little over the years? Rich cheerfully described himself as the "master of the hyperbole".

First off was the scandalous affair of the forged shopping list. Hilda was deputised to collect the groceries from the Co-op. Twice a week Ivor made out a list of purchases which Hilda dutifully read out to the shop assistant as tins and packets were gathered in from the shelves. There came the moment when Hilda realised the awful temptation of substituting an occasional purchase of her own choice. She succumbed. Instead of jam she asked for Cadbury's chocolate to the same value. The problem was what to say to Ivor when he asked for bread and jam for tea and found he had only bread. Never short of an answer, Hilda claimed she must have left the jam on the counter; she would collect it on her next visit. But then to buy jam she had to miss another item on the list. So for the next few days the family went short of — tea then butter — then sugar. Each time the discrepancy was spotted Hilda's excuses became more imaginative until, having bought yet more chocolate, she enjoyed one last fling. She told Ivor that by a dreadful accident, half the contents of the shopping basket had fallen over the side of the viaduct. What Ivor thought of that excuse was heard the full length of the street.

Hilda had better luck with the secret of the broken chair. It collapsed when, playing with her younger sisters, all three tried to sit on it simultaneously. With great care they refitted the pieces, then slipped the jacket of Verdun's suit over the back of the chair. They waited. Verdun came in, grabbed his jacket and watched in horror as the chair fell to bits. He was still staring when Ivor opened the door to investigate the noise. Poor Verdun was whacked all over the house for his clumsiness while the girls stood by wearing angelic smiles.

Rich and I were not witnesses to these adventures. We had our own quite different lives to lead. Soon after

Mam's death, I was taken in by brother Tom and his wife Cassie who lived three miles away in Cwmafan. Rich went to Cis who had set up home with her husband Elfed in Taibach, five miles to the sea side of Pontrhydyfen. Meeting regularly at weekends I thought of Rich as my best friend. But it took me some time to recognise a closer relationship. Just after my fourth birthday, Rich put me right. We were playing by the river one Sunday afternoon when suddenly he clutched my arm.

"You know we're brothers, don't you?" he declared solemnly.

I did not, but I was suitably overawed so I said nothing.

He gripped my arm harder. "We must never let the distance from Cwmafan to Taibach come between us."

What drama! I promised faithfully, of course.

But I still had not worked through all the family connections. Some time later I was asked to take some flowers to the cemetery. An old lady from the village came over to speak to me.

"You're Dic Jenkins' son, aren't you?"

I said I was not quite sure. "I think he's my grandfather."

"Oh, no, boy," she said. "You're his son all right. And that," she added, pointing to where the flowers rested on a mound of earth, "is your mother's grave."

Of all the influences on young Rich none was more powerful or lasting than that of Cis — his mother in all but name. In later years he showed his gratitude in many ways, not least by naming her the most important woman in his life. She was the standard by which all others were judged. No one relished the comparison.

Rich moved in with Cis on 25 October 1927, a few months short of her twenty-second birthday and a mere four months after she married Elfed James. For Elfed, who was already burdened with the insecurity of a miner's life, the financial and emotional challenge of caring for an infant brother-in-law was difficult to accept. But Cis was determined to do her duty — by both of her men. When Elfed lost his temper or spoke out of turn Cis was quick to shield Rich. He was never smacked. This could make Elfed feel as if he were second fiddle. "Nothing is good enough for that boy. Anything is good enough for me."

This was not true. Cis put her heart and soul into making a decent home, getting up in the early hours to prepare breakfast and see Elfed off to work before knuckling down to the domestic chores. At the same time she helped out with the Jenkins' laundry. With Rich in a pram or on her shoulder, she would walk the six miles to Pontrhydyfen to collect the dirty clothes, traipse home to Taibach to do the washing and ironing and then return the following day.

Cis divided her time with scrupulous fairness. Where, as she now admits, she might have been less than even-handed was in her show of affection. When it came to a choice between Elfed and Rich, as it often did, Elfed lost out. This assumed injustice may well have determined his attitude when Rich came to the first great turning point in his life.

More responsibilities came for Cis with the birth of two daughters, Marian in 1928, and Rhianon in 1931. Around this time she and Elfed put down a small sum of money loaned from his mother for a house of their own. On a mortgage of ten shillings a week the family moved into 73 Caradoc Street, a three-bedroomed 1920s semi built on "the Side", literally the side of the mountain. The back garden gave a complete view of Taibach — the Wesleyan chapel and the Eastern School facing each other just down the road, then the main street with the Co-op, more chapels and the library and, over the street, the steel mill which sent out showers of soot and metal splinters to blanket the town. A short walk from number 73 was a baker's shop run by the Hopkins family. In 1937 they had a son who, like Rich, was to become a fine actor. His name was Anthony.

Rich had his own bedroom which also accommodated a seafarer's trunk, a large black tin box handed down from Elfed's grandfather, who had taken it halfway around the world. It was used by all the children as a treasure house for their toys. One of the great treats at weekends was to embark on a ritual search of the box for toys which had passed unnoticed for so long they had regained their novelty. But Rich always ended up with his old favourites — a red and green railway engine, a Meccano set (from which nothing recognisable was ever made) and a set of skittles. The skittles were knocked down with a ball held to a pole by a length of string. Rich had great trouble finding a name for this game until a friend who was master at demolishing all the skittles in one, confided that older and more sophisticated players knew it as The Swinging Tit. Rich was delighted and lost no time in sharing his knowledge with the rest of the family. The reception was not what he expected. But undaunted by Cis's tut-tutting or Elfed's loud reproof, he and the girls referred ever after to The Swinging Tit, if always in hushed tones.

Rich's most treasured possession was a three-legged

stool. It cost two and sixpence from Bendalls and from a week after it was bought it wobbled under the strain of its many duties. The stool was variously a shop counter, the entrance to a mysterious cave, the steering wheel of a luxury car and, frequently, the platform for an impassioned oration on whatever subject happened to be uppermost in Rich's imagination.

Rich was quick to discover the power of language — the Welsh language to be precise since our patch of South Wales remained loyal to its mother tongue. Neither Rich nor I spoke a word of English until we were six and only then because we picked up odd words from the wireless.

The inspiration to stretch the use of language came from the chapel. Each Sunday along we trooped, spick and span, fresh from the zinc bath installed once a week in the kitchen for the highly organised routine of bath night. The chapel was our other world. Within that simple building we let our emotions rip. We sang lustily, prayed fervently and listened in awe to the thunderous declarations of moral judgement. A good preacher was a poet in action. He could spin words into a story of such power as to stop the mind.

Rich had a fancy to do the same. He had all the advantages — a fine, strong voice, a good memory and a sense of timing. With little encouragement he would give a front room sermon, declaring to the family, his congregation, the virtues of temperance and clean living. But he played for laughs, exaggerating the brimstone expressions of the inspired preacher and his readiness to point the finger — up towards heaven and down, down to everlasting damnation.

Once when we gathered to hear the self-styled paragon of virtue, we noticed that to one side of Rich was erected a pile of books. Their purpose was unclear until, at the climax of Joshua's triumph at Jericho, with a great crash, the books came tumbling down. The people of Jericho could not have been half as surprised at the collapse of their defences.

It was home entertainment of a high order and such was the demand — "Come on, Rich, give us a sermon" — that he extended the act to take in the rest of the service, albeit a shortened version which disposed of a hymn, a prayer and a lesson in three minutes flat. And this is where Rich first showed his ability as a performer — not so much in presentation, but in his sensitivity to the audience. He knew what they wanted and what they could take. He could adapt his routine to suit the mood of the moment — collecting laughs where none had come before, he stretched the joke; if the response was half-hearted, he immediately changed tack. But, best of all, he never outstayed his welcome.

His first appearance in front of an impartial audience was at chapel where, from the age of seven, he made regular appearances at the lectern to deliver a Sunday lesson. The curiosity here was that he gave more of a recitation than a reading. Instead of standing head down, with his eyes fixed on the big print of the bible, he lifted his face to the congregation to hold forth as if the words were his very own. It was assumed, and with every indication of approval from the more pious worshippers, that Rich had gone to enormous trouble to learn the verses by heart — closeted in his room, no doubt, for all of Saturday while other small boys were wasting their energy playing in the street. They could not have been further from the mark. Rich practised, it is true, but after running through the verses a few times he had no difficulty in remembering the extract almost word for word. It was the same with stories and poetry. Whatever took his fancy on the classroom or library shelves he learned off by heart to add to his repertoire of home entertainment.

Weekends at Pontrhydyfen were not complete without the juvenile talent show — Rich leading with a tall tale or recitation and the rest of us following with songs to make the heart swell. But in the week, when he was with Cis, his best audience was his two nieces, Marian and Rhianon, who were in awe of the older boy. Rich took advantage of his seniority to impose his choice of entertainment. Fear and horror came top of the list.

There was the strange case of the locked room, as investigated by the master detective, Charlie Chan. Rich went through all the motions of a terrified man incarcerated alone in his house. As the girls sat together on the sofa, biting their nails, he struggled with the window and rattled the door as, with mounting hysteria, the dreadful fear took hold — there was no way out. But then — what was it? — the sound of a key turning. Someone, out there, was unlocking the door. As Rich spoke these thoughts, he edged across the room until with an agonising burst of courage he grasped the handle, turned it, opened the door and slowly, fearfully, stepped out, closing the door behind him.

The girls waited — and waited — until it was obvious that if they wanted to know the rest of the story they had to follow Rich into the hall. But it was a winter's evening and there was no gas light out there. The door edged open. On a small table by the hatstand was a candle. Its thin flame illuminated the stairs where stood — Charlie Chan.

It was Rich with his pyjama coat on back to front. The Chinese effect was achieved by stretching his eyes into slits. It was not an award-winning impersonation, but in poor light it was strong enough to inspire terror in poor Marian and Rhianon. As a compliment to the actor, their screams were accepted as applause.

The time came when Rich and the girls grew apart. They took to dolls and he discovered rugby. They still played together but the occasions were invariably cut short by Rich suggesting a game of hide and seek.

"You count up to one hundred and then find me." When they opened their eyes, it was to find that he had gone off with the other boys to kick a football.

Rich was growing up.

CHAPTER
THREE

From about the age of seven to when he joined the air force at the end of the war, Rich had two great passions — and neither of them was a woman. His first love was rugby — and who could blame him? Rugby is the highest expression of Welsh culture. It requires exceptional physical and mental skills, with a touch of ruthless cunning. Not a bad training for life. Rich was suited to the game by build and by temperament. He was not the canniest player but what he lacked in artistry he more than made up for with raw energy. His enthusiasm for the game stayed with him all his life.

Along with rugby went a passion for reading. Rich gobbled up any printed material — books, comics, papers — which came his way. He solemnly informed Hilda that reading was the source of all wisdom. Some of his favourite authors might have been surprised to hear their work being described so loftily, but if, at an early age, Rich was not the most discriminating of readers, the sheer quantity of books which came his way guaranteed at least a passing acquaintance with some of the better writers. Cis and Elfed did all they could to encourage him though buying books was a luxury they could ill afford. Fortunately, the Carnegie Library, just down the road, was sufficiently stocked to meet the demands of the most avid reader. Rich went there every day after school. It was to be his favourite retreat throughout his life in Taibach.

Rich adapted quickly to the English language and took huge delight in the discovery of new words. As his less well informed, younger brother, I was the first to hear of the latest acquisitions in his vocabulary. "Sycophant," he said to me one day. "Do you know what a sycophant is?" I did not and he told me. But it was not so much the meaning of the word as its sound which fascinated him. With Welsh intonation, each syllable given its own emphasis, "sycophant" was a cruel and terrible word. We tried it out on our friends with devastating results. They may not have understood but they knew an insult when they heard one.

The power of words stimulated the desire to perform. His favourite prop was a brass candlestick. This served very well as a telephone, an aid Rich used to bring in characters who were never actually seen. The minister at the chapel, his schoolmaster, the librarian, all came in for gentle but well observed parody. The opening line — "This is Richard Jenkins speaking. Now, I want a few words with you." — became so familiar to us all, it was, in itself, a guarantee of a laugh.

The candlestick also functioned as a microphone, carried by Rich as an intrepid BBC radio reporter, sending back news of great events. He delighted Dadi Ni with a full-length commentary on the world heavyweight fight between Joe Louis and the Welsh boy from Tonypandy, Tommy Farr. It was a meticulously researched entertainment. Blow by blow accounts of the match in the newspapers and on the radio were sifted for the most dramatic imagery. When he was ready, Rich gathered us together in the front room. He sat behind a small table with his candlestick and an empty glass tumbler. Then he began, in an impeccable English accent.

"Good evening, ladies and gentlemen. This is the BBC. We are now taking you over to New York for a live commentary for the boxing match of the century."

Thereafter, it was a mix of Welsh and English, but all powerful stuff.

"And Tommy Farr has landed another blow to the jaw, and another. The champion is reeling, I can see blood streaming from his right eye. Can this be the end?"

Well, no it couldn't because there was the little difficulty of explaining how it was that Joe Louis snatched victory, albeit on points.

The glass tumbler was for sound effects. By pressing it against his mouth, Rich achieved the hollow atmospherics of a trans-Atlantic broadcast. Dadi Ni declared himself entirely convinced.

"Better than the real thing, boy," he told Rich who basked in the uncustomary show of approval from his normally reticent father.

Maybe this encouraged him to try his hand at impressing a wider audience. Without telling anyone in the family he entered a verse-reading competition — and won. We heard the news from Hilda who was told by a friend. "He has a beautiful voice," reported the friend. "They do say it's the best in the valley."

As a junior at the Eastern School, Rich did just enough work to get by. Apart from his feel for language he was not exceptional in a way that automatically marked him out for scholastic success. But then, in his last year, he encountered Meredith Jones, the teacher responsible for training the brightest and the best to win places at Port Talbot Secondary School.

Meredith Jones was a man of great power. A signal of

approval from him was the Taibach equivalent of the order of merit. More than prestige was at stake. Those who did so well in the exams as to be accepted for an academic education were virtually guaranteed a well paid and reputable job when they left school. And this at a time when jobs were hard to come by. For the lucky few there was the prospect of university and promotion to the ranks of the middle-class professions. Boys who defied the limitations of their environment to become doctors or lawyers were talked about in hushed tones of respect long after they had departed to make their fortune in Cardiff or the big cities across the border.

It was fortunate for Rich that Meredith Jones enjoyed talking. There were those who complained he did little else. Himself a scholarship boy, the son of a miner, he was passionate in his desire to awake the talent in young people. He achieved this by bombarding them with questions and arguments — anything to elicit a response that could be evidence of a lively mind. Facts took second place to imagery so that, reacting one with the other, Meredith Jones and his class would frequently launch off on some flight of rhetoric, far beyond the bounds of formal education. He had an opinion on every subject under the sun but best of all, he loved talking about his home and country.

"Gentlemen," he would thunder through his thick ginger moustache, "let no man despise Wales, her language or her literature. She has survived many storms; she has survived many empires. Her time will come. When the last truckload of coal reaches Cardiff, when the last black diamond is dug from the earth of Glamorgan, there will be men then digging gems of pure brilliance from the inexhaustible mines of the literature and language of Wales."

His impact on the young Jenkins hardly needs to be emphasised. Rich loved the man. But others were not so enthusiastic. Less flamboyant personalities were easily overwhelmed. Meredith Jones was seen by many as a tyrant, dispensing favours only to those who sought and met with his approval. That he could be harsh and insensitive was undeniable.

"I am going to teach you something important," he announced one day, "and Danny here will help me." Danny was the sort of boy who liked to stay hidden at the back of the class. For all I know he was able enough but he was made shy by a speech impediment which transformed every utterance into a high-pitched stutter. Meredith Jones led Danny out to the front and asked him to stand on a chair. "Now, Danny, I want you to recite."

Danny spluttered a few lines before surrendering to the barrage of laughter let loose by, among others, Rich and his friends. Meredith Jones rounded on them. "How dare you mock the afflicted. Are you so selfish as to take pleasure in the misfortune of others? Come out here, all of you." He then proceeded to give each of the miscreants a sound beating.

Long afterwards, Rich insisted that, for him, the experience was character forming, a lesson in humility. I did not doubt it. But I could not help wondering what Danny got out of it?

Rich took the scholarship exam in his stride and settled in at the Port Talbot Secondary School. But he did not lose contact with Meredith Jones. In 1940, his mentor left teaching to set up a youth club, the first to be sponsored by the local county council. Rich was one of the founding members. Provision for this venture was not exactly lavish. It was accommodated in a near derelict building on the edge of the Eastern School playground. It was gas lit and had a leaky roof. But the response from the youngsters was overwhelming. Suddenly, they had a place to call their own. It made a welcome contrast to evenings at home where every move was monitored by their elders.

The club had a drama group led by Leo Lloyd, a teacher of English who was a close associate of Meredith Jones. Rich was an eager participant, throwing himself wholeheartedly into any part which came his way. By professional standards he was hopelessly over-indulgent, giving all he had in every role, as if melodrama was the only bench mark. It was a mystery to me where he had picked up the exaggerated gestures, the staring eyes, the long pauses after every sentence — until I started going with him to the cinema.

The Taibach Picture Drome, known to its regular patrons as the Cach, had not quite caught up with the times. Even in the early part of the war, it was still showing silent films. But Rich was captivated. With a change of programme mid-week and a special children's matinee on Saturdays (actually a re-run of films which had all but exhausted their box office appeal) it was theoretically possible to visit the Cach three times a week. But the pocket money did not allow for such extravagance. A way round the problem was provided by a close friend of Rich's. Trevor George had an after school job in a barber's shop where he performed the duties of "wobbler". These included lathering up the customers who were there for a shave and sweeping up

44

the fallout from the short back and sides. As part payment Trevor collected the two free passes which the Cach awarded to the barber in return for displaying a window poster. Naturally, Rich was in on the deal.

One of the first films Rich and I saw together was Cecil B. De Mille's version of *Cleopatra*. It was billed as the most expensive film ever made. Who said that history never repeats itself?

A chance for Rich to demonstrate coarse acting as perfected by his silent screen heroes came when Leo Lloyd entered his drama group for Glamorgan's first Youth Eisteddfod. The production was a popular morality play of the time called *The Bishop's Candlesticks*, lifted from Victor Hugo's novel, *Les Misérables*. Rich had the meatiest role, that of the escaped convict intent on robbery who is transformed into a decent citizen by the artless generosity of his victim. Since the performance was in mime, Rich was able to concentrate all on body language, just like Rudolph Valentino. It was all there. The hand raised against the eye (fear), the arms outstretched (the appeal for mercy), the head bowed and shaking (guilt) and, finally, the eyes raised to heaven to signify the repentant sinner.

The club's supporters, a full bus-load of them, roared their approval. It was clear to them who deserved the first prize. The adjudicator was more difficult to please. He began by observing the virtue in restraint. A dramatic point, he argued, could sometimes be put across more effectively if it was implied rather than blazoned forth in a statement of the obvious. All this was too much for Leo Lloyd who interposed, in a loud voice, his own views on the quality of the adjudicator. "The man is obviously biased. He has no sense at all."

Thoroughly confused, the adjudicator hurried on to his conclusion which was really very favourable to the play and to Rich. The Taibach boys returned home in triumph.

Rich found in the activities of the youth club a stimulation which was absent in his formal education. Meredith Jones and Leo Lloyd treated him like an adult and he responded in a way which impressed them with his maturity.

"You have real talent in that boy," they told Cis.

The talent showed most obviously in his study of literature of which acting was a crucial element. Only too well aware of his club's limitations as a centre of dramatic excellence, Meredith Jones encouraged Rich to branch out. He commended his protege to Philip Burton, an English teacher at the grammar school, but more importantly, a rising star of the local cultural establishment. Here was a drama enthusiast whose reputation was so far advanced as to bring him offers of work on Welsh radio. Philip Burton had even visited the United States. He was a man of the world; and still only in his thirties.

Rich was already on slight acquaintance with Philip Burton who taught him English from his first year at grammar school. But Rich had failed to make an impression. His single appearance in a Burton production — as Mr Vanbatten in *The Apple Cart* — had attracted criticism for his atrocious American accent. "In any case," said the director, drawing attention to a feature of the young man others were too polite to talk about, "he has spots." There was no denying the fact. Rich had a skin so ravaged by acne as to suggest trench warfare. In his late teens, the pimples subsided, but their battlefield remained for the rest of his life.

Those who had faith in Rich were not so easily deterred by the blemishes of puberty. But by 1941, when he was fifteen, argument as to his real abilities was academic. The family had decided. Rich must leave school to earn his living.

The break in his education was not sanctioned without much heart searching. Cis wanted him to stay on; the family was sympathetic. But where was the money to come from? Like the rest of us, Rich was eager to pay his way. His morning newspaper round was a steady if modest earner which he supplemented by instigating a collection as well as a delivery. The old newspapers he accumulated were sold as wrapping paper to a local fish and chip shop. But it was nowhere near enough. A growing boy with a healthy appetite and a tendency to punish his clothes into early patchwork was an expensive item on the household budget. These were hard times for Cis and Elfed, as for the rest of the family. Hilda, who had left school at thirteen to help out at home, was now married with a baby son. Her husband, Dai, was off at the war. Tom's Cassie had died but he still looked after me and his daughter Mair.

Verdun, also married, had been badly injured in a mining accident. He was mending a coal cutter when some fool threw the main switch. The machine cut off half his foot. A year later he was back down the pit but it was a long time before he was on to full earnings. His only solace was the compensation which he used to buy a piano for his daughter, Ann. She had a fine voice and later turned professional.

Ivor was still looking after our two younger sisters,

Cassie and Edie, and Dadi Ni, a responsibility which forced him to postpone his own marriage until he was thirty-five — when he and Gwen had been engaged for twelve years.

Brothers Dai and Will were in regular employment, one in the police, the other in the army. Neither could be described as high earners. Nonetheless, Dai offered to help with Rich's schooling, as did brother Tom. His gesture was truly magnanimous since, as my foster parent, he was already paying for my education.

Perhaps with a little more effort a solution might have been found. Later Elfed was blamed for not trying quite hard enough, but it was asking a lot of him to continue supporting Rich into the years when the vast majority of young people were fending for themselves. It was not as if they got on particularly well. Elfed always harboured a resentment against his demanding and, in his view, disruptive brother-in-law. Unlike Rhianon and Marian who were polite and well behaved, Rich had a mischievous streak which put him at odds with all authority. Cis let him get away with it; Elfed was not so tolerant.

Only once as I recall was Elfed inspired to a burst of spontaneous praise for Rich. It happened on the day Rich went off to play his first game of cricket. He wore a pair of hand-me-down flannels which Cis had rooted from the bottom of the linen basket. They were baggy at the knees and thin on the rear, but Rich was delighted to have the conventional kit. Performer in the making he may have been, but in those days he was not that keen to be different.

Having made a few runs he returned in buoyant mood, tossing a coin. At first Cis imagined Rich had brought home a prize but when she saw it was a gold sovereign he treated so carelessly she had second thoughts.

"I found it in my pocket," Rich explained. "I guessed it might be worth something."

Elfed was summoned. He stared hard at the coin for a moment, then burst out, "My God, you've found it. This was my father's. He gave it to me when I was twenty-one. I thought I'd lost it."

Rich was the hero. Some time later, Elfed asked, "How did you know it was valuable?"

"That's easy," said Rich. "A man at the match offered me sixpence for it. I realised if he wanted to give me that much, it must be worth more." Elfed was impressed. For a time thereafter he conceded credit where it was due. But Rich quickly got through the residue of goodwill, and none of us were too surprised when we were told that Rich had, after all, left school. "He has a good job," Cis told me. "Mr Maynard's taking him on at the Co-op menswear."

The Co-op was the biggest store in town which was not saying too much. In wartime, its normally austere appearance was made yet more forbidding by the walls of depleted shelves. But for want of a livelier alternative and for the sake of the divi, the customers remained loyal.

Rich and the retail trade were ill suited. He simply could not take it seriously. When Mrs Jones turned up at the shop wanting to buy her Gareth a new suit, but not having enough clothing coupons, Rich was quick to oblige. "Don't you worry," he assured his nervous customer, "you can settle up next time." It was not long before everyone in town knew that, for Co-op bargains, Rich was the boy to make for.

I remember an effusive greeting from a neighbour who, hitherto, had hardly acknowledged my existence.

"That brother of yours," she confided, "there's a real friend for you. He won't let you down."

I found out later that Rich had supplied her husband and sons with a full stock of winter underwear, all off coupons.

When he was not needed behind the counter, Rich could be found in the library across the road. When he *was* needed behind the counter, Rich could be found in the library across the road.

Mr Maynard, who was a kindly man and not ill disposed towards his apprentice, gave a lack of progress report to Cis. "He's a bright lad," he told her. "No doubt about it. But he's not — well, how can I put it? — he's not quite what we expected. Perhaps you could have a word with him?"

Cis did have a word with him. Elfed had several words with him. Their conflicting approach to the problem made it worse.

"He's not happy at the Co-op," argued Cis.

"He's not paid to be happy," said Elfed.

Encouraged by Cis to believe that, maybe, there was a life beyond the Co-op, Rich poured out his resentment to others who might support his break for freedom.

Sympathiser-in-chief was Ivor — on the face of it an unlikely candidate since it was entirely out of character for him to play the patient and understanding adviser. Ivor was the tough nut of the family. A face miner who was proud of his record for shifting more coal in a day than any of his mates, he brought into the home the same rigorous standards that governed his life in the pit.

Stories abound of Ivor's exaggerated sense of fair play which he would defend against all comers.

There was the time when Verdun, still a boy and fresh into work, came home from the pit with his first trumps — the little extra paid by a miner to his young helper. Verdun put his week's wage — seven and sixpence — and his trumps — a threepenny bit — on the mantlepiece.

"What's this?" demanded Ivor.

"My pay," said Verdun.

"No," said Ivor, his voice getting louder, "*THIS!*" he pointed to the threepenny piece which Verdun had placed to one side.

"It's my trumps. Mr Davies gave it me."

"He did, did he," Ivor grabbed Verdun by the arm. "Then we'll pay a call on Mr Davies."

Together they marched out of the house and along the street to where the Davies family lived. Mrs Davies answered the door. She was a tiny woman, not given to resisting steamrollers.

"Is William there?" bellowed Ivor.

"I'll get him," said Mrs Davies and disappeared.

A few moments later her husband was at the door.

"Is this the boy who's working with you?" Ivor demanded.

"It is," said William, "and he's the best I've ever had."

"So is this his entitlement?" Ivor revealed the threepence in his hand. William became defensive. "I've had a hard week, what with the Co-op to pay and so forth."

"We've all had a hard week," shouted Ivor. "So you know what you can do with this." He threw the coin into the hallway. "Shove it up your arse."

After that, Verdun worked with another miner and his trumps increased accordingly.

Ivor's conception of justice was not always favourable to those closest to him. When Hilda set her heart on buying a wristwatch, she calculated the only way she could do it was to save a little each week on the house-keeping to pay for the watch on the never-never. The plan worked perfectly until Hilda was rushed into hospital with acute appendicitis. Before she departed she gave her younger sister, Cassie, some rapid coaching in delaying tactics. "All you have to say is . . ."

But Cassie got it wrong and Ivor found out. When Hilda came home from hospital it was to be told the watch had to go back. Years later when Hilda related the story to Rich, he made a shamefaced Ivor go straight out to buy her a splendid new gold watch. She wears it to this day.

From all this it can be gathered that Ivor was not an easy man to sway. No one certainly could describe him as a soft touch — except when it came to Rich.

For Rich he would do anything.

So when the novice shop assistant called round to his home to confess how unhappy he was at the Co-op and how he would do anything to get back to school, Ivor was angry on his behalf and promised he would do all he could to help.

Outside the family, Rich found his most powerful advocate in Meredith Jones. As a regular at the Youth Club, Rich had opportunities enough to persuade Meredith that he was in there fighting. His stage performances, though still a trifle over-dramatic, were a compelling display of individuality, a characteristic which he reinforced off stage by engaging in long, animated conversations on any subject under the sun.

Meredith was entranced.

When asked by Cis for an opinion on Rich, he answered promptly, "The boy is wasted in that shop. He should be back at school, finishing his education."

"Can you help?" asked Cis.

"I'm doing my damnedest," Meredith assured her. "But don't get your hopes up because it's not done yet."

Meredith Jones went out of his way to recruit some powerful sponsors for Rich. "What are strings for," he asked, rhetorically, "except to be pulled?"

Philip Burton was among the first to be roped in. He admitted he had been a little hasty in his assessment of Rich as a lightweight. A boy who was determined to break the mould — just as he and Meredith had defied the conventions of their upbringing — such a boy deserved support. Rich's former headmaster, Pop Reynolds, was sympathetic but saw difficulties. Teachers' recommendations alone would not work the magic. A reinstatement at the grammar school was a rare event. To achieve it, political muscle had to be exerted. Meredith Jones went to work on Councillor Llewellyn Heycock (later Lord Heycock), president of the youth club and a member of the Glamorgan Education Committee.

Every boy who made a success, argued Meredith, was a credit to the education service. Richard Jenkins had great promise, but it was likely to remain unfulfilled — unless he returned to school. Could the education committee, in all conscience, refuse the boy the opportunity to prove his talent? Councillor Heycock promised to speak to the school governors.

He encountered tough opposition from the chairman

who did not like bending the rules. Heycock argued that Rich would take his school certificate within a year along with his contemporaries who had not missed out on their education. What could be fairer than that? Moreover, if Rich succeeded he was certain to go to college to train as a teacher. And teachers were in short supply.

A few days later, Meredith sent a boy to 73 Caradoc Street to ask Cis if she could call in at the school. When she hurried round — expecting the worst but hoping for the best — she was greeted by Meredith in his most expansive mood.

"Good news," he boomed. "The boy can return to his rightful place."

Cis almost cried with relief and pleasure.

"But what about Elfed?" Meredith asked. "How will you handle him? Do you want me to come and have a chat?"

"Don't worry," said Cis, who feared that pressure from the short-tempered schoolmaster was more than likely to stiffen resistance, "I'll think of something."

But her hope of avoiding a row was misplaced because the only other advocate who could tackle Elfed head on was Ivor.

"Do try to keep your voice down," begged Cis.

Ivor said he would do his best. The conversation started well.

"The boy deserves his chance," they agreed.

"But there just isn't the money," Elfed put in. "It's all very well for you, Ivor, you're a face worker on piece rates. You earn good money, twice as much as me, I shouldn't wonder."

That did it.

"And what about the sacrifices I've made and Tom

has made?" roared Ivor. "Don't you think we've done our bit?"

"He's your brother. He's not my son."

By now the two men were standing glaring at each other. Cis tried a few soothing words.

"Very well, if that's the way it's to be, we'll all put our hands in our pockets.

But that was not the end of the story. "The strange thing is," Cis recalls, "that when it came to the point, Elfed would not accept a penny. He had his pride, you see."

A formal letter inviting Rich to resume his studies followed shortly. Years on, when he counted his income in millions, he told me it was the most valuable offer he ever received.

After ten months out on his own, re-adapting to the school routine was a curious experience for Rich. Academically he was a model student who worked hard to make up for lost time. But socially he had advanced much faster than his classmates. His ebullient personality was, in any case, ill suited to the formal discipline of not speaking until spoken to and always staying in line. Egged on by his less resolute friends who enjoyed the spectacle of authority under attack as long as they were not in the firing line, Rich could be relied upon to challenge the powers.

"Where's your gas mask?" Pop Reynolds demanded to know when he spotted Rich at the school gate without the regulation pack.

"I left it at home, by mistake," said Rich. "Where's yours?"

Pop Reynolds had the grace to admit he was equally forgetful. The rudeness went unpunished.

It was a trivial offence and a minor triumph for Rich, but was so uncharacteristic of the school as a whole that it was blown out of proportion. Questions were asked about his seriousness of purpose. Was he not seen drinking in a pub and smoking in the street? And what about these stories of his fondness for girls? There was nothing wrong with polite conversation between the sexes. But in the woods?

Among those who felt that Rich might be in danger of squandering his opportunities was Phil Burton. From his first day back at school, Rich had seen a lot of the man who was to be his cultural and professional mentor. Phil Burton was his English teacher, his commanding officer in the Air Training Corps and, with increasing frequency, his director on stage. In November 1942, Rich played his first major role in a Burton production, that of Owen Brown, younger brother of John, in *Gallows Glorious*, an emotional tribute to the hero of the American Civil War. In the closing minutes of the play Rich had a wonderful chance to grip the audience. Accompanied by an invisible choir celebrating victory over death "His Soul Goes Marching On", Owen was to be blessed with a vision of John Brown leading his army across the sky. Rich made the most of it. Alone on stage, arms outstretched, eyes lifted, he proclaimed the glory of the Lord.

Phil Burton made his by now customary plea for restraint ("You don't have to use a sledgehammer. A gentle tap will do the trick") but he was sufficiently impressed to offer Rich another role, this time in his own play, *Youth at the Helm*, written for the BBC Welsh

56

radio. Rich went to Cardiff for the recording. It was, he told me, like travelling to a new world. He was surrounded by people who were excited by what the BBC had to offer, the chance of reaching out to a whole population. The thrill of performing in a makeshift theatre to an audience of a hundred paled against the excitement of the studio and the hanging mike. There was no one to applaud but many to hear. Not having to act, physically, he concentrated on voice. And what a voice.

It was the first time I had heard the disembodied Rich. I was bowled over by the melodious, seductive tones of the Welsh Welsh, deeper and stronger than anything you will hear in the north.

Phil Burton too must have been impressed because it was after this that he began to take seriously Rich's now openly declared ambition to be a professional actor. The teacher was in need of a favourite, a young hopeful who could fulfil, by proxy, the dreams of a frustrated actor. His first protege, Thomas Owen Jones, was a clever young actor who had won a scholarship to RADA and appeared in West End plays and films before joining up as a fighter pilot. His death in the Battle of Britain came as a hammer blow to Phil whose sadness for a lost talent was compounded by a strong affection for the boy.

Rich appeared as a godsend. Here was the young Jones all over again, but with even greater potential. My brother had come a long way since the day Phil Burton had reported unfavourably upon his complexion. At seventeen, Rich had more than sufficient qualities to compensate for the after effects of acne. He had the rough good looks of a warrior, a stubborn jaw and compelling blue eyes. He was strong and intelligent and he could act. Phil knew that Richard Jenkins was capable of great things — just as long as he kept his mind on his ambitions and was not diverted by idle pursuits.

How could this be achieved? Phil called on Cis to talk about the future. He was worried, he said, that the education Rich was enjoying was not sufficiently intensive to bring him up to standard in the short time left to him at school. He needed extra tuition from someone who appreciated his abilities and was dedicated to his success.

Cis knew that anything she had to say was bound to be unhelpful. Ah yes, her Rich deserved the best but it was pie in the sky even to think about paying out for private schooling. The family budget was already stretched to its limit.

Phil reassured her. Money was not the obstacle. He, Philip Burton, would provide. But if he was to act as patron for Rich he had to be confident that his sacrifice was appreciated. It was necessary for Rich to live in an intellectually lively environment.

And where would that be? Cis wanted to know.

Well, as it happened, there was a spare room in the house in Port Talbot where Phil Burton had his own lodgings. If Rich moved in there, Phil could give him all the help he needed to achieve scholastic excellence while keeping a watchful eye on his protege. In short, Phil was offering himself as benefactor and mentor.

The proposition was enormously attractive. Cis was proud to think that a celebrity, respected throughout South Wales, should be prepared to put himself out for her Rich. And it was not as if he was about to leave the country. He would still be close at hand, she would still see a lot of him.

Others in the family were less inclined to take the offer at face value. Could it be that Phil Burton was attracted by more than intellectual qualities?

A bachelor in his early forties, he had led a protected life. After the death of his father when Phil was just fourteen, the prevailing influence of his formative years had been a strong-willed mother whose ambitions for her son were rewarded by a good honours degree at the University of Wales. That a career in teaching was not all he wanted was made evident by his dogged pursuit of a reputation as a writer and director. He never showed any inclination to marry. He used to say that his drama groups were his family.

As the youngest, my view on Rich's future was neither sought nor given. But looking back I can understand why my brothers were worried. Anyway, it was not as if Rich would be unchaperoned. Phil Burton's lodgings in Connaught Street were part of the household of a middle-aged widow and her two daughters. A pillar of the chapel, Mrs Smith was scrupulous in the management of her affairs. She was not the sort to tolerate any hanky panky.

Rich moved in with Phil Burton at the start of the Easter term in 1943.

The question must be asked. In that curious, close relationship between Phil Burton and Richard Jenkins, who led whom? On the face of it, Phil was the originator of ideas, the creator of opportunities and the master of technique. He worked Rich hard, teaching him all he knew of literature and drama, pointing the way to great writers. He showed by rigorous elocution training how English vowels could hone down the Welsh accent and make yet more memorable an already splendid voice.

But Rich too was demanding. He knew that he had a short time in which to prove himself. His final school exams were just months away. In other schools, in other parts of the country those of his contemporaries who hankered after an acting career were already planning their applications to RADA.

The change in Rich in the first months of his life with Phil Burton was apparent to everyone. Intellectually and socially he acquired a confidence which quite overawed the younger members of the family. He dressed well, at Phil's expense, adopted manners which some miners might have thought a trifle fussy and talked fluently on topics outside the normal run of conversation.

Phil Burton had a document drawn up assigning him as Rich's legal guardian. When he first raised the subject with the family the word "adoption" was used but no one took kindly to this and, anyway, the point became academic when it was realised that Phil was too young to meet the legal requirements. A guardianship seemed not so drastic but, still, some justification was needed. It was not good enough to say that it merely formalised what already existed. In that case, why bother?

Phil tried hard to persuade Cis, because he knew the rest of the family would listen to her, and Hilda who was also influential but for a different reason. It was she who looked after Dadi Ni and it was Dadi Ni who had to make the final decision. Phil told the sisters that he would be in a much better position to go on helping Rich if he became the boy's guardian. For example, he could use his influence to secure for him a decent higher education. Richard Burton, the foster son of a middle-class teacher, was more likely to be accepted than Richard Jenkins, true son of a retired coalminer.

Ideas on post-school education were already well advanced. Phil had looked into a scheme whereby volunteers for officer rank in the RAF could, at government expense, spend a preliminary six months at Oxford. Then after doing their time in the forces they could return to university to complete their degrees.

"I have every confidence," said Phil, "that with my support and recommendation as his teacher *and* guardian, Richard will be chosen."

It all seemed reasonable enough at the time, though in retrospect I do wonder if the social distinctions were quite as vital as he suggested. I have to say that Rich himself was dubious on this point — he had no great wish to fit in with middle class conventions. But he did go along with Phil's plans for him. And he was not at all averse to changing his name. As he subsequently admitted to any journalist who cared to ask: "Phil Burton didn't adopt me, I adopted Phil Burton."

But this did not mean that Rich was eager to walk out on the family. On the contrary, his lack of sentimentality on matters of appearance contrasted with his enthusiasm for holding on to the reality of family ties. To me, his younger brother, he gave generously of his time and attention. In the air training corps, where I was two years behind him, he taught me the Morse code and the rudiments of navigation. I remember listening with rapt attention as he explained the theory of flight, making an apparently complex subject appear ludicrously simple. He stimulated my interest in rugby, encouraged me in my reading and taught me to be loyal to my own. After a welcome favour, he turned away my thanks. "We have to look after each other. You would do the same for me."

On that clause of the family creed Rich and Dadi Ni were as one. But our father was of a more conservative generation. However often the advantages of the Burton connection were explained to him, he could never quite reconcile himself to Rich assuming another name. To him, it was a renunciation of a birthright. And the Welsh miners of the old school were very strong on birthright.

A meeting was arranged between Dadi Ni and Phil Burton. It was to take place at Hilda's cottage in Pontrhydyfen where Dadi Ni could at least feel he was on home ground. Phil was to bring the documents which Dadi Ni had to sign to make the guardianship official. But when Phil arrived, Dadi Ni was not to be found. He had popped out for a drink at the Miners Arms and was last seen heading in the direction of the British Lion. Along the way were several other pubs where he might have stopped off.

So Dadi Ni and Phil Burton never did get to talk to each other. The legend, repeated in so many books and articles, that Rich was signed away by his father, is utterly untrue. Instead, in December 1943, the family as a whole decided that Richard Jenkins should become Richard Burton. All it needed to work this transformation was an ad in the local newspaper. For us it was a small thing. For Philip Burton, as much as for Rich, it was a first claim to fame.

CHAPTER
FOUR

My born-again brother sailed through his higher school certificate and was duly awarded a place at Exeter College, Oxford. His last stage performance as a schoolboy was in the unlikely role of Professor Henry Higgins in Shaw's *Pygmalion*. He tackled the part as an exercise in elocution for himself as well as for the hapless Eliza. There was a gap now before Rich could resume his studies. He needed a temporary job. But not any job would do. On the lookout for a suitable enterprise for his prodigy, Phil Burton spotted an ad in the *Western Mail* inviting young Welsh actors to audition for a new Emlyn Williams play called *The Druids Rest*. The engagement almost exactly matched the time Rich had to work before starting at University. More to the point it was difficult to think of a better launching pad for the professional career.

Not yet forty, Emlyn Williams, actor, writer and director was recognised as a famous son of Wales. Two of his plays, *Night Must Fall* and *The Corn is Green* were in the front rank of popular quality theatre, attracting queues at the box office and praise from the critics. Like Terence Rattigan, he had a sixth sense for what the audience would like. *The Druids Rest*, a modest little comedy, was expected to make a decent profit on tour, but not to achieve a lengthy West End run. The story was of a Welsh family — Mum, Dad and their two boys — who were persuaded by the youngest son, Tomas, that the lodger they harboured under their roof was in fact a notorious murderer on the run. Rich had his sights on the Tomas role but this went to Brynmor Thomas who was the right age, almost fourteen, and already known to Welsh audiences as a cute boy actor. But Rich's journey to Cardiff was not in vain. For a start he met Emlyn Williams and Daphne Rye, the formidable casting director for H. M. Tennent, the leading West End theatre management. Both thought Rich had the voice and the presence to make a good actor. They were also impressed by Phil Burton — a restrained, sensible man, thought Emlyn, quite a change from the usual run of over protective and over indulgent parents, who filled the audition rooms with their nervous chatter.

The combined impact of the young actor and his guardian ensured that Rich did not come away empty handed. He was offered the part of Glen, the older brother. It was a minor role calling for a lot of standing about listening to the other actors. But Rich was over the moon. It was his first chance to test himself against the expectations of an audience of total strangers who were in the theatre because they had paid to be there and not because they were friends of the family. Rehearsals started in London in early November, 1943. The war battered city was not the most comfortable place to be but with the odds on an Allied victory shortening every week, there was a mood of optimism which favoured all types of entertainment. This counted two ways for Rich — the prospect of a receptive audience for *The Druids Rest* and the promise of a right-roaring time when he was not working. With his stand in, a fellow Welshman by name of Stanley Baker, Rich explored the pubs, the clubs and the dance halls. They made an exuberant pair, eager to lose their innocence and surrounded by girls who were really only too pleased to help.

But mostly the time was spent on hard work with rehearsals continuing late into the evening, with maybe supper afterwards to talk on about the play and to dream about the wider shores of acting. It was during one of these late-night sessions that Rich introduced Emlyn Williams to the words of Dylan Thomas. They were walking through darkest Soho (the blackout was still enforced) when Rich launched into an imaginative poetry recital right there in the middle of the street. It was a declaration of love for Welsh melody which Dylan Thomas could write better than any other and Richard could speak better than most. Emlyn knew then that this would not be the last time he and Rich would work together; not if he could help it.

The Druids Rest opened in Liverpool at the Royal Court. The furthest stop was the Prince of Wales in Cardiff. This called for a family outing but none of us had a car and anyway, petrol was in short supply. The train was ruled out because there were no connections late at night. Eventually, Ivor persuaded our local doctor to let us have use of his big black Riley and enough petrol for the sixty mile return journey.

What a night to remember. That the play was a sell-out was entirely attributed by us to the crowd appeal of Richard Burton. We said as much to all our fellow playgoers who showed an interest and to quite a few who did not. I sat with Tom, Ivor and his wife Gwen, a few rows from the front of the dress circle. We spent what was left of our sweet ration on a small box of chocolates which Gwen held in her lap and passed round during the interval. I read the programme six times. In bold type dwarfing all else except the name of the play was a warning of what to do in the event of an air raid. The nearest shelter, I recall, was in Wood Street. But I also remember thinking it would take more than a few German bombs to get the Jenkins family out of the theatre in the middle of the performance.

For those of us who were there for partisan reasons, the play was something of a confusion. By concentrating so hard on Rich, who had the least demanding role in the entire production, we lost track of what else was going on. We were nervous too. I suppose that stage fright is a common enough experience but surely not for the audience. We sat with hands clenched willing Rich not to forget a word or fluff a line.

After the show we found our way backstage for a small celebration. When Rich came over to give Cis a great big hug and kiss, the tears of joy and pride rolled down her cheeks. I met Stanley Baker who, responding politely to the question of a none too sophisticated man of the theatre, said that, yes, he would quite like to be an actor and that, no, he did not intend to be Rich's stand in for the rest of his career.

In the second week of January the play transferred to Swansea. A record family excursion was led by Dadi Ni whose experience of the theatre was slight but who appreciated, as he said, a good story. That he sat still throughout and not once asked the way to the bar suggested he was not disappointed. Then for Rich, it was off to London again, this time for the opening of *The Druids Rest* at the St Martin's Theatre off Shaftesbury Avenue. Just down the road at the Empire Leicester

Square, an eleven-year-old Elizabeth Taylor was making her debut in a weepie called *Lassie Come Home*.

The notices for *The Druids Rest* were at best lukewarm. One critic said it was less of a play than a number of amusing sketches of the Welsh character. Everyone agreed that Brynmor Thomas stole the show and there were a few kind words for the stars — Michael Shepley, who specialised in peppery colonel types (he once described himself as the last of the gentlemen actors) and Gladys Henson, the archetypal working class housewife. Rich had to be consoled by a paragraph in the *New Statesman* where he was described as showing "exceptional ability" in his struggle to play "a wretched part". There was praise too from Daphne Rye and her boss at H. M. Tennent, Hugh "Binkie' Beaumont, whose eye for a handsome young actor was not entirely ruled by hedonism.

The Druids Rest was taken off after two months. Before coming home, Rich saw Robert Helpmann's *Hamlet* at the New Theatre but missed out on the Gielgud version which opened at the Haymarket later in the year. By then he too was in Shakespeare — with the Oxford University Drama Society.

In the last month before Oxford, Rich did another radio play for Phil Burton, now a part-time contract producer for the BBC Wales. Rich was cast in the title role of Dic Penderym, a hero of the early Welsh labour movement who in addition to his other misfortunes (he was unjustly accused of murdering a policeman) had a bad stammer which the actor was called upon to reproduce. The day after the broadcast, Cis's daughter Marian was accosted in the street by a friend. "I heard your Rich on the wireless," said the girl. "Very good he was.

But with a stammer like that" (she sucked in her breath) "he can't have much of a future in the theatre."

Six months at Oxford was not long enough for Rich to achieve all that he wanted. So he took it at a rush, packing activity into all hours of the day and most of the night. If his exertions were largely outside the formal curriculum, this suited his RAF sponsors who were looking to their trainee officers to acquire social maturity more than academic excellence. But Rich was ahead of them. What with Phil Burton's tuition and his acting experience he was already possessed of enough maturity for a forty-year-old. Free from the doubts and inhibitions which usually afflict a teenager as he emerges into the wide world, Rich pursued his interests with single-minded determination.

The first objective was to gain a foothold in the Drama Society. In a sense this was easier than he could have imagined because his tutor, Nevill Coghill, was also director of OUDS. Coghill was a divided character. On one side was the brilliant teacher whose proudest work was to be a bestseller translation into modern English of Chaucer's *Canterbury Tales*. On the other side was the man of the theatre. Happy memories of his childhood games of charades spilled over into his adult life when the excitement of one of the great challenges, holding the attention of a live audience for two hours or more, was satisfied by staging high-calibre student productions. He was much respected in the professional theatre and later collaborated on a long running musical of the *Canterbury Tales*. But he never strayed so far towards the West End as to cut loose from academia.

Coghill was immediately impressed by Rich who, thanks to Phil Burton, knew the power of great literature.

And he had the voice to match the words, as the professor discovered at their first meeting when Rich launched into Hamlet's famous soliloquy.

"I want to act," explained Rich.

His tutor made encouraging noises.

"No I mean here, at Oxford. I want to act with the Drama Society."

It was the moment for restraint. "I don't see how that is possible. You are here for just six months. In that time we have only one production which is already cast and into rehearsals."

"You've cast every part?"

"Every part, I'm afraid."

Rich went away disappointed. But by their next meeting Professor Coghill had thought of a consolation prize. "Why not understudy? I know it's not like the real thing but at least you would be involved."

The play was *Measure for Measure*, one of Shakespeare's least successful comedies. Intriguingly, Emlyn Williams had tried and failed to bring it to life in an Old Vic production in 1937. Now, Rich went for the Williams role, that of the sanctimonious Angelo, master of Vienna, who condemns a man to death for the crime of lechery only to fall victim to the same temptations. His rival for the part, because from the very beginning this is how Rich saw him, was Halham Fordham who, post university, was to make a fine reputation as a radio actor.

Rich took to understudying in a way that was unsettling for his principal. By putting up suggestions as to how the role should be played, he invited comparisons that favoured his own interpretation. This and the constant enquiries as to the state of Halham Fordham's health brought an unaccustomed tension to what, after all, was an amateur production. Years on, Rich created some highly romanticised stories of how he got to play his first Shakespearian role. In one version Halham Fordham was taken ill on the first night just before curtain up: in another the unfortunate actor broke down in dismay when he realised he would not aspire to the Burton heights. Reality was a call up paper. Halham Fordham went off to fight the Germans leaving Rich to conquer the stage.

Playing in the open air, in and among the cloisters, Rich needed all his energy and passion to bring Angelo to life. Once, he overdid it. When Angelo comes to realise his quandary he suffers an agony of indecision:

"What dost thou, or what art thou, Angelo? Dost thou desire her foully for those things that make her good? Oh, let her brother live! Thieves for their robbery have authority when judges steal themselves."

At this point Rich cracked his fist against an ancient pillar which retaliated by shooting a stone splinter into his eye. When first I heard this story I was properly sympathetic but with repetition and embellishment ("I'm telling you Graham, it was a lump of rock as big as my hand") I descended to sarcasm. ("So you were blinded for the rest of the performance were you? That must have been very confusing for the other actors.")

Only brief notices of *Measure for Measure* appeared in the quality nationals but there were fulsome reviews in magazines favoured by the Oxford establishment such as *The Tatler* and *Horse and Hound*. At Nevill Coghill's invitation, Binkie Beaumont turned up and stayed long enough to congratulate Rich. "If after the war, you still want to be a professional actor," he told him, "come and see me. We should be able to find you something."

Another guest was Phil Burton who was enjoying his own run of success with the BBC. Having accepted an offer to take up a permanent job as a drama producer he was in the process of moving to Cardiff. Maybe with both in a state of high excitement they expected too much of the evening. Or perhaps Phil was heavy-handed in his detailed criticism of Rich's performance. In any event, there was some tension between them which led Rich to cut short their dinner and go on alone to a student party.

It was insensitive of Rich but it was symptomatic of his refusal to be held to account — by anyone. In the company of friends, Rich was generous in his praise of Phil Burton who, he maintained, was a superb director. He even tried to involve him in student productions. But he did not take kindly to the suggestions that he might in any way be dependent on the man he called father.

Of course it was out of the question that any of Rich's true family should visit him in Oxford. The indulgence would have been as excessive as it was inappropriate. We acknowledged, more readily than Phil Burton I believe, that like every youngster Rich needed the chance to find his own way. But there is no denying, social embarrassment played a part. None of us then would have felt comfortable in the tight little world of university manners. At the same time we feared that Rich might choose to disregard the family. It was a natural but unjustified anxiety. True, Rich did play the Phil Burton card when he wanted to impress the public school contingent but with those who were closest to him he never made any attempt to disguise his origins. Friends like Tim Hardy, better known as the actor Robert Hardy, who came from a prosperous, middle class background, knew all about us before we had even heard his name.

Rich's skill in playing the social conventions was more apparent in his eagerness to adapt to the interests of his companions. When he was with Tim Hardy, for whom rugby held no appeal, the talk was of great plays and the roles they were planning for themselves. But in the rugby pubs, with his own team, the University Second XV, known as the Greyhounds, it was all raucous songs and ribald stories. Rich liked to be liked.

Departure from Oxford to take up full time residence with the RAF was an occasion of great heart searching. Like everyone else on the brief journey into higher education, Rich pledged to return to Oxford after the war. For the rest of his life he regretted not sticking to his word.

But while there was no degree or any other formal recognition of achievement, he did not come away entirely empty-handed. Nevill Coghill predicted that Rich would be a successful, maybe even a great actor. For his private records, as Rich later discovered, his tutor was yet more fulsome. "This boy is a genius," he wrote, adding later, "I have had only two men of genius to teach — W. H. Auden and Richard Burton. When they happen one cannot mistake them."

After two short hops to the West Country and to Lancashire, Rich was posted to Winnipeg in Canada. If it was not exactly the centre of the war zone, remember, the worst of the fighting was over. Rich saw his period in uniform merely as an exercise in marking time. He would not be long for civvy street. But it was not as simple as that. International tensions in peace time meant that the numbers in the British forces had to be kept up.

This was achieved by adopting a policy of last in, last out. Rich had to wait nearly three years, until November 1947, for his freedom.

For the most part he kept his distance from forces' entertainment. Occupying his skills as a raconteur to gather a crowd in a pub was one thing but high jinks on stage in the tatty productions favoured by the ENSA (Entertainment National Service Association) were not to his liking. He was at one with the disgruntled trooper who jumped on stage at the end of an ENSA play shouting, "Three cheers for the audience".

Marking time for Rich was reading, rugby and riotous behaviour — usually in that order. When he left the RAF Rich was word perfect in all of the great Shakespearian roles. He was also a promising wing-forward. So much was declared by Bleddyn Williams who was soon to reach the glorious heights of a Cardiff and Wales and British Lions centre-three-quarter. With another rugby friend Dai, or Dinger Evans, a rock of a man, Rich toured the local bars. I cannot imagine that the landlords regarded them as a welcome sight. What profits they created in the consumption of beer they wiped out in damage to property and people. Fights with servicemen who were not RAF, or not Welsh, or even on occasion, not from the same part of Wales were the cause of frequent detentions. But Rich enjoyed his reputation as a jovial mixer. He had long since given up any idea of trying for a commission.

Serious theatre was a world away. He enjoyed talking about it to the interested friends like Mick Misell who had a hankering to act (and one day would come into his own as Warren Mitchell). And when he returned to Britain in late 1945 he was quick to renew contact with Tim Hardy whose enquiring mind was a spur to ambition. But the little I saw of Rich at this period made me think that, as an actor, he had lost his sense of purpose.

He told me about a fantastic hitchhike from Winnipeg to New York, one thousand miles on less than two dollars. "It was easy in uniform," he told me. "Every motorist thought he owed us something for helping to win the war."

American hospitality carried him along in New York. There were parties galore and an abundance of generous hearted girls eager to show him the city, and a lot else besides. As Rich talked, my teenage imagination, already made hyperactive by a chance adventure in the back row of the cinema, nearly cracked under the strain.

"And what about Broadway?"

"Broadway?"

"Yes, what about the theatres?"

Notwithstanding Rich's lavish descriptions of the good life I had assumed that it was the chance to see good acting which had principally attracted him to New York. But not a bit of it.

"Oh I got some free tickets. I went to see *Oklahoma*."

A light musical? Nothing else? Surely this was not the same Rich who had impressed Emlyn Williams and Nevill Coghill with his single minded devotion to the classics.

If I was surprised, Phil Burton was worried. He could see his prize slipping away from his grasp. When Rich had settled into his penultimate posting at Bircham Newton, in the remotest part of Norfolk, Phil made strenuous efforts to restore his protegé to the front rank of radio drama. But Cardiff, where Phil's influence was greatest, was too far from RAF Docking for the lifeline to hold for very long.

Fortunately, Rich had other friends who wanted him to succeed. In early 1947 Emlyn Williams asked him to play Morgan Evans in his television production of *The Corn is Green*. This was interesting on two counts. As the study of a young Welshman of poor background marked out for a brilliant career by a dedicated teacher, *The Corn is Green* had an obvious biographical significance for Rich as well as for the author. That the play was to be performed live on television was an added inducement.

Though still in its infancy and somewhat retarded by a wartime ban on output, BBC television was eager to test its appeal against other forms of popular entertainment. But confined to the studio with static cameras and set, it was natural for television drama producers to look to the stage for their inspiration. Plays which had done well in London were the first choice for adaptation to the small screen. At the same time stage actors who had to know all their lines on opening night were more likely to get work on live television than film actors who could mug up on their parts from day to day.

Though over-age for the part, Rich was one of the few actors around who had the experience and the ability to play Morgan Evans on television. He grabbed the chance to do something new and exciting. What he made of it remains a matter of conjecture. There were very few television sets in those days, certainly in our part of the country, and I have yet to come across anyone out of the potential audience of several thousand who actually saw the play. But the effect on Rich was undeniable. He was back in business and he was enjoying every minute of it.

He was also in love. The cause was a vivacious young lady who shared his television debut. Her name was Eleanor Summerfield. An independent spirit of great character, as her subsequent career as an actress and comedienne was to prove, she was attracted to Rich without allowing herself to be overwhelmed by him. After *The Corn is Green*, Eleanor went on tour with a company which seemed to take perverse delight in putting the greatest possible distance between her and Rich. He used up his quota of weekend passes hitchhiking to far flung outposts of the theatre circuit. Occasionally he wrote home.

"He'll not be here for Christmas," reported Cis. "He says he's spending his leave in Scotland. What do you think that means?"

Her brothers knew very well what it meant but thought it polite to remain silent.

"He's twenty-one," said Ivor. "He's old enough to look after himself."

The affair lasted eight months. Rich never told me why it ended but I suspect that Eleanor was too self-willed to make an ideal partner for Rich at this period in his life. Having recovered his ambition he, like all successful actors, wanted all the attention focused on him. Eleanor was not prepared for that. Rich had to wait another eighteen months for someone who was.

CHAPTER
FIVE

Within hours of his release from the military, Rich joined the queue of young hopefuls outside the offices of H. M. Tennent. It was, he told me, a spur of the moment decision. Having handed in his kit, and been given a rail warrant to take him home to Wales, he realised he had to change trains in London. Why not take the opportunity, he reasoned, to find out if Binkie Beaumont remembered him from Oxford days? He did and, more to the point, so did Daphne Rye who immediately offered to sign up Rich at ten pounds a week (a fortune for anyone used to RAF pay). As events were to show, she was also prepared to help his career in other ways. It was as if she and her boss, who could be equally attentive, were in friendly rivalry for the attentions of the curiously handsome young actor. I say "curiously" because Rich was not at all in the mould of the traditional matinee idol. There was nothing of the finely chiselled profile so beloved by the stage photographers. Rather, he had a puggish look — tough but at the same time warm and inviting. "The face of a boxing poet," said Emlyn Williams.

It was a first impression which could puzzle and disarm the competition. Richard Leech, also a contract player with Tennent who was to be a great friend, remembers the first time he set eyes on the much heralded discovery from the valleys.

"When he came in I thought, who is this? He's not

an actor. He's just a squat Welsh rugby player. I won't have any trouble here. But I was wrong. Oh boy, was I wrong."

Tennent's unwillingness to pay ready money extinguished any dream Rich had of returning to Oxford. Years on when he was disillusioned with blockbuster movies and disgusted with the inanities of the publicity circuit, he spoke lovingly of what he imagined he had missed. But at the time he poured scorn on Tim Hardy who went back to finish his degree, and on Warren Mitchell who won a place at the Royal Academy of Dramatic Art.

The family did not quite know what to think. The high value put on education caused regret for the opportunities Rich was passing up. But there was respect for his earning power.

"Ten quid a week, is ten quid a week, there's no denying it," said Ivor in the tautology of bar room conversation. "And he gets it whether he's working or not." For miners who had laboured a lifetime for less it sounded like a dream come true.

Rich's first Tennent role was little more than a walk on in an inconsequential play called *Castle Anna* at the Lyric, Hammersmith. But he also understudied the lead which gave him the chance in rehearsals to show what he could do. I missed this and his next play, *Dark Summer*, which went on tour in early 1948, because I was taking my turn in the forces, as a naval rating in the Far East. But I was home in time for the opening of Rich's first film, *The Last Days of Dolwyn*.

This was an Emlyn Williams project in every sense. He was the writer, director and the star with the meatiest role, that of an upstart bureaucrat who returns to Wales to execute a scheme to flood his native valley to make a reservoir. Out to thwart his plans is an old lady, played by Edith Evans, and her foster son, Gareth, who in the last scene accidentally kills the villain. Rich was cast as Gareth.

Viewed today, it must be said that Emlyn Williams let his sense of melodrama run away with him. *The Last Days of Dolwyn* did not measure up to Carol Reed's *The Fallen Idol* or *The Third Man* or Anthony Asquith's *The Winslow Boy*, all of which were made by London Films at about this time. But it brought in the audiences in Britain and in the States where, as *Woman of Dolwyn*, it appealed to the stereotyped image of the Welsh as a race of starry-eyed sentimentalists.

For Rich, *The Last Days of Dolwyn* was the luckiest of breaks, though as his acting friends observed, he behaved as if it were his due. The fact was that after six months on a Tennent salary he was impatient for action. Everybody told him he was good, so why could he not have the opportunity to show it? A camera test for a minor role in a film yet to be guaranteed a production date, was not what he had in mind. Rich was still very much a man of the theatre. The film business was a grey area for him. He did not doubt that he could make an impact on the screen, but was it worth the effort? He never did get to answer the question.

Emlyn Williams sought to allay his fears. The camera test was not the usual chaotic affair overseen by trainees. The legendary Otto Heller, director of photography on the film, was there alongside the director who gave Rich careful instructions on what to do and how to do it. A few days later, Emlyn Williams sent a telegram to the provincial theatre where Rich was appearing in *Dark Summer*. It read, "You have won the scholarship", a quote from *The Corn is Green* which needed no interpretation.

Rich was in. But still he did not realise what he was into. The backer for *The Last Days of Dolwyn* was Sir Alexander Korda, the great impresario of the British film industry and the only film maker on this side of the Atlantic who understood the American market. For part of the war, he had headed the British end of the MGM operation and though now running his own studios at Shepperton, he kept up his links with the US including a valuable distribution arrangement with Twentieth Century-Fox. Korda did things the American way which included generous budgets (he was often accused of extravagance) and big publicity billings for his actors. For the first time, the press was encouraged to show an interest in Richard Burton. Who was he? What did he want to do with his life?

Except in the barest detail Rich seemed unable to decide the answers to these questions. Take background. He was from the South Wales mining community, of that there was no doubt. But thereafter he could be working class and proud of it, or (courtesy of Phil Burton) middle class and equally proud of it. It all depended on the circumstances of the interview and what he thought the journalist wanted to hear.

In the early days, he tended to give Phil Burton more than his due asserting, for instance, that a formal adoption order had been agreed when he was only twelve. In fact, there was no adoption order and Rich was well past his seventeenth birthday when he moved in with his guardian. The glorification of Phil Burton meant a corresponding downgrading of the family. It was said that Rich spent his early years in penury, which was totally untrue, or that Dadi Ni was too fond of the booze to know what was going on. No one could deny that our father was a keen supporter of the local brewery, but then, it was difficult to find a miner who was anything else. But he was never roaring drunk and never lost control of his temper as Rich and Ivor were liable to do. Even when an overwrought friend pushed Dadi Ni into the canal, he emerged in a forgiving mood. If the same thing had happened to Rich he would not have felt peace of mind until he had flung the other man off the top of the viaduct.

The worst that could be said of Dadi Ni's drinking is that he used it as an excuse for avoiding unpleasant decisions. This is far short of the reports, often started by Rich in his jokiest revelations, of having to carry the old man home from the pub or of him finishing a session by sliding under the table.

No doubt it is unfair to blame Rich for all the misinformation and downright lies about the family which rolled off the presses over the years. But, at the same time, I cannot entirely blame the press. As Emlyn Williams often said to Richard: "You certainly gave them plenty of copy."

By the standards of Richard Burton's Hollywood debut, now a mere three years ahead, the promotion associated with his appearance in *The Last Days of Dolwyn* was modest indeed. But he was flattered by the attention of Korda's publicists who were far more adventurous than their colleagues in the theatre. Instead of relying on the critics for their press coverage they went out to create news and feature articles. Even before the film was released, Bill O'Bryen, casting director, nominated Rich as one of the ten likeliest stars of the future. For the record the other nine were: Jack Hawkins, Norman Wooland, Michael Gough, Jack Watling, Moira Lister, Honor Blackman, Sarah Churchill, Faith Brook and Rona Anderson.

I was back in Britain for the première of *The Last Days of Dolwyn*. It was an excuse for another family outing to Cardiff. Even to my untrained eye, Rich had what they called "screen presence". In a secondary role he held the attention wonderfully against such practised scene stealers as Edith Evans and Emlyn Williams. But for me seeing him on the screen larger than life was less of a surprise than hearing him sing. He had to get through a Welsh love ballad, "Ar Lan Y Mor", which was not at all his style of music. I heard he needed several takes to get it right but he remembered the words for ever afterwards. When I last heard him singing it, it was in duet with Elizabeth Taylor who adopted the song as her Welsh party piece.

Rich's leave of absence from Tennent to film *The Last Days of Dolwyn* was extended a month to allow him to play his most challenging theatre role to date — that of Constantine in *The Seagull*. For this opportunity he had to thank the actor and director Clifford Evans, who had persuaded the Arts Council to support a new season of fortnightly repertory at Swansea's Grand Theatre. Rich was heavily feted by the Welsh papers as a national celebrity. But unlike the London papers which quickly caught on to the mischief in Richard Burton, our own press portrayed him as a high-minded young man who spent his free time reading scripts and contemplating his next contribution to the living arts. Maybe on home ground Rich was more cautious about what he said to reporters but, with hindsight, his unnatural reserve probably had more to do with the fact that he was in love again — and did not yet want to admit it.

The girl was Sybil Williams, she was Welsh, nineteen and an actress who had played a bit part in *The Last Days of Dolwyn*. That much we were allowed to know before Rich returned to London. A few days later, on 5 February 1949, he sent a telegram: "Married this morning. Pity Wales."

The second sentence was not, as I first thought, a lament for all the single girls in the kingdom who now had to make do with second best, but a genuine cry from the heart for the Welsh XV who had unexpectedly lost against Scotland at Murrayfield.

Sybil and Rich had a lot in common. She too was from South Wales; she too had been brought up by an older sister, both her parents having died young. Much of her early life was in Northampton but her roots were in the Rhondda Valley where her father had been a pit manager. Like Rich, Sybil took to acting as an escape from the nine to five routine. She went to the London Academy of Music and Dramatic Art. But there the parallel ended for, whatever her qualities, Sybil was not a great actress. That she landed a bit part in *The Last Days of Dolwyn* was more a tribute to Emlyn Williams's generosity than to her raw talent. Yet, when she was herself, her personality sparkled. Sybil was the sort of person who would liven up a gathering just by walking in the door. She was ever cheerful, sympathetic and loyal. Add to this a period beauty which favoured the wholesome, good time girl and it was hardly surprising that Rich was hooked.

Though he never said as much, at least not to me, I feel certain that for Rich, marriage was a quick dash for security. Caught up in the swirl of celebrity games he needed a fixed point, a base where he could put up the shutters and feel secure. Just like Cis before her, Sybil was the ideal homemaker.

There was only one small problem. They had nowhere to start a home. This time the guardian angel in Rich's life (an overworked benefactor if ever there was one) materialised in the shape of Daphne Rye. At a nominal rent, she let the couple a small furnished flat at the top of her house in the Fulham Road. For good measure she threw in a champagne reception.

Chelsea in the fifties was the place to be for a rising young actor. Famous names of the profession were well represented in the smart Georgian and Victorian terraces. Just down the road from the Burtons lived the Williamses, Emlyn and Molly with their children Alan and Brook. In the belief that it was time for Rich to settle down, Emlyn had encouraged the relationship with Sybil. Now he was happy to use his influence to introduce Rich to powerful friends in the theatre and film. There were parties galore. They were great fun, if not always as useful as Rich hoped. He was still at the stage when he was prepared to sit at the feet of the great to hear words of wisdom. So often he was disappointed.

On the evening he met Terence Rattigan, the writer was seated room centre surrounded by young admirers. Rich was propelled forward by his host and introduced to him. Rattigan extended a gentle hand. "I was just saying," he confided to Rich who was anticipating a gem on stage technique, "I was just saying, when I was at Oxford I was quite the prettiest thing of my year."

The Rattigan connection was a disappointment in another context. In March 1949 Rich landed a small role in a new Rattigan play, *Adventure Story*, about Alexander the Great. The lead was Paul Scofield. Three years older than Rich and already a veteran of Stratford, he was well established in the public mind as one of the most exciting actors of his generation. For Rich, the temptation to challenge and thus overact in what was essentially a submissive role was irresistible. After three days' rehearsal he was summarily replaced by Robert Flemying, a quieter and more amenable actor, who, as it happened, was also blessed with a wonderfully deep, resonant voice.

Rich was furious, the more so because he genuinely admired Scofield and badly wanted to share success with him. He was angry too because he knew he was at fault. After a few drinks he would even admit the fact, though formally his excuse was that he was too young to play Paul Scofield's older brother. When, in all innocence, I suggested that he might have used heavier make-up I was rewarded by an icy silence.

Fortunately for Rich there were early compensations which soon wiped clean the memory of his humbling experience. His second film, *Now Barabbas . . .*, was an adaptation of a William Douglas Home play, his third for the West End and the first to be counted a success. The theme (uncharacteristically for a writer more at home with light comedy) was the destructive force of prison life on inmates and workers alike. Rich played an IRA saboteur, so convincingly as to come out best in the reviews, which were otherwise politely dismissive of the efforts of a distinguished cast led by Cedric Hardwicke. The trouble with the film was that it turned out to be such a lukewarm version of the play, which had some painful things to say about the inhumanity of prison life.

The theatre of the forties was not all French windows and swinging tennis racquets.

Praise for his work on the film set raised the standing of Richard Burton as a Tennent contract player. Soon after his departure from *Adventure Story*, Rich was signed up for the John Gielgud production of Christopher Fry's verse drama *The Lady's not for Burning*. With hindsight it is easy to see this as the chance of a lifetime. But in fairness to Rich, who to begin with was thoroughly dismissive of the entire project, the golden prospects were not immediately apparent. Fry was new to the West End where verse drama, unless it was by T. S. Eliot, was generally assumed to be commercially unviable. As star and co-director, Gielgud was the natural choice to give the play a distinctive style; who better to handle the author's verbal pyrotechnics? But this was a period when the Gielgud magic was thought to be fading. His name alone was no longer a guarantee of success.

Still, the role was bigger than any previously offered him and Binkie Beaumont was so enthusiastic on the actor's behalf, Rich thought it was about time he put in for a rise. Offered £15 a week he pressed for £20. Finally Beaumont compromised — £17.10s. Delighted with his negotiating skills Rich splashed out on a taxi all the way back to Fulham Crescent. As he got out he met Emlyn Williams who was the first to hear of the Burton triumph. He was not impressed.

"Go back and ask for £30," he ordered.

With enormous reluctance Rich did as he was told, pausing on the way to build up his courage in the only way he knew. The interview was long and heated but Beaumont gave way. As Rich left his manager fired a parting shot, "I suppose that old Welsh pit pony put you up to this."

The Lady's not for Burning was a triumph. The critics were full of praise for a play in which author and actors revelled in the joy of imaginative language. "An exciting night out for the brain" was a front-of-house review quote which, for once, accurately depicted the consensus view. Christopher Fry was proclaimed theatre personality of the year. Everybody in the cast had their share of praise though given the range of talent on parade, Rich was delighted to be hailed, yet again, as "an exciting new discovery". There was a scene in which all he had to do was to scrub the floor while John Gielgud and his co-star, Pamela Brown, for whom the play was specially written, worked with the dialogue. Rich was said by one critic to perform this dramatic task "convincingly". "So convincingly," added John Gielgud, "he attracted all the attention. The audience couldn't take their eyes off him."

The company was an extraordinary mix of ages with the senior level represented by Harcourt Williams, Eliot Makeham and Esme Percy, all in their seventies, and the junior by Claire Bloom, then just seventeen. Of Rich's generation were Peter Bull, who looked like a friendly version of his own name, and Richard Leech. Both liked playing jokes. A week before opening Peter Bull asked Rich if he had seen his front-of-house picture. Rich found himself looking at a middle aged stranger wearing a beret at a jaunty angle. The picture stayed put for the first month. So often was a story told of Esme Percy losing his glass eye, that he felt compelled to put out a statement that he was not inclined to divert the audience's attention by rolling a marble across the stage.

It was in rehearsal for *The Lady's not for Burning* that John Gielgud congratulated Rich on his radio portrayal of Shakespeare's Henry V. "So talented," he murmured. Rich was delighted. "And so like dear Larry," added Gielgud in one of his deflating asides.

Rich treasured the back-handed compliment. "It makes a better story. If he'd just said 'Well Done', there wouldn't be anything to tell."

The BBC *Henry V* was another project which, in the long-running mood of ill temper following his dismissal from *Adventure Story*, Rich was inclined to reject as an unworthy crumb of comfort. It originated with Frank Hauser, then a young director with radio drama who was commissioned to produce a celebratory offering for Shakespeare's birthday. Having chosen to present *Henry V*, albeit in a shortened version, it was simply a question of finding a suitably commanding voice to fill the leading role. Re-enter Tim Hardy who knew Frank Hauser from post war Oxford when both were finishing their degrees. He set up a meeting between Frank and Rich.

It was a boisterous evening with the three of them arguing like mad about how best to convey Shakespeare to a living-room audience. With the Rattigan lost opportunity fresh in his mind, Rich was over sensitive to criticism and angrily dismissed any opinion which did not coincide with his own. As the dinner progressed and the drinks bill lengthened Rich got louder and more aggressive. Frank Hauser might reasonably have called a stop there and then but, a Cardiff man himself, he knew a thing or two about the contentious Welsh and was not deterred. After departing the restaurant (to the plain delight of the other patrons) they collected Sybil from the Prince of Wales Theatre, where she was an assistant stage manager, and went on to the Burton flat to continue their debate.

"It was difficult," said Frank Hauser, "not to be won over by the Burton personality. It was a curious mixture of aggression and collusion. He was his own man and stood up for what he believed, which you couldn't help but admire. Yet at the same time he made you feel that if anyone was going to influence him it would be you alone — that you above all were so fascinating and stimulating, as to be worth his attention."

That Rich was not a beginner in radio weighed heavily in his favour. The rigorous apprenticeship with Phil Burton had taught him how to cope with the limitations of the sound studio such as the static mike. To shout a speech, as Shakespearian kings were wont to do, usually required the actor to stand well back from the mike. If he retreated too far he was liable to sound as if he were yodelling from a mountain top. Rich could magnify his voice without hollering, a skill which made his perform-ance all the more convincing.

Still, it was a big role to entrust to a relative newcomer and it was a tribute to Frank Hauser's powers of per-suasion that his BBC seniors allowed him to get away with it. The gamble paid off. *Henry V* was transmitted to an appreciative audience. What adverse criticism there was fastened on the BBC efforts to squeeze a quart into a pint pot — three hours of stage drama into a mere ninety minutes.

The West End run of *The Lady's not for Burning* brought a succession of Welsh visitors to London. I have to say that the play was not well liked by many of us because, for all its cleverness, it failed to grab the emotions. The comedy of manners had an underlying tension but it was difficult to work up any interest in the leading characters or in what happened to them. But it was Rich, not the play, we really came to see. And after Rich, who did all that his fan club could expect of him, including handing out drinks as if there was no tomorrow, we were eager to meet Sybil.

That she was the ideal choice for Rich no one had any doubt. She was pretty and astute and amusing and she knew how to handle him. Whether Rich knew how to handle Sybil was another matter. When he leaned heavily on her loyalty and patience in small matters, like turning up late at a restaurant or not turning up at all, we could not help wondering if sometimes he made more serious demands on her sensitivity.

Maybe it is always the same with successful people. Dedication to winning precludes many of the ordinary domestic civilities. Certainly Rich showed all the signs of a man working to get to the top. His workload was prodigious. When he was not at the theatre performing or rehearsing, he was to be found at Broadcasting House recording another play or at the film studios where he was now pretty well constantly in demand. For weeks on end his working day would begin at seven in the make-up room at Pinewood and end at ten-thirty as the audience filed out of the Globe Theatre. I know that stories abound of Rich's extra-marital affairs but, while I am the last to claim that fidelity was his strongest suit, I do wish that those who profess such close knowledge of his romantic exploits would explain where he found the time to satisfy so many demands.

Once or twice Rich and Sybil spent weekends with

the family. The local feeling was that they made the ideal couple, not at all spoilt by success. Rich responded cheerfully to the inevitable ribbing from friends and neighbours who had known him since childhood. One old boy who called him Douglas Fairbanks and thought he was cracking the most hilarious joke of all time, repeated the line often enough to be insulting. But Rich took it all in good part. He went to the same pubs he had known as a boy, sat talking in the same front rooms and went with the same crowd to the Saturday match. When he and Sybil were the guests of honour at a dinner dance in Margam, he told his hosts that "since he did not own a dinner jacket they would have to accept him in an ordinary suit". This went down well with those who were not invited. "He's genuine enough is our Rich," they told each other.

Professionally, Rich could do no wrong. His films were low budget affairs destined for screening as second feature. But so consistently good were his reviews that Korda put him under contract at a princely £100 a week. True to his central casting image as an actor of many accents, he played successively a Liverpudlian sailor, a Norwegian fighter pilot and a Romany smuggler. The first of these films, a docklands saga called *Waterfront*, was directed by a youthful Michael Anderson, who was just starting out on a career which would encompass *The Dam Busters* and Mike Todd's *Round the World in Eighty Days*. But *Waterfront*, his first solo effort, was not a success. What should have been an exciting adventure somehow turned out as a dreary melodrama which even Robert Newton at his villainous best could not save.

In *The Woman with No Name*, Rich had the chance to play opposite Phyllis Calvert, one of the most popular

British stars of the period. Their on-screen love affair was brief (Rich's character was killed off in the first reel) but memorable, not least for Cis who flooded out a Cardiff cinema with her tears. When Rich rang the following day to find out how she liked the film, Cis told him she had not cried so much in years.

"I'm sorry about that," said Rich assuming the worst.

"Yes," she sighed, "it was lovely."

Rich's next film appearance was in a light comedy which he hated. *Green Grow the Rushes*, an everyday story of smuggling folk, was not his style. A blatant attempt to cash in on the popularity of *Whisky Galore* (before its rapid descent into oblivion the film was actually renamed *Brandy Ashore*), everyone involved in the project suffered from an excess of good intentions. The money was put up by the film technicians' union, the ACT, whose members were made nervous by the apparent failure of the British film industry to fight on two flanks — against Hollywood on one side and BBC television on the other. It was a sign of the times that cinema attendance was dipping and famous studios were being sold off for development or commercial television. *Green Grow the Rushes* did nothing to reverse the trend. But for one rising young actor, it did help to concentrate his thoughts on his long term future. For the real money it looked very much as if America was the place to be.

Meanwhile, the Burton income was of a size to bring a smile to the face of his bank manager. Each film made him at least a thousand pounds for, at most, six weeks' work. I was staying with Rich when the cheque for *Green Grow the Rushes* was delivered. It was two thousand pounds. As a recruit to local government on three hundred a year with luncheon vouchers, I was wide eyed with admiration.

In early 1950 Rich and Sybil moved out of Daphne Rye's apartment into a house of their own. The Hampstead address — 6 Lyndhurst Road — sounded very grand but in fact, it was a bomb damaged property with only one habitable floor. The builders were told to start on the roof and then work their way down. Rich would probably have paid for the entire renovation out of his own pocket but Sybil was smart enough to know that there were generous grants for war repairs. Thanks to her, they created a very presentable home at modest cost. But they were not there long enough to enjoy it. Within a year they had decided to build a new house which became 10 Squire's Mount, also in Hampstead. Before it was half finished, Rich had departed for New York to appear with John Gielgud in the Broadway production of *The Lady's not for Burning*.

The offer came through when Rich was appearing in another Christopher Fry play, *The Boy with a Cart*, at the Lyric, Hammersmith. Written twelve years earlier for a Sussex Festival, this simple mystery play might never have got to London had it not been for the success of *The Lady's not for Burning*. When Gielgud had to withdraw from that play, so in effect closing it, to join Anthony Quayle for a Stratford season, he urged Rich to consider *The Boy with a Cart* as his next stage undertaking. If he, Rich, could persuade Binkie Beaumont to put up the money, Gielgud was prepared to come in as director.

It was a heaven-sent opportunity for Rich who recognised the value of playing his first stage lead under the guidance of one of the theatrical greats. But not for the first time the problem was in making the figures add up to a sensible business proposition. By no stretch of imagination could the play qualify for Shaftesbury Avenue. The prospective audience was limited to the intellectual side of the cultural establishment which reduced the likely box office take from the thousands to hundreds. If the prospect was to break even, a short run at a theatre outside the West End was called for. The Lyric was ideal. Moreover, it was available. *The Boy with the Cart* was booked in for six weeks.

I was there for the opening night and for the emotional scenes backstage after the final curtain. For the first time Rich felt like a star and he loved it. John Gielgud told him he had just given one of the most delightful performances he had ever seen in the theatre. Christopher Fry thought the part could not be better played. The feelings of gratitude were mutual. There and then Rich promised to appear in yet another Fry revival, *A Phoenix too Frequent*, for a short out of town season. With Gielgud about to take the London cast of *The Lady's not for Burning* to Broadway and Laurence Olivier playing in *Venus Observed* at the St James', Fry was at the summit of his popularity. Sadly for him the fashion for verse drama soon passed. Within four years Osborne, Pinter and Wesker were leading the way towards a realism in the theatre that precluded the high flown sentiments of poetic imagery. By then, Rich too was out of harmony with live theatre but for somewhat different reasons.

Towards the end of the second week of *The Boy with a Cart*, one of the company spotted Anthony Quayle in the audience. The significance of his visit was not lost on Rich. Quayle had lately taken over the direction of the Memorial Theatre at Stratford-upon-Avon where he had brought in star names such as John Gielgud and Peggy Ashcroft to rival the Old Vic in the quality of Shakespearian productions. Quayle was a man of enormous energy (which he attributed in part to the frustrations of time serving in the army), a gifted actor and director and an able administrator, a combination of qualities which immediately put him ahead of the game. But he had another quality, as important as all the rest put together. He was a great talent spotter. His entire repertory was blessed by a company of actors whose holding power could not be bettered anywhere in the country.

Anthony Quayle's third season at the Memorial coincided with the Festival of Britain, the year in which a war weary nation, brought lower still by years of economic austerity, was supposed to show the world that it could still measure up to the finest. From a leading classical theatre — Quayle himself would no doubt have said, *the* leading classical theatre — an extra special effort was called for. The decision was to put on four of Shakespeare's history plays — *Richard II*, the two parts of *Henry IV*, and *Henry V* — and present them as a continuing story. Curiously, this had never been tried before. Tradition held that each play was a distinct entity and so logically it must have seemed with the star roles in the Henries clearly identified as Falstaff and Hotspur. With Hal relegated to the second league of characters, it was not surprising that his advance to power, the crucial unifying factor, should have been neglected.

Quayle's idea was to bring a new understanding to Shakespeare's history cycle by restoring Hal to the centre of the action. But not everyone believed this was desirable or even possible. He needed an actor for Hal who had faith in the director's intentions and the power to realise them.

Having made his choice (when he saw Rich in *The Boy with a Cart* he said to himself "That's it. Let's do it"), there remained the problem of persuading the actor that it was in his best interest to spend a season at Stratford. For Rich the advantages were not clear cut. Against the prestige of the Memorial Theatre had to be set the glamour of an American debut and the opportunities that were likely to come from his Broadway appearance in *The Lady's not for Burning*. Rich was notoriously unsentimental in his attitude to Shakespeare. He had a hankering for the great roles but a nightly appearance in doublet and hose did not of itself appeal. Nor did he like competition when the odds were stacked against him. If he was to play Hal he would be up against the Hotspur of Michael Redgrave, an acclaimed Shakespearian actor and an established favourite with Old Vic and Stratford audiences. There was a risk that his inexperience might show.

The objections were anticipated by Anthony Quayle who thought of a nimble way around them. Instead of contacting Rich direct, he rang Sybil. Would she be interested in taking the minor role of the Welsh princess in the first part of *Henry IV*? Sybil, of course, was delighted. There was, said Anthony Quayle, just one other thing. He was thinking of Richard to play Hal. Perhaps Sybil would like to sound him out. Quayle himself had no doubt that the move to Stratford would give a mighty lift to Rich's career. But given that the money was not too exciting, persuasion might be easier if Sybil put in a good word as a preliminary to a formal offer.

Rich guessed immediately what Quayle was up to. But he was tempted almost in spite of himself. The challenge was formidable and he had no idea if he could bring it off but, he knew also, sooner or later he would have to try. Sybil was not alone in urging him to take the plunge. John Gielgud, who had spent two successful seasons at the Memorial, was strongly in favour. So too was fellow Welshman, Hugh Griffith, a larger than life character actor who had appeared with Rich in *The Last Days of Dolwyn* and in numerous radio plays. Griffith was already cast as John of Gaunt in *Richard II* and as Owen Glendower in the final part of *Henry IV*.

And then there was Tim Hardy who had been recruited to Stratford direct from RADA. In his case, it was not Anthony Quayle but his wife Dorothy who had acted as talent spotter. Having seen Tim and Robert Shaw in a student production she urged her husband to snap them up. Tim took great delight in proclaiming the Quayles' ability to pick out a winner. It was a gentle reminder of Rich's early judgement which he was now embarrassed to recall, that Tim did not have the steel in his character to fight his way to the top.

The deal taking Rich to Stratford was clinched when Hugh Griffith and his wife offered to share with the Burtons their rented manor house at Oxhill, just outside Stratford.

"We'll set up a little Wales in Warwickshire," promised Griffith. "What do you think of that, boyo?"

Rich liked the idea very much.

With their future settled for the year ahead, Rich and Sybil set sail for America. With minor exceptions the cast for *The Lady's not for Burning* was the same for New York as for London. This meant that Rich could be reunited with Peter Bull and Richard Leech, both first class actors who, refusing to take themselves too seriously, could always be relied upon to bring a sense of fun to the proceedings. Nor was there any shortage of amusement in New York. After the tension of the first night and the relief of the next day's enthusiastic reviews, came a succession of extravagant parties which had Rich trying to prove that when it came to hard drinking, he was Welsh champion and a world competitor.

I cannot say that in all this Rich gave much thought to Sybil. They were together for much of the day but at night after the show, Rich usually set off on his own, to return in the small hours. If there were no professional claims on his time, he slept through until lunch. Inevitably, there were rumours of an affair. Rich was strenuous in his denials. When the rumours persisted he had a talk with Richard Leech whose training as a doctor made him company friend, counsellor and father confessor rolled into one.

"You've heard what they're saying?" asked Rich.

The doctor confessed that he had overheard a word or two.

"Well it's not true. I may have a bit of fun but I'm not stupid. Why are they doing it? They're ruining everything, not just for me but for Sybil. She's no fool you know!"

Richard Leech agreed that Sybil was indeed highly perceptive.

"She's very upset. I don't think she can take much more of this. Will you help?"

"Of course," said his friend. "But what can I do?"

"I want you to stand up for me, boyo. When you hear gossip, tell them it's all lies. Just show a bit of faith in me, that's all it needs."

True to his word, Richard Leech dived in to defend his maligned colleague. "How dare you say that — what evidence do you have? Just think how hurtful this is to Sybil!"

A few weeks later on when Rich had left the cast to start rehearsals at Stratford, the girl linked with Rich ("Why are they doing this to me? Why?") took Richard Leech on one side.

"I need your help."

"Now if it's about those rumours," Richard assured her, "you needn't worry. I don't think anyone takes them seriously any more!"

Her distress mounted. "Do you think I worry about what people say? Anyway, the rumours were true. We *were* having an affair."

Richard thought he must have misheard. "What are you saying?"

"He lied to you for Sybil. He said everyone would listen to what you told them, but first you had to believe what *you* were told."

Richard was angry, then amused. He had fallen for the Welsh charm. He had no one to blame. But there was still a question. "So what do you want to see me about?"

The girl hesitated just for a moment. "Ah well. That's a bit more difficult. It's like this. Well, you see . . ." And then in a rush. "I think I'm pregnant."

When that little matter was finally cleared up, Richard Leech thought back to a conversation with Sybil. It was late at night when Richard and his wife were returning from a party to their hotel. Sybil, who was in a room down the corridor, was standing in the doorway.

"I thought Rich might be with you," she said.

Her friends made comforting noises. "Don't worry, he'll be back soon. He's probably been held up by some Hollywood mogul."

"Oh, I'm not worried," said Sybil. "I know Rich. I can take most things. It's just that I couldn't bear it if I believed he was unfaithful."

CHAPTER
SIX

Stratford was make or break for Richard Burton.

The advance notices showed that Anthony Quayle had put together a roll call of talent calculated to impress the most seasoned theatregoer. Rich was to invite comparison with Michael Redgrave as Richard II, Harry Andrews as Henry IV and Anthony Quayle himself as Falstaff. Backing them were a group of younger actors — Alan Badel, William Fox, Richard Wordsworth, Barbara Jefford, William Squire, Duncan Lamont, Robert Hardy and Geoffrey Balydon among them — all of whom could so highlight a secondary role as to magnify any inadequacies of the star performers.

Expectations were high all round. It was not just the regular theatre public who took an interest. Encouraged by the Festival of Britain to think proudly, the country demanded its heroes, in the arts as much as in sport and politics. With his much touted promise of greatness, Rich was a prime candidate for elevation.

The reinterpretation of the history plays as laid down by Quayle, favoured Rich in his now eager desire to attract a popular following. He was under orders to build up the role of Hal whereas Quayle and Redgrave were making a self-conscious effort to tone down their parts, a much riskier undertaking. It said much for the dedication of these actors who, incidentally, were also jointly responsible for directing the plays, that they stuck to their guns even when some notable critics accused them

of perversely misunderstanding Shakespeare's intentions. Thus, Anthony Quayle was not greatly thanked
for giving Falstaff some depth of character instead of
simply portraying him as a merry old soul. And Michael
Redgrave was told that his Hotspur was "overshadowed"
by Hal, as if this was a self evident fault in his performance.

For his contribution to the *Henry IV* double bill, Rich
walked away with the lion's share of the plaudits. From
Harold Hobson who, as the recent successor of the great
James Agate at the *Sunday Times*, assumed the mantle
of senior critic, there was embarrassingly extravagant
praise, but so overwritten as to be virtually incomprehensible to the ordinary reader. "Instead of a light hearted
rapscallion," said Hobson, "Mr Burton offers a young
knight keeping a long vigil in the cathedral of his own
mind." By which I think he meant that Rich fulfilled
Hazlitt's definition of a great actor as "the man who can
master stillness".

"Your eye picks him out and refuses to leave him,"
wrote Philip Hope Wallace. This ability to compel attention even when appearing to do very little, fascinated
the young Kenneth Tynan, then critic for the *Spectator*
and not, as Rich's other biographers seem to imagine,
The Observer, a paper he did not join for another three
years.

"His Prince Hal," observed Tynan, "is never a roam-
ing boy; he sits, hunched or sprawled with dark, unwink-
ing eyes; he hopes to be amused by his bully companions,
but the eyes constantly move beyond them into a time
when he must steady himself for the crown . . . Fluent
and sparing of gesture, compact and spruce of build,
Burton smiles where other Hals have guffawed; relaxes

where they have strained; and Falstaff must work hard to divert him."

Looking back after nearly forty years, Anthony Quayle believes that Hal remains in the front rank of Richard Burton performances. It was not just an actor's ability — though he had plenty of that; he also had a lively mind, a feeling for verse and what Quayle describes as the "heaven sent actor's mask", which derives in some mysterious way from the spacing of the eyes and the balance of the cheek bones and jaw. The extra quality which made for an exceptional performance was his intuitive understanding of the contradictions and conflicting emotions in Hal's character. "They were something of his own," says Anthony Quayle. "Like Hal he was not sure who he was or what he wanted to be."

This explains why Rich was less satisfactory as Henry V — a man who had come to terms with his own destiny. Rich, the private person, was very far from that idyllic state.

If his Henry V was not quite what the critics expected (it was too restrained for conventional taste) and if his last Stratford engagement as the lover Ferdinand in *The Tempest* was near disaster (Rich was entirely out of sympathy with the soppy youth), the wonderful and original portrayal of Hal entitled him, as Kenneth Tynan put it, "to swell the thin company of living actors who have shown us the mystery and the power of which heroes are capable".

But if his admirers in the quality press erected the pedestal for Richard Burton, it was their colleagues in the mass circulation dailies who gave him the lift which put him on top. Papers like the *Mirror*, the *Express* and the dear old *Daily Herald* were ecstatic in their praise.

"If the entire Festival of Britain can even approach this standard," said a *Daily Mirror* reporter, "the triumph over the moaners will be complete."

The other Welsh players at Stratford took pleasure in the reflected glory and used their advantage, in ways that could sometimes irritate the rest of the company, to promote the idea of a Welsh enclave responsible only to itself. The leading dissident was Hugh Griffith, whose house Rich and Sybil shared for the entire seven month season. Famed for his stage and film image as a wicked old man, Hugh Griffith tried for the same level of eccentricity in real life. In the Griffith household everything was Welsh including the three corgis — Branwen, Olwen and Matholwch. The Welsh dragon was on display in every room.

At his worst, Griffith would encourage the rebel in his young friend — "Go on boyo, you tell them" — so that Rich often made a fool of himself over silly misunderstandings. At best, he could think up a neat trick for showing that the Welsh — the masters of poetry — could bring something new to Shakespeare. There is a moment in the first part of *Henry V* when the chieftain Glendower (Hugh Griffith) and his daughter have a private chat. Shakespeare does not provide any dialogue, merely a stage instruction. Hugh Griffith thought he would try for a little variety in the proceedings by creating some lines in his native language. The actress who played opposite him fell in with the ploy. Her husband was appalled.

"Sybil may be Welsh," said Rich, "but she doesn't speak the language. The only word she knows is 'bach' and she can't even pronounce that properly." But never one to let the team down Rich laid on a course of what he claimed were superb elocution lessons. On the night, Sybil was word perfect. "The publicity," conceded Anthony Quayle, "was not unwelcome."

Rich made friends as well as admirers in his stint at the Memorial Theatre. Among them were several Americans and American based actors who journeyed to Stratford solely to witness the Burton phenomenon. When Rich had advance notice he sent out invitations to stay overnight at Oxhill. This made for some interesting and unusual parties. One weekend when Hilary, my wife, and I came to Oxhill, Rich said casually, "You'll have to watch yourself this evening. Humphrey Bogart is coming to dinner."

"Bogart? Are you serious?"

"You bet. And I'd be careful what you say if I were you. He can turn nasty when he doesn't like someone."

He gave no hint that he was anything but serious — and who was I to disbelieve him? Having sat through *Casablanca* and *The Maltese Falcon* I had a clear image of Bogart as a man not to be trifled with. So, playing for safety I was unusually quiet throughout the meal. I just sat there with damp palms, like Peter Lorre or Elisha Cook hoping to avoid a sock in the teeth.

Rich, I noticed, was not under the same compulsion to exercise restraint. He argued away on all manner of subjects, even banging his fist on the table to emphasise a point. Bogart gave as good as he got but not once did he lose his calm. I was impressed. Obviously, Rich had a way with this difficult character.

After the meal, Rich took me to one side.

"There's no need to overdo it," he said. "If you don't join in soon, I'm going to run out of things to say."

All right, I was only twenty-four and still mother

green. How was I to know that, in reality, Humphrey Bogart was just like any other successful actor — fifty per cent charm (rough or smooth, it still adds up the same) and fifty per cent insecurity. As the evening went on I realised he was not happy with what he was or what he had accomplished. He wanted more but had no idea how to achieve it.

"Have you ever heard of an American actor called Edwin Booth?"

"Wasn't he the man who shot President Lincoln?"

"No," said Bogart, "that was his brother James Wilkes Booth. Up to the time of the assassination Edwin Booth was one of the leading classical actors in the States. He travelled coast to coast playing all the great Shakespearian roles. Wherever he went he pulled in the crowds. And this was in the days when a theatre could be just a circle of lamps in the town square."

"And is that what you'd have wanted to do?"

"Hell," shouted Bogart. "It's what I want to do now. Play Shakespeare, I mean. I can do without the lamps in the square."

I was amazed. "You, play Shakespeare?"

"And why not?" growled the actor.

Suddenly I was under threat again. "Oh, no reason. No reason at all," I mumbled. I was back in the Peter Lorre part. "Can I get you another drink?"

Rich broke in. He sounded determined. "Well, now I'll tell you something. I'd give up Shakespeare tomorrow to play decent parts in films like *The Treasure of the Sierra Madre* and *Key Largo*." (These were two of Bogart's latest.) "We're all in a rut but yours is more comfortable than most. You're a lucky man."

But he did not mean all that he said.

"The problem for Bogie," he told me later, "is that like all American stars, he's typecast. His fans don't want to see him as anything but the all-American tough guy. Well, they're not going to do that to me. I want to be free to take any part I fancy."

Curiously it was not long afterwards that Rich was offered a film role he fancied very much indeed. He played Edwin Booth in the Twentieth Century-Fox production, *The Prince of Players*. The film was not a box office success but it gave Rich a lot of satisfaction and it remains one of the best testimonies to the Burton versatility in Shakespeare.

After seeing the film Bogart phoned his congratulations. "You were good," he said.

"Thank you," said Rich.

"Mind you," said Bogart, "I'm not saying I wouldn't have done better!"

Triumph at Stratford was followed by disaster on Broadway. To appear in Jean Anouilh's *Legend of Lovers* (called *Point of Departure* in London) must have seemed a good idea at the time. Anouilh was a distinguished and fashionable writer. Richard Burton was up in lights together with Dorothy McGuire whose theatre and film success in the matinee romance, *Claudia*, had brought her a popular following.

Heading the supporting cast was Hugh Griffith who could be relied upon to liven up rehearsal, usually at the expense of the director. Once, after numerous requests to repeat a scene, Griffith stormed out of the theatre.

"I will stay no longer," he bellowed as he marched up the central aisle. "I am going home."

Ten minutes later he was back. "I tried," he announced grandly, "but I found I could not walk the ocean."

Sadly, *Legend of Lovers*, an update of the fable of Orpheus and Eurydice, did not appeal to the critics who found it pretentious and wordy. The play opened at the Plymouth Theater on Boxing Day 1951. It closed on 12 January.

Rich came home to an offer to star in *Montserrat*, a Lillian Hellman drama with a capital *D*. It centred on Rich as a Spanish Army officer in Central America caught up in a rebellion. Six hostages are to be killed, if the whereabouts of the rebel leader are not revealed. The secret is kept, the hostages shot and the officer is left with a bad conscience. The play opened in Brighton, transferred to the Lyric, Hammersmith and closed, all within three weeks.

It was now about six months since Rich had taken Stratford by storm. In that time there had been no shortage of work or promise of work. But the results were a sad disappointment, even though Richard Burton the actor emerged from two theatrical flops with good personal notices. What was missing was the excitement of moving on and up in the world. It was all sub-standard Shakespeare.

The dull period came to an end with a summons to a meeting with Alexander Korda.

"I want you to go to Hollywood," boomed the producer.

"For what?"

Korda waved a fat cigar. "To be a star. A great star."

The intention was welcome but the details of how it was to be achieved remained hazy. What did soon become clear was that Korda, to whom Rich was still under contract, had made a lucrative sub-letting deal with Darryl Zanuck, production boss of Twentieth Century Fox. For appearing in three films, Rich was to be paid £100,000, of which twenty per cent was to go to Korda. It was a staggering amount of money — one million pounds in today's currency — and even allowing for Korda's share, Rich was set to become a very wealthy man. Korda's American contacts had paid off in a big way.

"But what parts are they offering me?" Rich wanted to know. The question was put many times and the response from Korda was always the same.

"Don't worry. Relax. They'll think of something."

The Burtons were packed and ready to sail when Rich discovered not from Korda but from a news item that his first Hollywood film was to be an adaptation of the Daphne du Maurier bestseller *My Cousin Rachel*. Rich did not need reminding that it was in another du Maurier film, *Rebecca*, that Laurence Olivier had consolidated his screen reputation. But that was ten years earlier. There had been a lot of changes in the film industry since then and Rich was not convinced that an old fashioned costume melodrama could still pull in the crowds.

Having decided to keep his thoughts to himself until he had seen a script, Rich waited for word from Korda. When it came it was to invite the Burtons to a grand send-off party.

"But what about the script?" pleaded Rich.

"Don't worry," said Korda and put down the phone.

The day of the party came and still there was no script. Rich began to feel the first pangs of desperation. The flow of drinks had a calming effect but as Korda shook hands to say goodbye, Rich made one last effort.

"Is there any chance of getting a script before we sail?"

"A script? A script?" Korda declaimed in his thick Hungarian accent. "The boy wants a script?" Then turning to an assistant, "You heard him. Give him a script."

The assistant rummaged in his briefcase and handed over a weighty manuscript. Rich was delighted and relieved. It was only later, at home, when he turned to the title page that he found he was looking at a well thumbed copy of *The Four Feathers* — a Korda production from 1939.

Without any lines to study, Rich spent the Atlantic crossing reading and thinking about his future. He knew enough about himself to recognise that while he could be a shrewd manipulator he was no businessman. Nor did he understand the subtleties of film contracts which could run to several pages of close typed gobbledygook. He needed someone to manage his legal and financial affairs.

He met the answer to his problem as soon as he got off the boat. Aaron Frosch was a young lawyer working his way up the hierarchy of Twentieth Century-Fox. His job when he first met Rich was to act as the official reception for visiting British actors.

That Aaron Frosch could go far soon became apparent to Rich. On the journey west aboard the Express Super Chief (this was in the days when to travel coast to coast by rail was to travel in style), they talked of little else except the intricacies of film finance with Aaron Frosch throwing out gems of advice on how to space out his earnings to minimise tax and increase income by taking advantage of studio perks such as chauffeur driven cars and five star hotels. For someone who knew what they were doing the possibilities seemed endless. Before they reached Los Angeles, Rich had made up his mind.

"I want you to represent me," he told Aaron Frosch.

"Fine," said Aaron. "But there are just two problems. The first is that to work for you I would have to set up my own office. This would cost a lot of money and I don't have a lot of money. The second problem is that I already have an employer — Twentieth Century-Fox."

Rich thought for a moment.

"If I solve the first of the problems can you handle the second?"

Aaron thought he could. And this is how my brother helped to set up a show business law firm which turned out to be the best of its kind. It was a partnership which, early on, made them both millionaires.

Rich was bemused by Hollywood. The flamboyant wealth, the wild parties, the sheer outrageousness delighted him. All these famous names! In a quick succession of handshakes one evening he met Elizabeth Taylor who was pregnant. Afterwards, he had to be told who she was. But despite the lavish hospitality, Rich was not yet a Hollywood convert. He was careful with his money (he and Sybil rented a modest house on the unfashionable side of town) and he was not taken in by the insincerity of so many he had to work with.

"They will say or do anything to protect themselves," he wrote. "They're all so bloody frightened."

In another letter a single sentence sprang out like a punch to the jaw. "To hell with all the sycophants."

Every way he turned there was someone waiting to

tell him what a brilliant actor he was. This might have been encouraging (no one is averse to compliments) if Rich's self professed admirers had actually seen any of his performances. But all they were doing, as Rich knew only too well, was to respond to the signals sent out by the studio publicists. Their bosses had decided Richard Burton was classed with Marlon Brando as a star in the making. And heaven help any one who wanted to argue.

"They flatter me rapaciously and obscenely," he told Richard Leech. "I am so great, great, great. It's like a new drink — Brando and Burton — guaranteed to go to your head if you stay too long in this town."

My Cousin Rachel did not get off to a good start. Rich's apprehension about the script — or lack of it — was endorsed by the director, George Cukor. When at last the screenplay was delivered, but without an ending, Cukor had more harsh words for the writer. He was not convinced by Nunnally Johnson's argument that there was time enough to settle on a denouement once they were into shooting. Cukor was a methodical director who liked to see his way ahead. He said as much to the producer who also happened to be Nunnally Johnson. Johnson immediately went to a higher authority who decided in his favour. Cukor was replaced by Henry Koster, the German-born director who was known more for his reliability in turning in a serviceable product than for imaginative award-winning film making.

Predictably, *My Cousin Rachel* joined the long line of torrid romances aimed at middle aged mums hot in pursuit of vicarious excitement. It was part of the film market which remained strong despite television. Early indications of a box office hit spurred the gossip and feature writers into action. As a du Maurier hero, Rich

112

was said to be a worthy successor to the fiery young Laurence Olivier. Even the *New Yorker* commended his sex appeal — "lean, handsome, troubled and upstanding,.

Rich was grateful to Henry Koster who was patient and considerate with the fledgling star. There was less understanding from Rich's partner in lust, Olivia de Havilland. Already an established Hollywood name (she had two Oscars and three nominations to her credit), Miss de Havilland was disinclined to share the limelight. But what she knew about playing to the camera Rich was able to match with an understanding of the mechanics of acting which came from his theatre experience.

"There was a scene," he told me, "where I had to run up a staircase, turn back at the top and then speak my lines. I did all this and when Henry said 'cut', the studio crew gave me a round of applause. I didn't know what it was all about until Henry let slip that most film actors couldn't do so many moves in one take. For a stage actor, it was the easiest thing in the world."

When the film was released Olivia de Havilland was asked what she thought of Rich.

"There is not another leading man like him," she said, just a trifle ambiguously. But in a magazine interview she, or her public relations counsellor, declared that "there was no limit to the fame awaiting Richard Burton". Privately, she could not stand the sight of him, an antipathy no doubt reinforced by the indelible memory of being on the wrong side of a block of scenery when Rich had a temper tantrum. He kicked it down on top of her.

For his part in *My Cousin Rachel*, Rich gained his first Oscar nomination, as best supporting actor. He lost out to Anthony Quinn (*Viva Zapata*) which was nothing to be ashamed about. Other trophies did come his way including a press award for the most promising newcomer to Hollywood. It was a sculpture about nine inches high showing a 35mm film encircling a globe. When he came back to Hampstead he used it as a doorstop in the lavatory.

"Can't you think of a better place to put it?" I asked him.

He shook his head. "You've got the wrong idea," he said. "I want people to see and admire it. Now what chance is there of that if I put it up on the mantlepiece with the other ornaments? But in the loo, what else have they got to look at?" I could not fault his logic.

The Welsh premiere of *My Cousin Rachel* caused great excitement and not a little patriotic fervour.

"It's a great day when a son of Wales conquers Hollywood," proclaimed the doyen of Cardiff cinema managers. "Something special is called for."

The "something special" required a telegram to Rich asking him to despatch a suit of clothes he had worn in the film. On the first night, some fifteen minutes before the end of the credits, I went backstage at the Capital and changed into the hero's costume. With the help of a full length mirror I hunched my shoulders and jutted my chin in a way that I hoped resembled a typical Burton stance. Then, holding that position, I made my way to the wings to hear the manager announce to the audience the arrival of an honoured guest. I walked on.

The applause was tumultuous. My first reaction was relief and delight that the impersonation had been so successful. But as the clapping continued I could not help wondering if this audience could take a joke. I had not wished to be hounded off stage by a fusillade of well aimed ice cream cartons. I held up my hands to beg silence.

"Ladies and gentleman," I began, "I am not Richard Burton."

But the trouble was, by projecting my voice, I even sounded like Richard Burton.

"Who are you then?" shouted someone. "Olivia de Havilland?"

That broke the ice.

"Truthfully," I said, "I am not Richard. He is working in Hollywood and cannot be here. But he has sent me along, his brother Graham, to thank you for this wonderful reception."

There was silence for a moment but as I turned to walk off, the applause was renewed. I breathed a sigh of relief.

Dadi Ni waited to see the film until it came to the Odeon at Port Talbot. Afterwards, Hilda asked him what he thought of it. He put on a glum expression. "Well I'm not sure I liked all that kissing and cuddling. It wasn't decent. What will Sybil say?"

Hilda tried to reassure him. "It's a film, Dad. It's only acting."

"Acting is it?" shrugged Dadi Ni. "Well, all I can say is, it looked real enough to me."

After *My Cousin Rachel* there was talk of Rich coming home for a spell to make a picture for Korda. The subject was the true life story of Richard Hillary, a Battle of Britain pilot who was hideously burned when his plane caught fire and crashed. Hillary's fight for recovery over a long painful succession of operations and an equally painful attempt to come to terms with his terrible scars, were recorded in a diary which became a bestselling biography, *The Last Enemy*. While the author was at the height of his fame and against all medical advice, he went back to the RAF and was killed on a routine training flight. It was the stuff of which legends are made.

Rich was fascinated by the inner man, a personality coming to terms with a new body which had none of the grace and beauty of its former self. But this was a theme which scared the film makers. We were still at a time when war stories were mostly about clean limbed heroes who fought and died without allowing too much introspection to interfere with the action.

So, instead of *The Last Enemy*, Rich made *The Desert Rats*, a war story in the traditional mould, for Twentieth Century-Fox. Later, he convinced himself that, in fact, Korda never intended *The Last Enemy* to go beyond a script outline. It was simply a ruse to force Darryl Zanuck to offer more to keep Richard Burton on his side of the Atlantic. When I showed surprise at this revelation, Rich persisted. "Korda never made *The Last Enemy*, did he? How do you explain that? If he had really wanted to do the film, there were plenty of other actors ready to play Hillary."

In the film industry, the cynical view was usually right.

The Desert Rats was a highly profitable enterprise for Rich — it brought him in over ninety thousand dollars for just seven weeks' work. There were other compensations, not least the opportunity of playing opposite James Mason who was repeating his now famous impersonation of Rommel, a role he had performed to great acclaim in *The Desert Fox*, released two years earlier. But though Mason gave the film a stature it might not otherwise have obtained it was Rich who indisputedly was the star. His soldier hero may not have had the depth of character of a Richard Hillary but there was no denying his appeal to audiences hungry for adventure.

There was a third name above the title — that of Robert Newton. His career had dived since he had appeared with Rich in *Waterfront* and it was as much for old times' sake as anything that he was still given star treatment. The problem was drink.

"I've told him," said Rich. "We've all told him. If he doesn't lay off, it'll kill him."

Twenty years on, many were to say precisely the same to Richard Burton.

Rich was less than halfway through shooting *The Desert Rats* when he clinched a deal on his third Fox film. *The Robe* was a biblical blockbuster, quite the most important Burton film thus far. But more was at stake than Rich's acting reputation.

Like every other Hollywood studio, Fox was suffering the pain of competition from the small screen. Between 1946 and 1951, five thousand cinemas closed in the US while ticket sales dropped by almost a half. It was the same story in Britain. Unkind critics joked that the trans-Atlantic film industry was kept going only by the sale of popcorn in one country and ice cream in the other. New ideas were needed to put life into the cinema. But instead of thinking about new creative ideas — putting the emphasis on quality — the narrow minds of the money men concentrated on technological wizardry to save their investments. First it was 3D, the process by which audiences could feel they were part of the action. But to experience the three-dimensional effect you had to wear coloured glasses, an encumberance which punters and management came to dislike once the novelty had worn off.

The next gimmick to astonish the public was Cinemascope. There was never any logical reason for the cinema screen to be square, argued the innovators. So why not widen the field of vision, allow the eye to wander over the panorama in a way that was quite impossible with television. The idea took hold but there was still much boardroom agonising before a script and a star were selected to launch the counter attack on home viewing. With an eye to the respectable middle-of-the-road audience — the former bedrock of the cinema — the choice fell on a simplistic religious fable which had already made millions for the book stores. *The Robe*, by Lloyd C. Douglas, was the story of Mercellus, a Roman tribune who carried out the execution of Jesus but who himself was martyred when he converted to Christianity.

To play Marcellus, an actor was needed who had a strong romantic image but who would not appear out of place in a religious epic. Vibrant young heroes who were following in the wake of Errol Flynn and John Wayne were not encouraged to apply. Richard Burton, on the other hand, might have been tailor-made for the part. That he had romantic appeal was undeniable. He also had what one critic described as a "rough sensuality" which made him believable as a Roman soldier caught up in a personal struggle between duty and conscience. But it was his acting experience which counted more in his favour. From the bewildered young lover in *The Lady's not for Burning* to the troubled Hal to brave Desert

118

Rat, his work combined star quality with seriousness of purpose. It was not a feature of his career that was to last much longer but for now it was his strongest card and he played it for all it was worth, which by today's values was close to one million dollars.

His director from *My Cousin Rachel*, Henry Koster, who was also to direct *The Robe*, spoke up strongly in Rich's favour. Nonetheless the offer took a long time in coming. Tyrone Power and Laurence Olivier were among several possible contenders who were sounded out and declined. Darryl Zanuck could be forgiven for wondering if a relative newcomer to films, with only two Hollywood roles behind him, was capable of leading the recovery of the entire industry. There was a lot of money at stake. It was not only the five million dollar production budget at risk but also the many additional millions needed to convert cinemas to Cinemascope. If the wide screen went the way of 3D, there might be nothing left of Hollywood except deserted back lots.

When, at last, Rich signed to play Marcellus, he was described by the formidable Louella Parsons as the "hottest thing in Hollywood". The other gossip columnists followed with ever more extravagant praise for the Welsh wonderboy.

Rich had another group of admirers — in their way more powerful than any press lobby. These were the self-appointed moralists for whom a religious film of such magnificent dimensions was the equivalent of a second coming. Rich did not welcome their attention. For one thing, he despised their cloying hypocrisy. He was, after all, acting in a film about Christ which was restrained by daft censorship laws from portraying the Saviour as a real person. Any attempt to introduce a note of realism into the proceedings was viewed with suspicion.

"I was told," said Rich, " 'When in doubt, look towards heaven. Be pious.' There were times when I wanted to throw up."

But if he had to do what he was told on set, he insisted on playing his own game away from the studio. He drank copiously, smoked heavily and fell in love with his leading lady. Sybil was tolerant of two vices and kept silent about the third. I fancy that by now she had settled on the philosophy of marriage that was to sustain her for the next ten years. This was to accept that Rich might wander but that sooner or later he would come home. Other women were an inconvenience to the smooth running of the Burton marriage but they were not a threat, least of all Jean Simmons, Rich's co-star in *The Robe*, who was only recently married to Stewart Granger.

Understanding as much about the film business as her husband, Sybil almost certainly took the view put to me years later by a very famous actress.

"You can't act falling in love without really falling in love — if just a little. There's no harm in it."

Ironically though this was said by the only woman who did threaten Sybil — and who finally defeated her — Elizabeth Taylor.

If I knew my brother, he treated his indiscretions as a game. Like Sybil, he did not think of them as a hazard to marriage, except in so far as he had to keep silent about his many escapades. He told me, as he told many friends, that his involvement with a certain actress led him to a nasty encounter with the husband.

"He invited me over for a drink. When we were alone he told me he had something important to say. Then he went behind a desk, opened a drawer and took out a gun. He put it down in front of him, all the time talking about me and his wife, accusing me of forcing her into an affair. He wanted me to swear on the Bible that I would never see her again!"

"And did you?"

"Of course. What do you think I am?"

"And did you keep your word?"

"Ah well . . . you know what they say about a promise made under duress, don't you? It's not really a promise at all. Still, I was more careful, I didn't want my head blown off."

True or false? Movie buffs will know that his story bears a close resemblance to a scene in *The VIPs*, when Rich, playing a super-rich businessman, accuses Louis Jourdan of stealing his wife. All I can say is that Rich told me the story many years before the film was made. Perhaps he also passed it on to Terence Rattigan who built it in to his script.

Rich was quickly bored by *The Robe*. "It is," he wrote, "like all epics; indifferent."

That his frustration did not often spill over into ill temper ("I've had only four screaming fits in this picture") was entirely to the credit of Victor Mature, a veteran of Hollywood potboilers who refused to take himself or anyone else on the set too seriously.

Some of Rich's favourite anecdotes featured Victor Mature. Legend had it that this muscle-bound man, described by studio publicity as "a beautiful hunk", would never take a risk which might lead to physical injury, however minor. Rich asked him if the story was true.

"You'd better believe it," said Mature. "I think twice before walking up a wet step."

When he starred in *Samson and Delilah*, he was asked to wrestle with a lion.

"No way," he told the director.

"But Victor, this is a very old lion."

"No way."

"But Victor this is tame; it's so gentle it wouldn't harm a baby."

"No way."

"But Victor, this lion has no teeth."

"So what do you want, for me to be gummed to death?"

Another story from *Samson and Delilah*. When, in the famous dinner scene, they brought on the head of John the Baptist, Victor Mature ruined the take by shouting out, "Dig that crazy dessert."

Rich was intrigued by the sheer professionalism of Mature. The temptation was to underrate this self depreciating performer.

"But when it came to cinematic technique," said Rich, "he knew the business from A to Z. I learned a lot from him."

When filming started on *The Robe*, no one quite knew what to expect. They simply hoped for the best and worried incessantly about not getting it. After the first rushes were viewed by the production chiefs, there were murmurs that Rich was too wooden (a criticism that was to dog his film career) and that there was not enough action. Rich was understandably nervous. He knew that his future was riding on the audience reaction to this film. Seeking reassurance he took advantage of a party invitation to approach Spyros Skouras, Greek-American

president of Twentieth Century-Fox and the chief instigator of Cinemascope.

"What will you do," asked Rich, "if *The Robe* is not
a success?"

Skouras was thoughtful. After a pause he growled,
"We start by hanging you by your thumbs."

But as the production advanced with all the actors
doing their best with a limp script, studio opinion shifted
towards Rich in a big way. The word was out that
Richard Burton was turning in a magnificent performance which would make Fox a killing at the box office.
Without waiting for solid evidence of achievement, Darryl Zanuck decided he wanted Rich on a studio property — before anyone else tried to cash in. He offered
Rich a ten-year contract worth something over one
million dollars. This was in 1953, remember, when you
could buy a fine out-of-town house in its own grounds
for less than twenty thousand dollars and a luxury Cadillac for eight hundred dollars. With Rich's approval
Aaron Frosch tried for better terms, and got them.

"It's fantastic" he wrote home. "They are offering as
much as fifty thousand sterling per picture and are
absolutely convinced when I turn them down that I'm
a clever boy after more money."

But Rich was serious. He had every intention of
rejecting the offer. Even Aaron Frosch could not believe
it. So confident was he of settling a deal, he encouraged
the Fox lawyers to draw up a contract. When they
realised a signature from Burton was not theirs for
the asking, the recalcitrant actor was summoned before
Zanuck to explain himself.

Zanuck was used to getting his own way. A favourite
Hollywood story had him shouting at an assistant who

was careless enough to interrupt him, "Don't say yes until I've finished talking."

But Rich was not to be bullied. He wanted to make films but at the same time he was determined to shape his own career. For a man of just twenty-seven it was asking too much to sign over the next decade to one studio, however prestigious. As Rich was leaving the meeting, Zanuck warned him, "You know I could stop you working in Hollywood. But for me, you might never make another picture."

"I believe you," said Rich. "But I can go back to the theatre. I have an offer from London. I might very well take it. You can't stop that, can you?"

What Rich did not point out was the value of the offer — a mere fifty pounds a week. Still, it came from the Old Vic, a world centre of artistic excellence, and from Michael Benthall, one of the best directors of his day, who had worked with Richard at Stratford.

Benthall rang the Burton home from New York where he was visiting Katherine Hepburn. She was sitting by his side when he made the call.

"I think it's time you tried Hamlet," said the director.

Rich was cautious.

"Oh, I don't know about that. I'm not sure I'm ready for it."

Katherine Hepburn snatched the phone from her guest.

"Now look here. You are going to play Hamlet. And that's final."

It was an order so compelling as to be almost certainly the determining factor in Rich's decision to reject Twentieth Century-Fox.

But his career was not all that concerned him. After

124

a year in Hollywood, he was homesick, Sybil likewise. They were longing to get back to London and to Wales. When after fifty-eight days shooting, *The Robe* was completed, he could not wait to escape to New York and on to the first boat to Southampton. Sadly, it was not as easy as that. He had to wait for at least a month while the film was edited, in case any retakes were needed. Rich and Sybil decided to make the best of it by renting a beach house in Santa Monica. They felt they could both do with a rest, lounging and swimming and frying in the sun.

In the evenings they set off on the social round or entertained visitors, one of whom was Emlyn Williams.

"He was in great form," Rich reported to a friend, "and made me more homesick than ever. He played the part of the eternal Welsh lodger, sly and odiously polite and agreeing, and always trying to create trouble between husband and wife: 'Never mind Mrs Burton bach, your husband may be late coming home and perhaps with spirits on his breath but I'll be here, Mrs Burton bach. There! There! There!' "

But they had fun together.

"We went out almost every night and escorted the master to parties at one of which I had to be left the night. To Emlyn's delight."

As the time for departure approached so Rich became more nervous and difficult to live with.

"I'm looking forward to the Old Vic with a kind of belligerent apprehension," he wrote. "I wake up sweating with fear in the middle of the night and smoke and walk myself and mutter myself back into some semblance of confidence. Hamlet is the mischief, of course!"

There was another cause for apprehension. With a

release date for *The Robe* still to be agreed, no one was eager to pre-empt the critics' verdict. In fact, Rich had to wait until he was back in London before he knew the fate of Hollywood's "most ambitious picture in the fourteen years since *Gone With the Wind*".

The verdict was to become tiresomely familiar over the years. The critics on the tabloids liked the film and liked Richard Burton. The critics on the heavyweight papers liked Richard Burton but disliked the film. It "contains more piety than wit and more spectacle than humanity," said *Time*, but "it is ably served by a competent cast, headed by Richard Burton". C. A. Lejeune, writing in *The Observer*, praised Rich's "attempt to put some real character into the tribune", adding, "If his attempt is not crowned with very great success, it is not the fault of the actor who does his best with the material."

Happily for all concerned the studio bosses were more at home reading the box office returns than press reviews. The popularity of *The Robe* was undeniable. This was partly thanks to Cinemascope which on the whole was favourably received and which gave the film a curiosity value. But Richard Burton was the star they all came to see. In one hundred and thirty-five minutes running time, he was scarcely off the screen. Someone calculated that of seven hundred speeches, Rich had to deliver three hundred and thirteen.

Hardly surprisingly, most of the publicity for the film centred on Rich. It did him no harm at all when he reopened negotiations with Fox (he eventually settled for a non-exclusive contract for seven films at a base fee of one hundred thousand dollars a picture plus a share of the profits). And the almost daily press coverage boosted the appeal of the Old Vic company and filled the home of Shakespeare with audiences who might not otherwise have been attracted to the classics.

But Rich still had mixed feelings about Hollywood. When he felt low he talked about the "mean time" he had there. But it was his own character, not that of his American hosts, which disturbed him.

"I didn't do many favours," he told me. And then brightening up. "Oh yes, there was one. A stuntman who was getting on a bit came to me one day to talk about a scene we were doing together. We had to fight our way up a flight of steps so that he could fall off the top of the battlements. 'It's simple,' he said, 'but please make it look difficult.' I asked him why. 'Because I get a hundred bucks for every retake and I could do with the money.'

"So on the first take I dropped my sword; on the second I had a sneezing fit and on the third I was the one who nearly fell over the side. After that I couldn't think what else to do except get it right. So my friend walked off with four hundred dollars. He was very grateful. It was my one good turn at Hollywood."

It is true that in this period of his life Rich could be enormously self-centred. His reputation for selfishness was reinforced by a tendency to keep a tight hold on his pocketbook. Maybe it was insecurity, the fear that what he had gained so early in life he could just as easily lose.

But signs of the later extravagantly generous Burton were beginning to appear. On her birthday, Sybil woke up to find a red ribbon in her hand. It stretched off the bed, across the floor and out of the door. She followed it — down the stairs, across the living room, into the hall and out through the front door. There she found her present, tied with a bow of red ribbon — a red MG sports car.

This story came to me by Rich's friend and fellow actor William Squire and I cannot resist adding his postscript. Having told his wife about Sybil's present he awoke on his own birthday to find a red ribbon leading down the stairs and out the front door. At the end of it was a red MG — the Dinky toy version.

CHAPTER
SEVEN

As soon as they were back from America, Rich and Sybil spent a week with the family. It could so easily have been a disaster. As the local boy made good in wicked Hollywood Rich was a prime target for gossipmongers and fortune hunters. But he was so unlike what everyone imagined a star to be. He stayed with Hilda (not in a fine hotel), he visited the pubs he had known since he was a boy (not the country club) and he enjoyed the company of old friends (instead of making a beeline for the nobs). Even if there was a certain amount of calculation in this playing the ordinary boy from the valley, it worked a treat. The bores were seen off before they had a chance to get in on the act, leaving the rest of us to enjoy the rare chance of a family reunion.

Every evening there was a gathering in the Miners Arms or the Copper House, both just a short walk from where Hilda and Tom lived. Both pubs did good business that week. Rich had to put up with a lot of ribbing but he took it all in good part. There was a worrying moment when he was approached by a young miner who had had one pint too many.

"I want you to come outside."

Rich himself was too high to refuse. In the cold air, he asked, "What's all this about?"

"Over here," asked the miner pointing to the gents. Rich followed him in. They stood side by side at the strip of guttering which served for a latrine.

"Well?"

"Nothing," said the miner. "It's just that I wanted to tell my friends that I've had a piss with Richard Burton."

At the end of a glorious seven-day celebration, Rich and Sybil returned to London, he to start rehearsals for *Hamlet*. Notwithstanding the challenge of Anthony Quayle, the Old Vic was still the most famous Shakespearian theatre in the world, with a long list of triumphs and honourable defeats to back its claims. Edith Evans, the first West End star to perform in the Waterloo Road, went there, she said, to learn how to play Shakespeare. That was in the mid thirties when Laurence Olivier, Ralph Richardson and John Gielgud were asserting their talents.

Rich was determined to join the elect. But there was a division of opinion as to whether Hamlet was the best way to start. For the convention of the time, Rich at twenty-seven was thought by some to be a little young to tackle the role. Olivier had been thirty and Robert Helpmann thirty-five before they had taken up the challenge. A student of Old Vic history had wickedly pointed out that Frank Benson, a doyen of the pre First World War theatre, was over seventy when, by his own estimate, he got the true measure of the part. But Gielgud had done it at twenty-six and Alec Guinness, in a modern dress production at the Old Vic, at twenty-four.

A more serious objection to the prospect of a Burton Hamlet was his well known impatience with the surly Dane. There was too much posturing to suit his restrained style of acting. And yet the great soliloquies appealed to his reflective nature. As Richard Harris, a great friend of later years, has said of my brother, "He was always Hamlet. He became a middle aged Hamlet, ever introspective, easily disillusioned.''

In the cast were Claire Bloom, whom Rich had got to know when they were together in *The Lady's not for Burning*, Robert Hardy whose meticulously practised skill as a sword fighter was to be put to good use and other friends like Michael Hordern and William Squire who made good company on and off stage. Wendy Hiller played Emilia and Rosemary Harris, Desdemona.

The only slight tension was between Rich and Claire Bloom. Though an actress of enviable experience she was a mere twenty-two, a reserved young lady who was naturally wary of playing opposite a man whose slaphappy ways with women she had witnessed at first hand. She confessed her fears to William Squire.

"You should have seen him in New York. He's a terrible man. Will you protect me?"

William said he would be delighted. With the two of them seen together so much the rest of the cast made the obvious deduction. In his usual blunt way, Rich put the question to William.

"Is there something between you two?"

He was rewarded by a suitable shocked reaction.

"There's nothing between us. Nothing at all."

"Well it bloody well looks as if there is," said Rich.

In the following weeks, William fulfilled his pledge and stuck close. Until the day when he was sitting in the stalls with Claire Bloom while Rich was rehearsing on stage. After listening for a while in awed silence, Claire whispered, "He is wonderful, isn't he?"

William leaned over to give her a kiss on the cheek.

"Goodbye Claire," he said, and departed.

It was, he claims now, his best exit line ever.

Hamlet opened at the Edinburgh Festival in August 1953. The critics were kind but not wildly enthusiastic. It was said that Rich gobbled his words as if he was in a hurry to finish the play. Robert Hardy was among those who missed the feel for the great poetry while admitting that Rich brought dash and energy to the role. Part of the difficulty was the venue, a theatre created within the Assembly Hall, an imposing manorial style Church of Scotland edifice just below Edinburgh Castle. Less from choice than from the need to accommodate the perimeter columns blocking the view, the actors' space was a platform stage, with the audience on three sides. There was little in the way of scenery. Michael Benthall hung the fourth side of the hall with looped curtains but otherwise there were just a few heraldic shields dotted about. The main entrance to the stage was a broad flight of stairs which also served to carry the actors out into the audience. J. C. Trewin of the *Illustrated London News* who was seated at the end of a row, recalls how "courtiers might brush past you, or Ophelia would dart out in her madness, or you would turn to find their Majesties of Denmark coming down behind the bier".

There were moments too of dire peril. A critic sitting beside J. C. Trewin was all but impaled on a sword. When he came to write his review he began, "Last night I sat transfixed . . ."

Rich found the setting and the style of production disconcerting and was unable to disguise his uneasiness. Phil Burton made the pilgrimage to Edinburgh to reinforce Michael Benthall's plea for a more measured performance. Once he had an idea fixed in his head, Rich did not take easily to directions but the old magic of Phil Burton, even though it had not been much in evidence in the last year or two, seemed as powerful as ever. By the time *Hamlet* opened at the Old Vic where Rich felt much more at home, he had tempered the pace of his delivery but without losing any of the passion or excitement of the role.

But the critics were still not entirely happy. While praising a performance which, to quote Harold Hobson, "was as satisfying as any that memory can recall for a good many years", they pointed out the "lack of subtlety and even variety" which stopped it short of a triumph. Rich was left with a nagging worry that he had not quite cracked the part. It was the reason he came back to it fifteen years later when he was invited to try his luck on Broadway.

When a reviewer described Rich as a "rugger playing Hamlet", he was closer than he might have imagined. It was at this time that my brother made his last appearance on the muddy turf. In defiance of his contract which quite sensibly ruled against parachuting, big game hunting, mountain climbing and rugby football as unreasonable insurance risks, he rose to the challenge of a local game. After his muscle-building course of weight lifting, decreed by the producers of *The Robe*, he was confident he could put on a decent show. But he reckoned without his celebrity status which, to the opposing team, was like a red rag to a bull.

"I knew I was in trouble," said Rich, "when I was in mid scrum and I heard someone shout, 'Never mind the bloody ball, where's the bloody actor?!' "

He emerged with multiple bruises to his pride. His body suffered less even if he did claim to spend the next week at the Old Vic playing Hamlet like Richard III.

He was certainly in good enough shape to lead the post-match celebrations with favourite stories of great rugby characters like Annie Mort from Taibach who before a home match at Aberavon would drop goals from around forty yards with either foot to entertain the crowd. Annie, explained Rich, wore what we used to call "sensible" shoes. Then there was Five-Cush Cannon who won the sixth replay of a cup final (the previous five encounters having ended with scores 0–0, 0–0, 0–0, 0–0, 0–0 with extra time) by throwing the ball over the bar from a scrum ten yards out in a deep fog and claiming a dropped goal. And getting it.

But the most unlikely hero ("It's all as true as I stand here," protested Rich) was Jimmy One Arm who, despite his affliction suffered in the First World War, played for Cwmavon in the 1920s.

"He was clever, you see. He used the misplaced sympathy of innocent visiting players who didn't go at him with the same delivery as they would against a two-armed man. How were they to know it was just a ploy to lure them on to concussion or other organic damage? I tell you, going easy on Jimmy One Arm was first cousin to stepping into a grave and waiting for the shovels to start."

By happy accident Rich's early appearances at the Old Vic coincided with the British premieres of *The Desert Rats* and *The Robe*. It was an impresario's dream. While the press lined up for interviews, the fans blockaded the box office. The gallery at the Old Vic, where a perch on a wooden bench could be had for two shillings, was packed night after night with youngsters out to catch a glimpse of the real Richard Burton. Not that he had it all his own way. Playing opposite Rich was a contemporary whose build up as a potential theatrical great made him a close rival for the victor's crown. John Neville had much in common with Richard Burton. Born into a working class family he came to drama encouraged by an older friend, not quite a Phil Burton figure, but one who was sufficiently appreciative of the living arts to take John on frequent visits to Stratford. Instead of Oxford and the RAF, John Neville chose the Navy and RADA followed by an intensive apprenticeship at the Birmingham Rep. and the Briston Old Vic where he attracted respectful notices and popular acclaim. His was the more conventional route to the Shakespearian summit, as mapped out by John Gielgud with whom he was often favourably compared.

So it was that having started from much the same point, John Neville and Richard Burton ended up as contrasting actors — the one classical and melodic, the other brooding and dangerous, more in the fashion of the young Olivier. As the season progressed and John Neville came into his own with a stunning performance in *Richard II*, the fans divided, Burton versus Neville. It was not the way the elders in the stalls liked to judge their Shakespeare but they could hardly deny that teenage hero worship had its commercial compensations. Michael Benthall was among the first to see the possibilities. For the third year of his five-year plan, he pencilled in Burton and Neville to alternate as Othello and Iago. It was an audacious scheme which neither actor could resist.

"It's mad," said Rich. "Let's do it."

Meanwhile, they had to get through the current season. For Rich who began and ended with *Hamlet*, there were three other major roles to confront — Coriolanus,

Caliban and Sir Toby Belch. He was also cast as Philip the Bastard in *King John*. For this he had little to say but was on stage a lot, a feature of the production which delighted his teenage followers but disconcerted the rest of the cast who had to work overtime to hold the attention of the audience.

As Caliban, the "savage and deformed slave" of *The Tempest*, the miracle was in the make-up. It took over two hours to transform Rich into a hideous beast, an endurance test which caused him great anguish because it was virtually impossible for him to lift a glass. It was worth the effort. His descent into bestiality was acclaimed as further evidence of what one critic described as his "vigorous versatility". But there were some doubters who, knowing Rich's dislike for dressing up, judged that he was leaning too far toward farce. Their opinion gathered strength when Rich tried out his Sir Toby Belch, a padded and painted freak with a stick-on bald pate who looked less out of Shakespeare than a refugee from Bertram Mills' Circus with a slapstick talent to match.

But all was forgiven for his Coriolanus, by far his greatest contribution to Shakespearian acting. It was a role wished on him by Phil Burton who knew that his Richard was one of the few young actors capable of portraying the divided personality that was Coriolanus, not as a savage thug, but as a tragic hero. The production owed much to Laurence Olivier's interpretation, also seen at the Old Vic, which was the talk of the theatre year in 1939. Taking his cue from Lewis Casson, his director, Olivier had revealed his patrician as a victim of arrested development. Here was a mother's boy who, damned by his insufferable snobbery, arrogance and pride, had enough in him of loyalty and even generosity to hint at unfulfilled greatness. The testing moment is the final death scene when Coriolanus is roused to a suicidal frenzy by Arfidius' gibe — "thou boy of tears". The long remembered climax as performed by Olivier had him shrieking his rage as he ran a flight full of stairs to a platform there to meet his assassins' spears. A pause, and then he toppled backwards to be caught and held by his ankles, like a carcass above the stage. Curtain. It was a difficult act to follow but Rich managed it. As Harold Hobson said of his Coriolanus: "Nothing in his life becomes him like the leaving of it . . . Mr Burton has this foul mouthed Roman traitor clad in a great scarlet cloak, that is like a splash of blood on the world's face, stand with arms outstretched in front of the dark city doors of Corioli and, in the attitude of a priest celebrating some tremendous ritual, is stabbed to death by his envious enemies. He falls with a crash of an empire."

The ambiguity of the character entranced audiences. Again, from Harold Hobson, "Mr Burton tries to soften Coriolanus, not in his voice which has the authoritarian ring all right, but in his face, which is frequently suffused with a smile of singular sweetness altogether belying the savagery and insolence of what he was to say."

Olivier himself was full of praise. It was, he said, the best Coriolanus he had seen, a compliment which, strictly interpreted, excluded his own performance. And rightly so.

The catalogue of backstage visitors was heavily weighted towards the great and the good. His peers he recognised but even with advanced warning from the stage door and introductions from those in the know it was impossible for Rich to keep track of the politicians, business tycoons, ambassadors and other dignitaries who came to shake his hand and wish him luck.

One visitor who did not require an announcement was Winston Churchill who came to see *Hamlet*. Rich was bowled over. He could be naively susceptible to flattery from those he regarded as giants in their craft. And the Prime Minister was undoubtedly of that category. After the event Rich wove a thick web of fantasy round the evening. Stories of what Churchill said or did were a regular part of his bar room entertainment and not to be taken too seriously. There is little doubt that Churchill congratulated Rich on showing him a "very fine, virile prince" or that they managed a rapport which, unexpectedly for Rich, was to serve him well in his subsequent career. But the often repeated anecdote of Churchill going into competition with Rich by audibly mumbling Hamlet's lines from the front stalls, must be counted as pure fancy. As told by Rich after a few drinks it sounded convincing enough. But judged in cold print, was it even remotely feasible?

Humphrey Bogart and his wife Lauren Bacall came to see *Hamlet*. Afterwards they took Rich and Sybil back to their Dorchester suite for dinner. It was the first time Rich had been into the hotel. Within years it was to become a second home to him. William Squire also went along that evening. As a young man he attracted the visitors' admiration for his ability to age so convincingly on stage.

"And without make-up," exclaimed Bogart. "Would you believe it?"

Embarrassed by so much attention from the great man, and scrabbling for nice things to say in return,

William let slip that he thought Bogart's pyjamas, flung over a chair, were splendid, quite the most luxurious he had ever seen.

"Take them," said Bogart. "They're yours."

Which is how William Squire came into possession of blue silk night attire monogrammed HB. It was an act of spontaneous generosity which made its impact on Rich as well as on the recipient of the gift. It surprised, it impressed, it left a lasting memory; it was the way for a star to behave.

"You like it? Take it. It's yours," was to symbolise Burton's hospitality to family, friends and not a few passing acquaintances.

CHAPTER
EIGHT

In between rehearsals and performances at the Old Vic, the likeliest place to find Rich was Broadcasting House where his distinctive voice was much in demand. A drama producer once told me, "Richard can bring out a depth of meaning that even a writer doesn't suspect." Another said, "He speaks the English language better than almost anybody else."

The admiration was mutual. Rich loved radio. It gave him enormous opportunity to create imagery outside the close confines of stage or film. The disembodied voice could take its listeners anywhere, do anything. Then again, radio had its practical virtues. It slotted in conveniently to the life of a stage actor and it did not overstate its claims on time or effort. Radio could be hard work but the labour came in short, intensive bursts and when one job was finished, there was always something new to enliven the spirit.

Actors whom Rich admired but might never otherwise have encountered — like Donald Wolfit — felt the same way. Radio was fun and even if it did not pay very much it was a great boost to education and experience. I was often surprised at the names Rich associated with great acting. One such was Ernest Thesiger, a veteran of stage and screen, whom I first saw as the elderly Emperor Tiberius in *The Robe*. A shrunken skeletal figure, he wore a blond wig which made everyone laugh every time he walked on the set. But he overcame the indignity to turn in a convincing performance. To this day, it is memorable against a parade of excellent cameos. But Ernest Thesiger did not steal the picture as he did twenty years earlier as the effeminate mad scientist Dr Praetorious in *The Bride of Frankenstein*. From then on he was unrivalled as the elderly eccentric, ever threatening to surprise or shock. It was a role he relished in real life as much as in fiction. Rich told me that when Thesiger was invited back to his school, Marlborough College, as a guest of honour he enlivened a dinner with the senior master by casting a lascivious eye on some of the senior boys. After taking a more than usual pleasure in a close conversation with a well built sixth former, he turned to his host to express his admiration: "I'd give *anything* to be that boy's mother."

On radio, his spindly voice was much in demand to represent frailty — usually with a strong measure of deviousness.

"He was always around somewhere," said Rich. "Everybody made jokes about how tiny and shrivelled he was. I was in a studio once when an actor was playing about with an umbrella, trying to furl it properly. As he opened it someone shouted, 'Don't do that, Ernest Thesiger might pop out.'"

The danger of radio for Richard Burton was the tendency of some producers to let him get away with second best. The younger ones, particularly, could be slightly in awe of the Shakespearian wonder boy and disinclined to put him right when he really needed it. But Rich knew when he was being lazy and, despite his reputation for stubborness, was ready to accept direction. Frank Hauser, who had introduced him to radio, knew this only too well. When Rich sat down to record a selection of the work of the First World War poet Edward Thomas, it was immediately clear to Frank Hauser that he had not done his homework. The verses, of elaborate construction, were read without understanding or true feeling. To make matters worse, sitting next to Frank Hauser, listening with embarrassment, was the poet's widow. Ten minutes in, Frank stopped the recording, took Rich aside and give him a piece of his mind. My chastened brother went away to study the script, returning several hours later to give a near perfect performance.

"He always respected those who stood up to him," said Frank Hauser. To which I might have added, "Well, nearly always."

The radio production which brought out the best in Richard Burton, and a host of other Welsh actors, was *Under Milk Wood*. The starting point for Rich's involvement was the death of Dylan Thomas at the ludicrously early age of thirty-nine. It happened in New York where Dylan had stopped off on the way to Hollywood where he was to complete work on a film script. Rich was saddened but not surprised by the news. He loved Dylan for what he was, a writer of genius and a Welsh writer at that. Though he did not speak the language, Dylan possessed a full measure of that peculiar Welsh literary talent, described by James Agate as "putting the truth of its own imagination higher than other, more easily recognisable forms of truth". The power of words, their imagery, counted for all, which led to curious syntax and to unforgettable art.

But however much Rich admired Dylan as a writer, as a private person he found him all but overwhelming. His personality was on automatic pilot to self destruction.

He lived to excess in a way that Rich might have found curiously familiar if he had been able to look into the future. But at that period of his life, while he lived boldly and was just discovering the joys of extravagance, he was still young enough and ambitious enough to fear going over the top. Dylan had long since made the jump and was off and away into his own world.

Rich was one of the last people here to see Dylan alive. He stayed with Rich and Sybil in Hampstead a few days before leaving for America.

"He was on the cadge," he told me. "But then, he was always on the cadge."

They had drunk heavily and invented wild schemes for combining their talents.

When I talked to Rich about the tragedy he rejected my synonym for wasted opportunities.

"He sought his own death and found it. I don't call that a tragedy."

The script for *Under Milk Wood* — "a play for voices" — was delivered to the BBC a few days before Dylan Thomas left for America. Elements of the play were known to Rich who had seen earlier versions and had been sufficiently impressed to incorporate extracts into his impromptu Dylan Thomas recital which he would give at the drop of a hat. The complete *Under Milk Wood* was delivered to the Old Vic by the producer Douglas Clevedon who was charged with the awesome responsibility of making radio history. Rich agreed immediately to head the cast. He took over First Voice (originally intended for the author), allowing the Second Voice (originally intended for Rich) to go to Richard Bebb.

"In fact," said Rich, "Dylan wrote the whole damn thing for himself."

Just about everybody who was anybody in Welsh acting was roped in to play the other sixty-seven parts. Hugh Griffith appeared as Captain Cat, Meredith Edwards as Second Drowned, Mr Waldo, Utah Watkins and Butcher Benyon, and Rachel Roberts as Mae Rose Cottage, Mrs Dai Bread Two and sundry other parts. For anyone who does not know *Under Milk Wood*, the very names of the characters must give a fair idea of the richness of the dialogue. Sybil was in there, as Miss Myfanwy Price among others and so was Phil Burton who was the Preacher and Fourth Drowned. It was all great fun and it was a resounding success. *Under Milk Wood* was repeated endlessly (quite unlike any other radio play) and praised extravagantly. It was said by Watford Davies in his retrospective study of Dylan Thomas, to be "quite simply, the best radio play ever written". Interestingly, he stopped short of calling it a work of literature. Apparently such a grandiose term was inappropriate for a play which had no plot and reduced "a view of life to immediately entertaining details". Ah, well, the Dylan Thomas devotees could live with that. Having heard the broadcast they rushed out to buy the book and next to see the stage production and eventually the film starring Richard Burton, which opened the 1971 Venice Film Festival.

Under Milk Wood was thought by Rich to be one of the best things he did on radio though, that year, he was equally proud of his voice-over for a documentary feature. *Thursday's Children* was a government information film on the teaching of deaf children to speak. It won an Oscar and Rich could not have been better pleased if he had taken off the best actor award.

For sheer fun Rich appeared in "The Frankie Howerd Show". As nearly always in broad comedy he was stilted and uncomfortable, winning laughs simply as a good sport, willing to play the idiot. But he came away with a huge admiration for Frankie Howerd, a funny man who did not need a book of jokes to hold an audience. He did it all on nods, winks and innuendo.

"If I had his talent," said Rich, "I'd drop Shakespeare tomorrow."

I have never asked Frankie Howerd but I rather suspect he would have reversed the compliment.

1953 ended with *Hamlet's* traditional excursion to Elsinore where, said Shakespeare, the real history book prince plotted to kill the wretch who murdered his father. Rich was not in the best of health. The workload in London had been a strain, he was drinking too much and was nervous about his imminent return to Hollywood. On the boat he was at the centre of a drunken scene when he accused Michael Hordern of consorting with the critics. "Traitor," he shouted across the bar. "The man's a traitor."

The idea that Michael Hordern could not have a drink with journalist friends without betraying the cause was patently ludicrous and afterwards Rich apologised profusely. But his display of bad behaviour set the nerve endings tingling. How would he perform in a role in which he knew success had so far eluded him? In the event he performed wonderfully. Before the crowned heads of Denmark, Sweden and Norway he discovered another side to Hamlet's character.

The Times critic said it all. At Edinburgh and the

Old Vic, he wrote, "Richard Burton appeared to have selected from Hamlet all the most unsympathetic traits he could find. His playing had power, but it was curiously without charm. He has since come by a charm which sits extremely well on youthful melancholy; and in gaining charm, the performance has lost none of its original power." Rich came back to London feeling more confident. He was determined that one day he would have another crack at the elusive Royal.

From the Old Vic, Rich went off on his one-year tour of duty on behalf of Twentieth Century-Fox. In every way except financial the experience was infinitely depressing but it had a lasting influence on him and, in my view, marked a turning point in his career.

The first of three successive films, *Prince of Players*, was thrown together round the life of Edwin Booth, the nineteenth-century American actor whom Rich had first heard of in conversation with Humphrey Bogart. The studio must have thought of it as a great opportunity to exploit Richard Burton's upmarket appeal as a leading Shakespearian actor while holding to a familiar story line of the single-minded fighter snatching victory from the jaws of defeat. (For Edwin to make a comeback after his brother had shot the president was, after all, quite an achievement. "Almost," said Rich, "as remarkable as surviving a bad review in *The New York Times*.") But trying to have it both ways was a recipe for disaster. The Shakespearian extracts were pitched in like songs in a musical (Shakespeare's Greatest Hits) but without the same appeal. It was not entirely the director's fault. Rich as Edwin Booth on stage put on his best Stratford and Old Vic manner — restrained, thoughtful, pent up. The style simply did not come across on the big screen which needed an actor of the old school, with booming voice and violent histrionics, to make an impact. Rich knew he had got it wrong. On one of his brief visits to London when we met for a drink he ended up slamming his fist on the table in sheer frustration.

"I'd give anything to do the whole bloody thing again!" he shouted.

A few weeks later when I saw *Prince of Players* in a near deserted Aberavon cinema, I realised what he meant. The film was just dull. The critics tried hard to be kind though C. A. Lejeune delivered a hefty backhander when she said of Rich that he portrayed Edwin Booth "as a plausible understudy for the young Laurence Olivier". The general view was that more Booth and less bard would have done the film a lot of good.

The mood of dark depression soon passed. When Rich and Sybil came home for Christmas 1954, all the talk was of a new blockbuster movie which was to repeat the success of *The Robe*. Rich had been handed the title role in *Alexander the Great*. The budget was enormous, the attention to detail meticulously strict and the dedication to a high standard of acting and direction made evident by the choice of Robert Rossen to oversee the project. The location was to be the rolling sierras outside Madrid where the Spanish army was ready to fight Alexander's wars with the Persians as part of their training to defend the fatherland.

"Believe me, Graham," said my brother, "we're on to a winner. Hollywood history is crap but I've got a feeling this once could be different."

He was wrong.

"Why?" I asked when he came back to admit another disaster. "What happened?"

Unless you take the view that all epics are doomed by the weight of their own pretensions (and I would have thought David Lean has proved this not to be so), the likeliest explanation for the failure of *Alexander the Great* was the inability of the screenwriter, producer and director to hold the story together. Robert Rossen, who did all three jobs, was a gifted director of social dramas with a well deserved Oscar to his credit (*All the King's Men*). But a historical saga was not his element. He did his best to prove otherwise but though he professed great interest his attention wandered and he soon lost grasp of events. A large part of the reason was back in Hollywood where Rossen had lately come through a gruelling interrogation by the infamous House Committee on Un-American Activities. A self-confessed former Communist who had long since severed his links with the Party, Rossen had backtracked on his earlier refusal to name names. Consequently, he was ostracised by former friends on both sides of the political divide.

"He was a troubled man," said Rich. "He would say one thing and mean another. After the first few weeks he seemed to lose heart in the film."

Rich took the easy way out. He did what he was told when he was told but otherwise played the game for laughs. Stanley Baker, one of his closest friends, kept the humour bubbling and Claire Bloom was there to provide excitement of a different sort. When he was not needed on set, Rich set off on the tourist trail, followed by a bevy of autograph hunters. Sometimes Sybil went with him; sometimes not.

Alexander the Great became Alexander the Bore. Three hours of closely studied military history was too much for audiences, let alone the critics. The best notices went to the Spanish cavalry and lancers who, with Cinemascope to help them, managed to hold attention while they engaged in pitched battle.

By now Rich had not too much faith in the artistic judgement of his Hollywood masters. But by his own estimation there was little he could do about it. The money was good — too good to pass up on a matter of principle when no immediate alternative was to hand. He might have tried to change studios but it was foolish to imagine that as an easy option. *Alexander the Great* was, after all, the responsibility of United Artists who had Rich on loan from Fox. One seemed to be as bad as another.

He could find refuge in the theatre. In fact, he would find a refuge there; he was booked to reappear at the Old Vic for the 1955–56 season. But he did not fancy a lifetime stint at perhaps one hundred pounds a week. The Burton problem, as described by Richard Harris after Rich's death, was already in evidence. "Half of him wanted to be the best actor in the world. The other half didn't care enough."

His third film of the year was the most desperate of the trio. *The Rains of Ranchipur* was a remake of the 1939 Tyrone Power vehicle, *The Rains Came*. The excuse for its revival was the impact of nature taking its revenge in the form of a massive tidal wave, massive flood and general mayhem blown up to Cinemascope proportions. It was difficult to understand why actors were needed at all except as endorsement for the technical wizardry. Incredibly, Rich was cast as an Indian doctor. Not even the make-up was convincing. They imported an elocution expert to help him with his accent but after a couple of lessons they agreed his case was hopeless. Dr

Safti, as portrayed by Rich, must be the only Indian doctor on screen to sound as if he came from Cardiff.

Co-starring was Lana Turner, the original Sweater Girl pin-up of the war years, who thrived on romantic melodrama. Miss Turner overplayed her role while Mr Burton underplayed his, a combination which led to a less than satisfactory relationship on and off the screen.

When Rich came home he needed the rest. His moods were unpredictable, veering from undisguised glee at his financial success to weary contempt for the film industry for its apparent inability to deliver worthwhile parts.

"They can do it for Alec Guinness and James Mason," he complained. "Why not me?"

There was an easy answer often given as a compliment. Richard Burton was one of the small group of actors who possessed all the qualities of the screen hero. The strength of Guinness and Mason was in their talent for character acting. This gave them a wider choice of roles including, in the case of James Mason, some wonderfully villainous parts, but it reduced their star rating and earning power below that of Richard Burton.

I do not believe for a moment that Rich needed me or anyone else to spell this out to him. He had a shrewd idea of the way Hollywood was moulding his career and though he had a desire to be trusted as a more versatile actor the will to fight for a change in the rules was fast receding.

For one thing he was beginning to enjoy the privileges of wealth. Who could blame him? It was quite something for a miner's son to return to the valley in a smart new Jaguar and with a roll of banknotes thick enough to buy out every beer cellar in the country. If he was looking for signs of approval from those who gave him his start, the show of wealth, solid proof of success, was more important than flattering reviews in the smart papers.

But to the extent that he also needed the approval of his peers, he calculated that it was possible to work a compromise which would give him the best of both worlds. To limit himself to one film a year in Hollywood would bring him in at least fifty thousand pounds, enough to meet all the demands on his pocketbook. Therefore, he could afford to live in Hampstead and play at Stratford or the Old Vic as the fancy took him.

It was a pipedream, as he was soon to discover, but while he played his second season at the Old Vic, the prospect looked real enough. He was to open in *Henry V*, a role he had not quite made his own four years earlier at Stratford. To be offered another crack at the elusive monarch was an exciting prospect.

When rehearsals started in late November, three of the six productions planned for the season had already been seen by the critics. Their comments did not inspire excitement at the box office. John Neville was praised for his Mark Antony but otherwise *Julius Caesar* was greeted with polite reserve. *The Merry Wives of Windsor* provided a jolly evening but was thought by many to deserve more respect than a knockabout farce. It was withdrawn prematurely just before Christmas. As for *The Winter's Tale*, no one could find a good word for it. The play was said to be the nearest to a complete failure the Old Vic had known in five years.

Stratford too was going through a dull patch. "It is all so deadeningly anonymous," wrote Kenneth Tynan. "What Stratford needs again is an actor or director to set the tune for it, to bang a tuning fork against the text as Richard Burton did four years ago."

Well, this time it was the Old Vic which revived on a strong dose of the Burton magic. Opening on 13 December, *Henry V* ran to full houses for seventy-one performances. The critics were ecstatic. "It was," said Philip Hope Wallace, "the turning of the Old Vic's long run of ill luck."

On one level it was old-fashioned performance with Rich giving full measure to the patriotic speeches. But he also managed to convey the brutal ruthlessness of the ambitious monarch, refusing to dilute the character with false charm.

"He gives a cunning warrior, stocky and astute, unafraid of harshness or of curling the royal lip," declared Kenneth Tynan. "The gallery gets no smiles from him, and the soldiery none but the scantiest commiseration."

With Richard Burton's return to the Old Vic, the rivalry with John Neville was immediately reasserted. Those who favoured John Neville as the consistent star of the Old Vic (he was there for the full five-year cycle of history plays) felt that the title role in *Henry V* was rightfully his. Richard Burton was the usurper. But in making do with secondary billing as Chorus, John Neville turned in an extraordinary virtuoso performance which delighted his fans. Sadly, it also rocked the centre of the play. As Kenneth Tynan pointed out, "The compere who steals the show is by definition a bad compere."

Rich took it all as a great joke believing, with every justification, that if anyone was trying to upstage, it was the bobby soxers in the gallery who roared their approval whenever their favourite actor made a move.

The Burton–Neville duel of talents reached its climax with the Michael Benthall production of *Othello* in which the two actors alternated the leading roles. The press needed little encouragement to write up this contest in terms more appropriate to a wrestling match. "The Fans make it Fight Night at the Vic" and "Bobby-sox War over the Moor" were typical headlines. Rich was described as "the Pontrhydyfen Profile"; Neville as "the Barnet Barrymore". Publicity of this order naturally provoked the teenagers towards greater excesses. There were evenings in the Old Vic when the roars of encouragement and approval from the gallery drowned out what was happening on stage. You needed a copy of the text to follow what was going on.

The strain on all the actors, but on Rich and John Neville in particular, was tremendous. To play Othello one night and Iago (the largest part in all of Shakespeare) the next was bad enough, but to perform in circumstances more appropriate to a rock concert could bring on a state of nervous exhaustion. On more than one occasion I discovered Rich slumped in a chair in his dressing room, drained of all energy, unable to move. I would help him out of his costume, clean off the greasepaint, load him into the car and drive him to Hampstead, all without a single word spoken.

Of all the many times I saw Rich as Othello and Iago, I cannot recall a single disaster of confused speeches or scrambled lines. The odd misplaced word, maybe, but never anything serious. However, there was one night when he suffered an identity crisis. We arrived late at the theatre. As Rich crashed in through the stage door he shouted to one of the other actors to ask what part he was playing. Either he misheard or the information was wrong because ten minutes before curtain up two Othellos appeared in the wings. There followed a frantic cleansing operation as various ladies with little sponges tried to get the black off Rich's face. They were not entirely successful. This Iago was not exactly coloured but he did look as if he had spent too long in the sun.

Possibly irritated by the hooray style of theatre promotion, the critics were not greatly impressed by the production. Mostly, they took the line that the exchange of roles was nothing but a publicity stunt to disguise the fact that neither actor was ready to play Othello. There was some justice in this. At thirty, Rich and John Neville were the youngest actors in living memory to attempt a role demanding, in the words of Kenneth Tynan, "that unfeignable quality which some call weight and others majesty, and which comes only with age."

But Rich as Iago won many plaudits. The calculated holding back of energy and emotion in a way that suggested a scheming mind in overdrive, building up to a climatic eruption, served him well as the treacherous lieutenant to Othello, as it had when he played Hal at Stratford. Whatever their differences both characters were enticed by power, wanting it for its own sake.

Friendly or no, the critics made little difference to the box office appeal of *Othello*. Every performance was a sell-out. The play was withdrawn on 12 May 1956 after Rich had played Othello twenty-four times. Had he stayed with the company the play could have continued its run for a year at least.

In fact, Rich departed the Old Vic earlier than originally planned. The reason was partly exhaustion with the sheer drudgery of theatre work. (Rich was not one of those who enjoyed the security of the routine; once he had mastered a role he was eager to get on to the next challenge.) But there was also an unhappy interlude

154

when, for the first time, Rich came under the direction of Tyrone Guthrie. It was for a production of *Troilus and Cressida* which Guthrie, ever the seeker after novelty, set in the world of Ruritanian costumes and manners. Guthrie had a great admiration for Rich, describing him as "one of the six gentlemen who mean anything in the box office and also can even begin to make a showing in the great parts". But he was not at all sensitive to the delicate matter of actor's status. For Guthrie there was no such thing as a star, only bigger or smaller roles.

From the word go Rich was out of sorts with his part and with his director. As Thersites, "a rascal; a scurvy railing knave; a very filthy rogue", Rich was asked to dress up like a bookie's runner which made him look more foolish than devilish. After a day or two of rehearsal, he backed off pleading doctor's orders.

He took his final bow at the Old Vic as Henry V, a suitable gesture of farewell since it was for this part that Rich won the prestigious *Evening Standard* award for best actor. It was, said the judges, an easy choice, quite unlike the play of the year which turned on a long drawn-out debate over the relative merits of *Waiting for Godot* and a piece by Jean Giraudoux called *Tiger at the Gate*. The fact that Samuel Beckett lost out to the now-forgotten Giraudoux should tell us something about the value of show business awards.

Holding to his conviction that it would not be long before he returned to the London stage, Rich used the break before his next film commitment to sort out his finances to his own and his family's best advantage. Some time earlier, at the instigation of Aaron Frosch, he had made himself into a company known as Atlantic

Productions. Among the shareholders were all the senior members of the family who, twice a year, were given a gift — £750 in August and £250 just before Christmas. These were known as our "fotos", the Welsh slang for cheque, and they arrived punctually right up to the year of Rich's death. (Incidentally, the last foto I received was accompanied by a note from Valerie Douglas saying that because the bank transaction had actually taken place a day or two after Rich had died, the value of the cheque would be deducted from any gain I might make under Rich's will.)

There were other outgoings which he claimed against tax but at a time when tax rates were steeply progressive Rich was keen to find ways of holding on to a higher proportion of his earnings.

"As it is," he said, "it's not worth bothering after the first fifteen thousand. Most of it goes straight to the Inland Revenue."

The obvious solution, the one adopted by so many other high earners in the entertainment industry, was to become a tax exile.

"Look at it this way," he said. "As a resident abroad I can work three months a year in this country without getting into trouble with the Inland Revenue. That gives me plenty of time for stage acting. The rest of the time I would probably want to be abroad, anyway, in Hollywood or on film location. So why don't I make the best of it?"

It was then only a question of finding a place to live where the authorities were amenable and the surroundings tolerable. The offshore islands were immediately discounted. "I would feel cut off," said Rich.

This left Switzerland as the likeliest prospect. It was

close, convenient and offered a secure and unfussy style of living which appealed to Rich and Sybil.

They made their first sortie in early 1957 when they rented a small villa at Celigny. Within weeks they had bought Pays de Galles with its view of Mont Blanc. Their neighbours included the Aga Khan, Charles Chaplin, Peter Ustinov and Jean Anouilh. Rich opened his first Swiss bank account with the proceeds from *The Rains of Ranchipur* and *Alexander the Great* — it added up to close on one hundred thousand pounds.

With the move to Switzerland, Rich set up a family trust fund from which all of us benefited at one time or another. That we were able to buy our own homes when none of us were particularly well-off, was thanks entirely to our brother's generosity.

Just before he left to film in Jamaica he offered me use of his Jaguar.

"You've need of a car," he said. "Why not take this one?"

"No," I said, "it's a bit too grand for me, especially with petrol at three shillings a gallon. But I tell you what. Since you're offering, I wouldn't mind driving the MG."

He laughed. "I don't care what you do. But you'd better ask Sybil; it's her car."

I drove it for a full year and cared for it like a baby. I have never had a better car since.

Whenever any one of us hit a bad patch, Rich was the first to help out. It was always done in a jokey way, almost as if he sought to deflect a show of gratitude.

A long letter to brother Tom, at a time when life was showing its rough side, had buried within it this short paragraph:

"Enclosed is a little cheque. I hope you will accept it. I know how a few weeks' unemployment cripples your finances, and I don't want you to scrape through Christmas. You can pay me back sixpence a week out of your old age pension! If Wales beat the All Blacks I'll give it to you as a present."

Rich took a lot for granted but he was never crude in his giving. He recognised and respected working class pride.

In between thinking about Switzerland and actually moving there, Rich went off to make two modest films. The first, *Sea Wife*, was yet another of those ventures which must have looked all right on paper. It was a wartime love story of a shipwrecked sailor who falls in love with another survivor who just happens to be a nun. Despite exotic locations (the filming was in Jamaica) the story was made weak by the absence of any real passion and the perverse casting of Joan Collins as the religious novice. Already enjoying a reputation as a wicked lady, Miss Collins needed strong direction to steer her away from her self-imposed image. She might have got it from the first choice director, Roberto Rossellini, the leader of the Italian new wave, but with the break-up of his marriage to Ingrid Bergman and hotly publicised affair with an Indian screenwriter, he had too many problems on his mind to give much attention to the picture. Barely had filming started than Rossellini walked off the set, not to return. After that it was downhill all the way.

Joan Collins is on record as having livened up the proceedings by virtuously rejecting the advances of her co-star. But Rich denied he ever made the effort.

"She had a much exaggerated view of her own importance," he said. "But so did everybody else on the picture, including me. We deserved our disaster."

The other film was *Bitter Victory* with Curt Jungens and Ruth Roman. For Rich it was a return to the desert war, with a love interest thrown in. So adverse was its reception that Columbia withdrew the film before it went out on general release.

Rich returned to Switzerland to lick his wounds. On a visit to Wales he told me he thought his film career might be finished. The disappointment of his latest venture was compounded by the knowledge that he had thrown away at least two good chances to make amends. Yet neither was rejected heedlessly. *Reach for the Sky*, the story of the legless war hero, Douglas Bader, looked set to be a re-run of the disappointment over *The Last Enemy* which Korda had promised but failed to produce. In the event *Reach for the Sky* was a box office hit and a triumph for Kenneth More who played the indomitable flyer with style.

Even more of a heartbreak was losing out to Peter O'Toole, then a virtual beginner in films, on the casting for *Lawrence of Arabia*. In the critical week or so when the part was his for the asking, Rich could not bring himself to sign away a year of his life on another historical epic. The torture of *Alexander the Great*, not to mention *The Robe*, was too fresh in his memory.

It was some time before he could bring himself to see the film which made Peter O'Toole an international star. When he did, his verdict was characteristic.

"Peter has a streak of wildness that makes him entirely believable as a mad genius. It is, in itself, a sort of genius. I don't know that I can match it."

He was soon to find out. But for the moment Rich

was content to distance himself from the movies. "They sure to hell don't want me. And I sure to hell don't need them."

The spur to his reviving confidence was the offers coming in to tempt him back to the stage. It was an exciting time in the British theatre with a new generation of writers led by John Osborne, Harold Pinter and Arnold Wesker leading the attack on conventional middle-of-the-road drama. Hardly a day passed without the delivery of a script that was worth the effort of reading. The welcome mat was out at Stratford and at the Old Vic and at other theatres like the Royal Court and the Oxford Playhouse (Frank Hauser's latest venture) where the sparks of originality were flying. But Rich was in no hurry to commit himself. For a while I assumed it was his artistic judgement which was running on slow time but various comments he let drop soon led me to realise that financial considerations were uppermost in his mind.

"When there's a lot of money going out," he told me, "you need a lot of money coming in."

The tautology was not without force. Rich was beginning to take on the style and extravagances of a big star. Apart from an agent and financial adviser, he needed at least one secretary and a manager to handle his day-to-day arrangements.

Into this last role stepped brother Ivor. It was one way of keeping the money in the family but otherwise I was not over the moon about the appointment. My reservations were chiefly personal. While I admired Ivor as the driving force in the Jenkins family in the years after our mother's death, I was never able to get close to him, at least not until the last months of his life

160

when circumstances dictated a dramatic change in our relationship.

Ivor was the strong man of the family — tall, powerfully built and something of a fitness freak. He was always immaculate. Even in his working clothes — after being invalided out of the army, he made a living as a bricklayer — his trousers had a razor edge crease and his shoes were sparkling. As a child I lived in awe of him.

That he could be a steadying force in Rich's life was undeniable. His down to earth talent for practicalities was bound to ease the running of the household while his common sense might help to put a brake on some of Rich's wilder flights of fancy. But Ivor was not one to admire or argue on professional matters. Though an intelligent man he knew little of the theatre or films. For him, Rich was the creative genius who could do no wrong.

By mid summer 1957 Rich had decided on his next engagement. He was to return to the stage, after all, but not in London. The charms of the West End stage paled to a shadow against the bright inducements offered by Broadway. *Time Remembered* was another overweight fable from the pen of Jean Anouilh. No matter. Bolstered by Richard Burton and Helen Hayes, one of the grand dames of American theatre, the production brought in advance sales of six hundred thousand dollars, a record for a straight play in New York. The critics were polite without getting over-excited. Normally, they would have damned with their faint praise but this time they were overruled by ordinary theatre-goers who were drawn less by the show than by the desire to find out what this young Richard Burton was all about.

Rich was thrilled by his reception and comforted by

the feeling that, on stage, he was back on home ground. When I met him for dinner late one evening, I was amazed at the transformation from the restless and nervous character I had known in Wales not two months earlier to the assured and contented star performer, seemingly at the height of his powers.

After a few drinks he leaned across the table and tapped me on the arm. "Gray," he said, "remember when we were boys? From the very first day I kicked a rugby ball, I had two ambitions: to play for Wales at Cardiff Arms Park and to play against England at Twickenham. Well, it hasn't worked out that way. But why should I worry? Stratford and the Old Vic have been my Cardiff Arms Park and Broadway my Twickenham. I haven't a complaint or care in the world. Life has been good to me."

CHAPTER
NINE

As a family, the year started sadly with the death of Dadi Ni and ended happily with the birth of Kate Burton, named after Katherine Hepburn. Rich declared total delight with his daughter but this did not stop him launching into an affair which proved to be a near fatal hazard to his marriage.

Dadi Ni died at eighty-one. The event should not have been unexpected yet he had come through so much it was difficult to accept that he was no longer with us. The news was cabled to Rich in Switzerland. Ivor was with him. We assumed they would come back for the funeral but they decided against it. Their absence naturally created some gossip locally and in the press, which thankfully was treated lightly by Rich. He told reporters that Dadi Ni would never have approved the extravagance of a plane ticket — just to attend a burial.

But there was more to it than that. All his life, Rich tried to keep his distance from suffering and grief. I do not mean by this that he did not care. When sympathy and help was needed, he was quick to offer both, whatever the cost. But you were not likely to see Rich at the side of a hospital bed or at a funeral. It was almost as if he was frightened of letting himself go, of revealing too much. For all his build-up as the indomitable hero, Richard Burton was very easily moved to tears.

There was something else with Dadi Ni. Rich was never altogether sure what his father thought about him.

163

As he wrote to me, "I didn't know Dadi Ni very well — he was always an enigma to me — but blood is blood and I feel very empty today. Ivor has been hit much harder of course, but is as taciturn as a rock. Feels a lot, says nothing."

It occurred to me then that Ivor and Dadi Ni had much in common.

It was in the character of Dadi Ni to play his cards close to his chest. Compliments did not come easily from him. Yet Rich lived in a world where everybody told everybody, "You were wonderful, darling". He did not want or respect such effusiveness, least of all at home, but the contrast between all embracing warmth and what seemed to him to be chilly incomprehension made it difficult for him to get close to Dadi Ni. He assumed, wrongly, that Dadi Ni took no interest in his work. Certainly, the old man stayed away from Stratford and the Old Vic (at his age he could be forgiven for his dislike of long journeys) but he went to most of Rich's films.

When we were a lot older, stories about Dadi Ni often came into our conversation. Rich was surprised when I told him how our parent had enjoyed *The Robe*.

"He never even saw the film," Rich protested.

"He did so. I should know, I took him. We went by bus to Swansea and stood in the queue. As we came up to the ticket counter, the cinema manager recognised me or Dadi Ni. He said it was a huge privilege to see us there and offered us the best seats, free of charge. But Dadi Ni wouldn't have it. 'Oh no,' he said, his eyes twinkling, 'I couldn't accept. It would be like taking money out of my son's pocket.' "

I was laughing all through this but Rich listened in

silence. When I had finished, Rich thought for a moment. Then he said quietly, "I didn't know," and I could see there was a tear in his eye.

Early 1957 brought a summons to another funeral. It was for his friend Humphrey Bogart who was killed by throat cancer at fifty-eight. Again, Rich declined. But the memories stayed on.

"Can you believe it? The tough guy gone. He came from such a posh family. There was nothing tough about his upbringing. We used to joke about it. He said I had to give him lessons on how to look poor."

I murmured something about how sorry I was.

"It was his real name, you know, Humphrey Bogart. But he had a middle name. DeForest. Imagine it. *Casablanca* starring Ingrid Bergman and Humphrey DeForest Bogart. I told him, with a name like that, you could make a career in soap opera."

His favourite story of Bogart was of a party which had Cole Porter and Jack Buchanan among the guests. Each provided a little entertainment before Bogie turned to Rich.

"Spout some Shakespeare, kid!"

He did so and as he went into full voice, Cole Porter improvised an accompaniment and Jack Buchanan swept into a dance. What an act!

The following morning, Bogie was on the phone.

"I've just had a call from an agent," he told Rich. "He can get you eighteen thousand dollars a week if you do your act in front of a paying audience."

"Great," said Rich, "what's the catch?"

"He wants Cole and Jack too."

Kate was born on 11 September, weighing in at 6lb 4oz. She arrived a week prematurely which pleased Rich enormously because he was able to see her before flying to New York where he was to start rehearsals for *Time Remembered*. Playing opposite him in romantic mood was Susan Strasburg, at nineteen a seasoned Broadway actress who had earned her launch in *The Diary of Anne Frank*. Temporarily unaccompanied in New York, Rich took to inviting Miss Strasburg to parties and restaurants.

It was an exhilarating time on Broadway. Peter Ustinov was there with his play *Romanoff and Juliet*; Rex Harrison and Julie Andrews were appearing in *My Fair Lady*; and Laurence Olivier was startling his admirers as *The Entertainer*. Other party companions like Hugh Griffith and Donald Houston were in frequent attendance. Even Phil Burton was in town, pursuing his vocation as a guru of acting skills.

Pitched into this heady environment, my brother parted himself from any remaining vestiges of discretion. Susan Strasburg followed in his wake while creating a few waves of her own. She was no stranger to the bright lights. As the daughter of Lee Strasburg, founder and director of the Actors Studio and a titanic influence on American theatre and cinema, she had enjoyed an advanced upbringing and the company of lively minds. But she was still a girl with all the emotional extravagances of her age. Her affair with Rich was, for her, a matter of deadly seriousness. Rich was warned of this, by Ivor among others, but he ignored all the danger signals until it was too late to disentangle without great distress all round.

The arrival of Sybil and Kate allowed Rich the chance to play the devoted husband and father but by then he found it all but impossible to switch roles convincingly.

The gossip writers simply did not believe him, Susan Strasburg likewise.

Of all the principals in this sad saga, Sybil alone retained her dignity. This she achieved by flatly refusing to believe that anything untoward was happening. She even had the courage to return to Switzerland before the end of the run, leaving Rich in New York to sort out the problems of his own making.

Immediately Sybil was out of the way, Susan Strasburg moved in for the kill. There are many versions of what happened but my conviction is that Rich stalled to prevent a crisis. He had no intention of running off with Susan Strasburg (as he repeatedly told any of us who asked) but he held back from saying anything quite so emphatic to the lady for fear that she might throw a fit in front of the paparazzi. When she saw him off at the airport, it was in the fair hope that before many days had passed he would be back waving his divorce papers in one hand and a shiny new wedding ring in the other.

The reality was a sailor's farewell — passionate and permanent. Whatever he promised to the contrary, after his departure from *Time Remembered*, Rich made no effort to make contact with Susan Strasburg. A few months later when he was filming in London, Susan came to see him but was turned away. The panic was over. I assumed, too readily, that Rich had learned his lesson. He was at the end of one sad little affair. But the tragic love story of his life had yet to begin.

The success of *Time Remembered* and the renewed press interest in Richard Burton as a box office star, gave the film producers something to talk about. Maybe his screen career was not finished, after all. One offer Rich liked the look of very much indeed. It was to appear in the film version of John Osborne's play, *Look Back In Anger*. When it was first put on at the Royal Court in 1956, *Look Back In Anger* created more interest — and controversy — than any other new play since the war. By exposing the savage frustration of a young intellectual caught up in the web of British class values, Osborne departed radically from tried West End conventions of what made a good play. The critics welcomed an entertainment which struck close to the core of British political malaise and young audiences responded vigorously to a writer who could demonstrate their grievances.

On the crest of *Look Back In Anger* and his next play, *The Entertainer*, which introduced Laurence Olivier to the new drama, John Osborne joined with his director, Tony Richardson, to set up Woodfall, an independent film company, as the vehicle for carrying their revolution to the cinema.

Rich was by no means a political animal. Though vaguely socialist by tradition, he had no difficulty in reconciling ideals of equality with great personal wealth because, in truth, he did not think about it a lot. But he was attracted to originality of ideas and when these coincided with the opportunity to test his range as an actor, the bait was irresistible. Well, maybe only when the money was right. *Look Back In Anger* on screen paid so much better than *Look Back In Anger* on stage.

A fine cast was assembled to match the quality of the product. Along with Rich as the anti-hero Jimmy Porter, were Mary Ure as his wife Alison (the only survivor from the Royal Court production), Claire Bloom as Helena and Edith Evans, who gave one of her most moving performances, as Ma Tanner, a character referred to but never actually seen in the stage version.

At thirty-three, Rich was thought by some to be too old for his part (the American critics were particularly strong on this), but for me his age counted in his favour because it made the character more vulnerable. The callow Jimmy Porter of the theatre, ever whining about injustice, made you want to scream in frustration. If he felt that strongly about social inequality why didn't he get off his arse to do something about it? But in the film, Rich played a more mature and thoughtful Jimmy Porter whose anger drew sympathy because it conveyed a sense of time passing and opportunities lost. It was the first time I had seen Rich expose weakness and emotional inadequacy. *Look Back In Anger* was, for my money, the best thing he had done on stage or screen. The pity was that because the film was not a financial hit he failed to recognise the importance of what he had achieved.

I saw a lot of Rich during the filming of *Look Back In Anger*. He seemed to want family and friends around him. It was as if he was making a deliberate attempt to reinforce the domestic security he had so nearly lost over the affair with Susan Strasburg. When she appeared on the set at Elstree, the lack of warmth would not have shamed a November morning. Claire Bloom was also given the cold treatment which, I suspect, made the film an unhappy experience she felt she had done nothing to deserve.

Less easily deterred was Mary Ure, whose undisguised determination to get Rich into bed was all the more embarrassing because she was married to John Osborne. More than once I heard her proposition Rich in a way few men could have resisted.

"It's an occupational hazard," he told me.

For the first time I could see that the problems were not all one way.

After *Look Back In Anger*, the fortunes of Richard Burton went down and up like a yo-yo, and just as fast. Two bad movies followed in quick succession. The first, *The Bramble Bush*, was a low grade soap opera about a doctor involved in the mercy killing of his best friend; the second, *Ice Palace*, took Rich to Alaska for a tepid yarn about fishing against the elements. According to him the dip in the reputation was more than compensated for by the lift in his bank balance. When shooting overran on *Ice Palace*, the fee to Rich, set at a basic fifty thousand pounds, more than doubled.

The upturn started with the first ever production of the John Osborne play, *A Subject of Scandal and Concern*. Directed by Tony Richardson, it was shown on BBC television in 1960, three years before the play was adapted to the stage. Once again, Rich proved that he could show vulnerability without losing his grip of the role.

He went on to another television venture, this time a collaboration between the BBC and ABC to record a twenty-six-part documentary on the life and times of Winston Churchill. It was called *The Valiant Years*. As the off-screeen narrator, Rich had to be Churchill. But to imitate that distinctive voice was to invite ridicule as a second-rate impersonator. Instead Rich allowed his own deep mellow delivery to suggest the Churchill style while at the same time sticking close to the Churchill rhythm of pauses and inflexions. It was a superb display of acting which viewers on both sides of the Atlantic found entirely convincing. Churchill himself gave his unqualified approval.

"The actor and the politician have a lot in common," said Rich. "It takes one to know one. I was successful with Churchill because I knew his secret. He was the greatest actor of them all."

With that thought in mind and knowing what was to come next for Rich, I could not help wondering how Churchill, in his prime, would have fared in a Broadway musical. Rich, I have to say, took it in his stride.

The idea was put to him by Moss Hart, one of the legendary Broadway writers and directors, who had worked with Rich on *Prince of Players*. Higher on his credits was the direction of Lerner and Loewe's *My Fair Lady* for which he had picked up an Tony award. After the triumph of *My Fair Lady*, Alan Jay Lerner and Frederick (Fritz) Loewe had followed up with the equally successful film musical, *Gigi*, which won ten Oscars, the largest number ever received by any film in the history of Academy Awards. Now they were back with the live theatre and reunited with Moss Hart for a muscial adaptation of the story of King Arthur (he of the Round Table), his marriage to Guinevere and Guinevere's romance with Lancelot.

It was a tall order because the hero had to win sympathy while losing his wife, which was not the usual way of doing things on the musical stage. But the team who could win over middle America to a Parisian man-about-town who falls in love with a pubescent schoolgirl (Gigi) was not easily constrained by tradition.

Even so, Rich thought long and hard about *Camelot*. Was he really the sort of actor who could feel comfortable trilling pretty lyrics across the footlights? He put his fears to Alan Lerner and Fritz Loewe who assumed he was worried about his singing ability.

171

Alan Lerner was encouraging. "We had the same problem with Rex Harrison in *My Fair Lady*. Rex said he couldn't sing. But he learned to talk in tune and everyone thought he had a wonderful voice."

Rich was appalled. "But I can't do that. What would they say at home to a Welshman who was in a musical and wasn't allowed to sing? I'd be classed as a traitor."

His prospective employers were not convinced.

"But do you have a singing voice?" they asked dubiously.

Rich cleared his throat.

"Listen to this," he said and launched into a sturdy rendering of "A Cry in the Wilderness" — in Welsh.

At that point it was still open to the producers to say "Thank you" and "Next please". But instead they told Rich they wanted to go ahead, while reserving judgement on the musical virtues of the Welsh Presbyterian hymnal. For his part, Rich had built himself up to a level of enthusiasm where all his earlier worries were forgotten. He would play King Arthur and he would damn well make a success of it.

Rich quickly developed an affection for the triumvirate. Moss Hart he had got to know quite well over the years but he soon came to realise why this bubbly, talented man enjoyed working with Alan Lerner and Fritz Loewe. They had great style and humour.

I would love to believe Rich's version of the Rolls-Royce story.

"On a stayover in London, Alan, who had this great passion to own a Rolls-Royce, dragged Fritz along to a Bond Street showroom. 'Which do you want?' Alan asked Fritz. 'But I'm not buying,' said Fritz. 'You're the customer.' 'Don't be silly,' said Alan. 'Now you're here you might as well get one. You'll regret it if you don't.' 'OK,' said Fritz warily, 'I'll take that beauty.' 'Good,' said Alan, 'I'll have that one. Now we'd better find out what we do about paying.' Fritz put a hand on his friend's shoulder. 'Don't worry,' he said, lifting his cheque book from his pocket, 'I'll get this. You bought lunch.' "

Honesty compels me to add that Alan denied the last part of the story though he did buy a Rolls-Royce and he did persuade Fritz to follow his example.

Good humour and singleness of purpose were at a premium on *Camelot's* run up to Broadway. The chapter of accidents would have stopped any other show in its tracks. Alan Lerner, whose third marriage had just broken up, suffered a haemorrhage brought on by depression and overwork. No sooner was he out of hospital than Moss Hart had a heart attack. Meanwhile, frantic efforts were being made to reduce *Camelot* to a presentable length. When it opened at the new O'Keefe Center in Toronto, the final act was still in full swing at midnight. One critic praised the show for "helping considerably to shorten the winter".

Cuts and further cuts were made. By the time the show reached Boston it was down to four hours — manageable but still overlong. Throughout these tribulations Rich, by common consent, gave magnificent support.

"God knows what would have happened had it not been for Richard Burton," wrote Alan Lerner. "If ever a star behaved like a star in every sense of the word, it was he."

Rich led by example, learning new lines without complaint (before New York he had to rehearse what was virtually a rewritten second act) and offering encouragement to the rest of the cast. When there was time to spare he gave Shakespearian classes which became so popular as to attract recruits from outside the *Camelot* circle of actors. With Rich about, the inevitable moods of depression did not last very long. He had faith in the show and in the ability of the company to turn it round.

And he loved the challenge. "It sounds perverse," he admitted, "but when you're given a perfectly written part, like Hamlet, there's not much you can do with it after the first few performances. The Burton Hamlet is the Burton Hamlet and that's that. But in a show like *Camelot* when the changes are coming thick and fast, all things are possible. You can make something of the part that is yours and yours alone."

His co-star, Julie Andrews, though less of an extrovert, was equally supportive. She remained calm even when asked to learn a new song one day before the first New York preview.

If they were looking for reasons to be optimistic, the strongest was the advance booking. It was phenomenal. Even lurid press stories of disasters out of town could not stem the queue at the box office.

But the opening at the Majestic Theater in New York was another matter. All the celebrities in the world — and most of them seemed to be gathered there — and all the glitter of first night razzamatazz could not disguise the fact that, even now, all was not well. The show was still too long and too heavy. It also suffered by comparison with *My Fair Lady* which was in its fifth year on Broadway. There were more joyous, hummable tunes to be had in the company of Professor Higgins and Eliza Doolittle.

A quick glance at the reviews suggested that *Camelot* would close in six months, after it had exhausted its advance booking. But this was to fail to take account of the persistence of Alan Lerner and Moss Hart, who was now back in action as director. Once more the surgical knife was brought out. Twenty minutes was lopped off the running time.

Then came the big break. "The Ed Sullivan Show", the most popular on American television, devoted a whole hour to the music of Lerner and Loewe. No doubt the network expected a reworking of old favourites from *My Fair Lady* and *Gigi*. What it got was all the best from *Camelot* — "If Ever I Would Leave You", and "Where are the Simple Joys of Maidenhood?", Rich singing "Camelot" and Rich and Julie together singing "What do the Single Folk Do?".

The following morning the bandwagon started rolling. It was helped on its way by President Kennedy who declared *Camelot* to be his favourite musical. Earlier hostilities were forgotten. Everyone in the know said that *Camelot* was set for a very long run indeed.

I went out to New York for the opening of *Camelot*. It should have been one of the great moments of my life but no sooner had I arrived than I went down with 'flu which turned to pneumonia. I was promptly rushed off to Mount Sinai Hospital which can only be described as a luxury hotel for invalids. After I had been tucked up in bed by a pretty nurse and visited by a succession of doctors who looked as if they specialised in diseases of the rich, I fell to wondering about my health insurance.

The limit I could claim was two hundred and fifty pounds which, on a rough calculation of the value of my surroundings, meant that I had to recover by nightfall.

In fact I was in Mount Sinai for three weeks. I never even saw the bill. Rich paid it on my behalf telling me that when I got home I had to claim the insurance and use it for a family holiday. I must have been the first patient to come out of Mount Sinai at a profit.

From hospital I was taken to the Burton apartment on Central Park West, a palatial residence with as many rooms as a whole street of houses in Port Talbot. On the mat outside the front door was printed a large B which I thought was just a touch ostentatious for short-term residents. Sybil explained.

"It's not us. This is the Bogart apartment. Lauren Bacall has let us have the place for as long as we're in New York."

My hosts were under strict orders not to let me out of bed but I was desperate to see *Camelot* and threatened to be a difficult patient unless my wish was granted. So after a few evenings of frustrating inactivity, Sybil took me to the theatre. No effort was called for on my part. I did not even have to press the elevator button. Bob Wilson, a charming and gentle black American who was the latest addition to the Burton entourage, helped me in and out of the car, up and down steps and virtually lifted me into my seat in the centre stalls.

It was a magical evening. As the severest critic of my brother's singing I have to say that he confounded all my fears. His voice came across magnificently. But he was so much more than a singing actor. He had to impart love, joy, sadness and in the end, hope and strength of spirit. It was all very sentimental but none the worse for that. Lavished on the audience as only the American theatre knows how, the splendour of *Camelot* was, as a critic put it, "the timeless dream of Broadway".

Rich was so much at home in his portrayal of Arthur that he could work the audience as he wished. T. H. White, the author of *The Once and Future King*, on which *Camelot* was based, told me how Rich had proved to him his command of the script.

"In the speech about how he became a king while still a boy, he talked about the sword in the stone and how he thought it was a war memorial. It was, I thought, a hushed speech but Richard played it for a laugh. I objected to the treatment in a mild way saying, 'Why break the pathos?' Richard said, 'Very well, Tim; tonight just for you I'll play it straight.' And he did. Until then, I didn't know an actor could compel an audience to laugh or not, as the fancy took him."

I had my own evidence for Rich's ability to ring the changes. On that first evening, I was startled almost out of my seat when I heard King Arthur greet his crusty old friend Pellinore with the question,

"How goes it with my kinsman, Sir Graham? Word comes to me that he was gravely ill. I trust he is now in better health."

Pellinore, played by Robert Coote, an actor of military style and bearing who did not welcome any departure from the rules, blustered a response. From where I was sitting it sounded like a vague indication that poor Sir Graham was on his way out. But on stage, the words of Pellinore came over with stark clarity.

"What the bloody hell are you talking about?"

Rich threw an arm around Robert's shoulder and boomed with laughter.

"No matter, no matter. We will talk of this again later."

Pellinore looked understandably nervous.

In the weeks I stayed with Rich and Sybil, the routine was for me to drive with Rich to the theatre and stay with him in the dressing room until curtain up. Then I would watch the show from the wings.

Each day the car was ordered for just after five, earlier than was strictly necessary but Rich hated sitting in the rush hour traffic. Once at the theatre and having bounced our way through the crowd of autograph hunters, Rich did the round of the dressing rooms greeting the rest of the company. This was not just friendliness on his part. He liked to be sure there were no problems like an unexpected sickness before he started his own preparations for the show.

Rich never ate before going on stage but he drank copiously, starting with vodka and ending with a can or two or three of Budweiser beer. This was in the days when my brother's drinking was treated as a joke. Because however much booze he got through it never seemed to affect his performance, colleagues who might otherwise have delivered a friendly warning indulged his choice of relaxation. I remember someone telling me, "For Richard the bottle is like a second wife; and who wants to break up a happy marriage?"

While his dresser bustled around, Rich and I filled the hour before curtain up with talk about family and rugby, anything but show business chatter. In the last moments he went over the opening scene in his mind while humming a couple of lines from the first song. But even in the early weeks of the show he never rehearsed in his dressing room.

"If I don't know it now," he said, "I never will."

After a good show, Rich was in high spirits, eager to go out on the town. It was not at all like Stratford or

178

the Old Vic where often he was too exhausted to change out of his costume. Standing ovations were not uncommon and when the cheering was loud and strong, Rich would come out with a phrase we had heard from our brother Tom.

"I reckon I've filled my ten drams today."

Ten drams, or trucks, of coal justified a bonus.

Dinner with Sybil or some of the cast or with visiting celebrities seldom ended before two or three in the morning. But Rich was no longer a late riser. He was usually up at seven, planning a morning in the recording studios (he was still working on *The Valiant Years*) or meetings with producers and agents.

It was a hectic year, one in which he never missed a single performance and which culminated in a Tony award for best actor in a musical.

If, professionally, Rich was enjoying one of the best periods of his life, on the domestic front all was not well. It was difficult to understand why. If he had been a faithful husband it might have been said of Rich that he was suffering the seven-year-itch. But Sybil was reconciled to his philandering which he no longer sought to disguise. I suppose they both thought that after the Susan Strasburg affair any lesser indiscretion could be treated as incidental.

Drink was more of a problem in so far as Rich in his own home was liable to become argumentative and abusive. It was a side of him that most of his friends in the theatre had yet to see, though from comments made to me I suspect they guessed what Sybil had to put up with. That she did tolerate wild bouts of temper and even excused them says much for her.

Sybil, said Tim Hardy, "was born to flower with

Richard''. How true. She never did anything that was not with his interests in mind, but in a curious sort of way she gained strength from giving so much.

Rich was a lucky man and I told him so, adding, ''What did you use to say? You hadn't a care in the world. So what's happened to you?''

He hunched his shoulders and lowered his head as if he was about to wrap himself into a ball.

''I don't know, Gray, I don't know. It's just that, well, all this, it's not what I expected.''

He stopped there. There was nothing further to get out of him. It was clear that he had not yet found contentment. Why, I could only guess.

One possibility was the tragedy of his second daughter. Born on 26 November 1959, Jessica was a pretty dark-haired baby. Outwardly she appeared a normal, healthy child, if somewhat withdrawn. She never smiled or showed pleasure in the silly games children enjoy. In New York she spent all her waking hours staring, uncomprehending, at the flicker of the television screen. Rich was incensed.

''Why does she do that? It's not natural.'' And to Sybil, ''Why the hell doesn't she do something, say something?''

Just before I returned home, they discovered the answer. Jessica was autistic.

When Sybil told me the medical verdict, I was lost for anything constructive to say.

''What does it mean?'' I asked. ''Can she be helped?''

Sybil was tired and, unusually for her, clearly depressed.

''Nobody knows what autism really is. That's the hell of it. It's a sort of mental illness, I suppose. Jessica lives

180

in a world of her own. She doesn't recognise me or Rich or anybody. There's no way of telling just how much she understands."

Rich turned for advice to doctors and psychiatrists. The answer was always the same. There was very little that medical science could do. The only hope was that Jessica would eventually respond to the unselfish and undemanding love of those around her.

It did not have to be spelt out to Rich that the home of a busy actor who was out at odd times and travelling a lot was not best suited to the needs of an autistic child. Except in one respect. Ivor and his wife Gwen were on hand.

Not having any children of their own, Ivor and Gwen doted on the young Burtons. Nothing was too much trouble. I cannot say if Jessica might in the end have acknowledged their unstinting devotion. When Rich and Sybil parted, there were hints of possible breakthrough. Gwen, who was the most gentle and motherly of women, told everybody she was making headway and was devastated when Jessica was taken away. The break with Kate was equally hard to bear though here it was Ivor who took the hardest knock.

Kate could not pronounce Ivor so she called him Eye-Eye and she wrote a poem saying how much she loved him. Ivor had the poem framed and kept it by his bed. It stayed there all his life.

Jessica was eventually put into a special home where she remains to this day. Sybil and Rich often went to see her until the doctors advised against any more visits. It was too upsetting for the girl, they said. As part of the divorce settlement with Sybil, Rich set up a trust

181

fund which guarantees proper care for Jessica as long as she lives.

But this is to jump ahead in the story. When I left New York in early 1961, there was no thought in Rich's mind of breaking up the family. He was restless and discontented; maybe even feeling a little guilty now that he knew the seriousness of Jessica's illness and how little he could do to help her. But what he wanted was a distraction, not a disruption in his life.

The opportunity came with a phone call from producer Walter Wanger. He had seen *Camelot* and had enjoyed the show enormously. He wanted to have lunch with Rich to put an idea to him. Rich said he would be delighted. He hoped the idea was an exciting one. Oh yes, said Mr Wanger, he could be sure of that.

When they met, the producer lost no time in getting to the point. The offer was for Richard Burton to co-star, on second billing, with Elizabeth Taylor in the Twentieth Century-Fox blockbuster, *Cleopatra*. Perhaps, suggested Walter Wanger, Rich had heard a thing or two about the film. He was indulging in irony. Not to have heard of *Cleopatra* was akin to saying you lived on the moon.

Already a year into production, *Cleopatra* was less a tragedy than a disaster. No sooner had shooting commenced than the picture was deprived of its major asset. Elizabeth Taylor was rushed into hospital with a near fatal bout of pneumonia. Studio politics caused the resignation of the director and contractual limitations led to the premature departure of leading actors. Peter Finch who was to have been Caesar and Stephen Boyd, cast as Antony, dropped out to pursue other less stressful roles. The budget debit stood at five million dollars with nothing to show for it. Meanwhile, it had been decided to abandon filming in England where, belatedly, it was discovered that the climate was ill-suited to the recreation of ancient Egypt. Not for nothing was *Cleopatra* known as the film that fell flat on its asp.

But the latest news, insisted Wanger, was more encouraging. Elizabeth Taylor had all but recovered and was ready to begin work, Joseph Mankiewicz, installed as a director of calming influence and sensitive touch, was heavily into rewriting the script, Rex Harrison looked set to play Caesar and the budget had been replenished. In fact, so much money was swishing around that it was possible to advance highly attractive terms; like a quarter of a million dollars plus generous living expenses including a family villa outside Rome (the latest choice for the location) and two chauffeur-driven cars on permanent call plus a share of the profits.

As an exciting diversion, *Cleopatra* was irresistible. The film took Rich into a higher earning bracket, which was success of a sort, it offered another chance to conquer the big screen and it was a way out of family preoccupations.

"Anyway," he told me, "I've always wanted to play Antony. This is maybe not quite what I had in mind but it's a good second best."

There was one problem. Rich still had three months to go on his *Camelot* contract. Walter Wanger thought the matter could be settled amicably. Recognising someone who was determined to get what he wanted (Wanger, who was not a fit man, saw *Cleopatra* as a final glorious chapter in his career) Rich advised Alan Lerner to demand of Twentieth Century-Fox what he thought his star was worth. Alan conjured up a figure and put on a percentage to allow for bargaining. Fifty thousand dollars was what Alan Lerner suggested by way of compensation and that was precisely what he got. It was, he said, an easier way of making money than writing musicals.

As the outgoing star of *Camelot*, Rich had the biggest say in choosing his successor. He put forward the name of William Squire, fellow Welshman and Shakespearian actor whose career had spanned all the leading classical companies.

"But a musical," queried Moss Hart, "can he play in a musical?"

"If I can, he can," declared Rich. There was really no answer to that.

William came over to New York and was given the full treatment. Rich took him to meet the cast, ending up at his own dressing room.

"And this," he boomed, waving expressively, "is all yours." Shell-shocked by hospitality, William took in what was by far the most spacious and comfortable dressing room he had so far encountered. He was impressed but also a little bemused at a style of living to which few serious actors ever aspired. "Richard had moved out of reach. We couldn't quite get to him any more."

But there was a single welcome note of normality. After the show, Richard and William had dinner at Sardis. William spent some time studying the five-star menu, eventually coming up with a choice exotic enough to suit the occasion.

"And what are you going to have?" he asked Rich.

"Me?" said Rich, having thrown the menu aside without giving it a glance. "Oh, I'll have a plate of chips."

The waiter took the order without a blink. William

half wondered if the man knew he was one of the few remaining links between Richard Burton and ordinary life.

I went to New York for Rich's final night in *Camelot*. It was an extraordinary experience which had me in tears when, after a dozen curtain calls, the company disappeared into the wings to leave the king alone on stage to abdicate his throne. At the farewell party, Moss Hart led the toast to the future of Richard Burton.

"Great actors like you," he said, addressing himself to Rich, "are born once in a lifetime. You are as big a personality off the stage as on the stage and you are, in every sense, larger than life." He paused to raise his glass but instead of finishing on that high note he continued in softer voice, "I beg you not to waste your wonderful gifts. You must know you have it in you to be one of the greatest stage actors of this century."

Sadly, this plea was only heard. It was not understood.

CHAPTER
TEN

And so to Elizabeth Taylor, alias Cleopatra.

At twenty-eight she was the nearest America had to a princess. She was photographed whenever she stepped out and quoted whenever she opened her mouth in public.

Her film career went far enough back into childhood for the entire country to have witnessed her maturity from winsome juvenile to stunning beauty. Devoid of privacy, her every action was open to public judgement. The devastation she suffered when her third husband, producer Mike Todd, died in a plane crash set off a tidal wave of sympathy which promptly receded when the tabloids blazoned the love of Elizabeth Taylor for the singer Eddie Fisher, her late husband's best friend.

The preliminary to their marriage was Eddie Fisher's much publicised divorce from Debbie Reynolds, whose prim ways made her favourite of the bible belt. Elizabeth was blamed, unjustly, for wrecking a partnership which was already heading for the rocks.

Elizabeth married Eddie Fisher in May 1959. By then she had completed her best film to date, *Cat on a Hot Tin Roof*, and had embarked on another sweaty piece from Tennessee Williams, *Suddenly Last Summer*. Her director, Joseph Mankiewicz, not one to dispense compliments lightly, described her as "close to being the greatest actress in the world."

Back on her pedestal as America's favourite actress,

Elizabeth saw off the competition for Cleopatra with a deal which promised her one million dollars, ten per cent of the gross and a small army of paid servants. Meanwhile, she collected an Oscar for her latest film, *Butterfield 8*. Elizabeth Taylor was at the height of her very considerable powers. She had much to lose.

Her long illness and slow recovery put a strain on the Twentieth Century-Fox accountants but they were up against the publicity people who could produce a mileage of press coverage to show how their girl would, to the benefit of all, shine at the box office. The more money poured into *Cleopatra*, it was argued, the more would eventually come out. The budget was reworked to add up to a staggering one hundred and twenty-four million dollars.

Enter Richard Burton. Plucked from *Camelot* where he had ruled as undisputed star he was now part of a film package in which the only vital constituent was Elizabeth Taylor. However generous the rewards to Rich or to Rex Harrison or to anyone else who appeared in *Cleopatra*, it was clear that their contribution was secondary to the overriding need to maximise Elizabeth's earning capacity.

Rich's place in the pecking order was confirmed by the casual way in which he and Sybil and the family were installed in their villa and then left to kick their heels for three months until he was wanted on set. (Wanger might have saved his money.) He made light of the experience — he wrote home letters saying how much he appreciated the enforced rest — but the idleness had more than a recuperative effect. The frustration of waiting rekindled his ambition. He was determined to win.

So it was that in the first scene with Elizabeth, shot in January 1962, he came almost as an adversary, an actor possessed with the desire to dominate. The effect was electrifying. Among those who crowded the set that day was Ron Berkeley who, as make-up artist for Elizabeth on most of her films, had seen her capitulate, on screen, to a succession of leading men. But this was new.

"Elizabeth was not used to assertive men. Oh, they might put on an act for a while but they nearly all ended up showing love by deference, paying tribute to her beauty. Only one other man had taken her by sheer force of personality. When she encountered Richard Burton it must have seemed to her that she had rediscovered Mike Todd."

There were striking similarities between Richard Burton and the flamboyant showman producer. Both had tough, sometimes aggressive personalities, both enjoyed the pleasures of wealth and both were capable of phenomenal extravagance. But more to the immediate point, both had it in them to face Elizabeth on equal terms.

From their first meeting (excluding the early chance encounter at the Hollywood party when he was over for *The Robe*) Rich was neither frightened nor overawed by Elizabeth. This in itself must have come as a surprise to the lady. But he was also attentive and intrigued. How could he not have been? Elizabeth was, after all, a fascinating woman.

One reason why film production is so expensive is that it requires a lot of skilled people sitting around doing nothing, waiting for their turn to work. Not only is this method of organisation costly; it also creates an environment in which gossip thrives. Much of it is good humoured tittle-tattle about who is sharing a bed with whom and goes no further than the well stocked dinner table. But when the film is a projected world beater, the stars are front page favourites and rumours abound as to the unsatisfactory state of their current marriages, that is where the trouble starts. It quickly gathers pace if the location happens to be on the home ground of some of the sharpest, hardest and most cruelly devious scandal writers and photographers in the business. It was thus with *Cleopatra*.

One week after the first clinch, director and producer were discussing the probability of a Burton-Taylor affair and its likely impact in terms of adverse publicity. One week after that there were nudge nudge stories and suggestive pictures in every show business column at home and abroad.

In our little enclave in Wales, the rumours were greeted with disbelief and anger. But as the rumours persisted, anger turned to fear that after all, something was seriously wrong.

Many years afterwards Rich told me that he and Elizabeth had been thrown together by events. I knew then what he meant though if the comment had been made much earlier I might have dismissed it as an easy excuse for adultery.

The problem for them both was to do what they were paid to do — which was to fall in love on screen — and yet to keep their distance away from the set. With an actor of more celibate reputation and an actress of less obvious charms, this might have been possible. But they weren't and it wasn't.

And so what started as a harmless — or more or less

harmless — flirtation soon became a matter of public concern. Sybil behaved with her customary dignity. She refused to panic and stayed loyal to Rich, but after many inconclusive challenges which showed her husband to be troubled and confused, she departed with the children to Switzerland.

"It is best," she said, "for Rich to be free to work out his own future."

As Sybil flew out, Eddie Fisher flew in. Already made insecure by the challenge of trying to be something more than Elizabeth Taylor's husband, he made the fatal mistake of presenting himself too obviously as the aggrieved party. From the popular press he got the sympathy he expected but couched in such patronising terms as to make him look foolish. Elizabeth was privately furious at his anguished protestations while publicly asserting her determination to hold together her marriage. Likewise, Rich declared his love for Sybil and a refusal to countenance a break-up of his family.

Under some pressure from my relatives I tried to put through a call to Rich but either he was not available or he refused to speak to me — I suspect the latter. Whenever Rich was in trouble his first inclination was to try to ignore it. Instead I spoke to Ivor.

"What's going on, then?"

"What do you mean?"

"Oh, come on, Ivor. You know what I'm talking about."

"If it's those newspaper stories, there's no truth in them."

"Are you sure?"

"Would I be telling you otherwise?"

"It's just that it's difficult to believe they make it all up."

"Well, they do. There was an article last week. It said that Rich had been to Elizabeth Taylor's villa a dozen times. But I know for a fact, he was there just once and that was to tell her it was all over."

So there *was* an affair. What else was going on? I knew Ivor well enough to realise that he had two priorities — to protect Rich and to shield the family, expecially Cis, from hurtful news. He was not going to make it easy for me to find out the truth.

In another phonecall, I got out of him that he had persuaded Sybil to return to Rome to talk over the future with Rich. Leaving the two of them alone in the villa, Ivor and Gwen had taken a long weekend in Naples. That was in early February. On the same weekend, Elizabeth and Eddie Fisher met in Paris to try to sort out their lives.

From all that I discovered subsequently I do believe that Rich wanted to save his marriage but could not bring himself to cut away cleanly from Elizabeth. Anyway, given that they had a picture to make, his problem could not be solved by a straight choice.

Elizabeth argued much the same with Eddie Fisher. But neither he nor Sybil were prepared to accept half measures. Why, they must have asked, should we make sacrifices?

Sick to death of the humiliation piled on him by the press, Eddie Fisher retreated to Switzerland to the house he and Elizabeth had bought recently at Gstaad. Sybil decided to go to New York. She did not tell Rich of her plans but left Ivor to break the news after she had gone.

Rich, meanwhile, had some travelling of his own to

do. He was to spend two days in Paris filming a cameo role for a star-spangled chronicle of the 1944 D-Day landings called *The Longest Day*. It was more than two years before I saw this film and, my, how it brought back memories of the turmoil of his private life. He played an RAF pilot as if the character was suffering from more than battle fatigue. In the scene where he and Donald Houston crouch over their drinks lamenting the friend who did not return, the pauses are so long as to suggest either that Rich had his mind elsewhere or the director of an otherwise very noisy film had suddenly been converted to the dramatic effect of the extended silence. I take the former to be the likeliest explanation.

I know that Rich intended flying the long route to Rome via New York where he hoped to persuade Sybil that their marriage could yet be saved. But the pulling power of Elizabeth Taylor proved too strong.

On 18 February, the world press carried the story of Elizabeth's attempted suicide.

Rich caught the first plane direct to Rome. So did Eddie Fisher.

The truth, as they discovered soon after landing, was not quite as dramatic as the morning's headlines. Elizabeth had indeed been taking sleeping tablets, but with the innocent intention of getting some sleep. No doubt she was piling on the agony as the misjudged victim of a romantic tug of war. But those around her heightened the tension by their cloying concern and melodramatic gestures. So when Elizabeth's hairdresser, Vivian Zavits, took her some sandwiches and milk, saw her stretched out on the bed and screamed "Oh, my God, she's taken pills", it was simple reflex for one or other of the staff to summon an ambulance, doctors and the US cavalry.

While the ambulance roared across town to the Salvator Mundi Hospital another friend obligingly rang the press and told them where to wait to get the best pictures. Poor Elizabeth, befuddled by sleep, hardly knew what was going on. It took less than an hour for the doctors to report there was nothing at all wrong with Elizabeth Taylor but by then the press was in no mood for good news. They wanted to hear the worst and when they did not get it they suspected a cover up.

Support for this jaundiced view came when Walter Wanger put out a barely plausible story of how he and Elizabeth, having shared lunch, had eaten something which disagreed with them. This begged the question as to why Wanger was not also in hospital. Why he had to lie when he could just as easily have told the truth I cannot say, but the effect was to cause further confusion. Rich flew in to a barrage of reporters demanding to know his version of the story. When he said he did not have one, they shouted their disbelief. Rich was furious.

As his press agent, Chris Hoffa, hurried him out to his car, Rich heard for the first time that Elizabeth was all right.

"So what the hell else is going on?"

Chris Hoffa had no idea. The studio was refusing to make any statements, assuming, with scant regard for the perseverence of bloodhounds, that silence would end speculation. Predictably the reverse happened. Readers of the popular press had a wider choice of contradictory stories than at any time since the first day's shoot.

Rich determined that if no one else was willing to act,

he would. On the journey from the airport, he and Chris Hoffa worked out a statement. It began:

> "For the past several days uncontrolled rumours have been growing about Elizabeth and myself. Statements attributed to me have been distorted out of proportion, and a series of coincidences has lent plausibility to a situation which has become damaging to Elizabeth."

There was more on the same lines, all well intentioned but too vague to achieve the aim of cutting out rumour and speculation.

Sadly, Rich did not consult the studio before issuing his statement so that the first Walter Wanger knew of it was when the press started bombarding him with telephone calls. Totally at a loss as to how to respond, he fell back on a straight refusal to believe that Rich had said anything at all. He even tried to persuade Rich to deny he ever made his statement.

The chaos off the *Cleopatra* set was matched by the chaos on the set. With thousands of extras milling about, it was virtually impossible to film any scenes with Elizabeth and Rich without someone smuggling out an unauthorised picture. Large sums of money were offered for the most intimate shot of the two stars together. One woman who was keen to make a fortune and her career in photojournalism, constructed an elaborate, fluffy hairpiece which served as a nest for a miniature camera. She was caught when a crew member noticed her predilection for manipulating her left breast like a bell push. The control mechanism was strapped to her bra.

With the entire Twentieth Century-Fox production terrified of adding fuel to what was obviously a blazing fire, Joe Mankiewicz was asked to postpone filming any scenes which might be judged controversial. This left Rich and Elizabeth little to do except concentrate on avoiding the press and sorting out their private lives.

The first rule, they decided, was to stay well away from each other. Leaving Elizabeth in Rome to celebrate her thirtieth birthday with her long suffering husband, Rich set off for Pays de Galles for a family conference. Ivor and Gwen were there; so too were our second eldest brother Tom and his wife, who went along to represent the views of the home base. If this sounds as if we were pushing our noses into affairs that did not concern us, I can only re-emphasise that we were all touched by Richard Burton's notoriety. There was no intention of giving uninvited advice but we did feel we had a right to know from Rich what was going on and to explain to him the upset and wrong caused by the sensationalist press.

By all accounts Rich put on his best act of contrition. He admitted an affair with Elizabeth but claimed it was a passing fancy common enough in the film business, which the press had exaggerated out of all proportion.

"I don't want to break up my marriage," he insisted. "I don't want to leave Sybil. Everything will be all right if only she'll listen to reason."

A clear impression brought away by Tom was that Rich was actually frightened of what he had started. For the first time the prospect of losing Sybil was real. And not just Sybil. With her would go his confidence and his stability.

"He won't take the risk," said Tom. "He's not that much of a fool."

But we reckoned without Elizabeth Taylor. She was

a tough young lady who was not easily deflected. I guess that at this point she had still to fasten on Richard Burton as the man for her. But she had made another decision which was every bit as significant. She had decided that her marriage to Eddie Fisher was over.

When Rich arrived back in Rome he found a changed Elizabeth. The heartache she had been carrying around had disappeared. She was a lighter, happier Elizabeth, beautiful and great fun to be with. Rich soon caught the mood. Even the paparazzi seemed less threatening.

"Why should we hide away?" Rich demanded to know. "What have we to be ashamed of?"

Elizabeth came up with a plan for thwarting their pursuers.

"They want pictures, so let's give them pictures. Let's give them more pictures than they expect, more pictures than they could ever want. Let's give them so many pictures, they'll never want to point a camera at us again."

The idea appealed to Rich. It was outrageous, it was a laugh and it might just have worked. Never once did it occur to him that Sybil or anyone else in the family would misinterpret the rush of scurrilous publicity. They would know it was just good old Rich having his game. Wouldn't they?

On the evening of 31 March Rich and Elizabeth went out on the town. Forewarned, the photographers turned up in force. The couple was photographed hand in hand, joking and laughing. Short of a lingering embrace, whatever they were asked to do, they did.

The gossip writers claimed that Richard Burton and Elizabeth Taylor were in love. Now, they had the pictures to prove it.

The following day, the story made the front pages round the world.

The studio bosses did not know whether to laugh or cry. The Burton–Taylor affair was creating vast publicity for *Cleopatra*, more than any previous film had ever enjoyed. But was it good publicity? Among those who thought not was the Pope. A bulletin from the Vatican condemned the "caprices of adult children" which were said to "offend the nobility of the heart which millions of married couples judge to be a beautiful and holy thing."

For a Presbyterian, causing offence in Rome was not such a dreadful thing. When it came up in a phone conversation, Rich was dismissive. "He's never been on my party list." Even so, the dishonourable mention from the Pope made its impact on public opinion, especially in the States where, once again, the moral minority turned against Elizabeth. Wagging tongues kept up a chorus of disapproval which hit a crescendo of absurdity when an eccentric far-right Democrat tried to persuade his colleagues in the House of Representatives to support a banning order on Richard Burton's entry into the United States. Backed by a weird assemblage of campaigners for righteousness, Congressman Feighan, who was not used to being taken seriously, fed the neurosis at Twentieth Century-Fox. Trembling for their jobs, the studio executives talked of nothing else but *Cleopatra*. Had they got a sellable film? If yes, would "The Scandal" help or harm its prospects?

The fact was, nobody knew. But that did not deter speculation. Rich and Elizabeth tried to block their minds to what was going on around them. This was easier for Elizabeth who was more in control of herself and less inclined to take kindly to moral platitudes. Rich was at the other extreme — confused and, out of deference to Sybil, feeling that he had to listen to everyone. He was not short of choice. When the family had done with him — and we were all adamant in our desire to see him make a clean and final break with Elizabeth — the heavy guns such as Emlyn Williams were hauled to the front. He flew to Rome to urge his young friend to return to Sybil. Rich listened politely, agreed that Emlyn was talking good sense and said he would think about it. He told us all he would think about it.

I have no doubt he kept his promise. But he was a prisoner of his own emotions. He loved Sybil and was spellbound by Elizabeth. To act decisively was beyond him. He lived from day to day hoping decisions would be made for him, willing the fates to direct him. He was confused, uncharacteristically obtuse and contradictory, all without appearing to notice the change in his own character.

Just how muddled he had become was revealed to me a few months later when Rich was interviewed by Kenneth Tynan for *Playboy* magazine. By now filming on *Cleopatra* was finished and Rich and Elizabeth were in London working on their second film together, *The VIPs*. As a general rule, Rich was refusing press interviews but Tynan, who had sought him out for stardom and more than once had nominated him as Laurence Olivier's successor, was an obvious exception. The meeting was at the Dorchester where Rich and Elizabeth had adjoining suites overlooking Hyde Park. Possibly anticipating misunderstandings, Kenneth Tynan sensibly took along a tape recorder.

The talk began with a re-run of Burton the stage actor

with some neat jibes at his eminent rivals ("Olivier frequently dries up; John Gielgud never stops drying up") and a bilious attack on modern playwrights. Of Samuel Beckett — "*Waiting for Godot* is playable, I suppose; it doesn't make sense, but it's playable"; of Arthur Miller "totally humourless"; of Tennessee Williams — "There is only one line in all his plays that I consider memorable" (it was a stage direction in *A Streetcar Named Desire*); and of Eugene O'Neill — "Hopeless. No good. The phoniest playwright I've ever read." Only John Osborne escaped unscathed.

After this warming up session during which, no doubt, a fair amount of alcohol was consumed, Tynan steered the discussion towards personal matters.

"What," he asked, "are your views on the sanctity of marriage?"

Rich took the bait and was soon floundering in shallow waters.

"Monogamy is absolutely imperative." (Yes, he really did say this.) "The minute you start fiddling around outside the idea of monogamy, nothing satisfies anymore. Suppose you make love to an exciting woman other than your wife. It can't remain enough to go to bed with her; there must be something else, something more than the absolute compulsion of the body. But if there is something more, it will eventually destroy either you or your marriage."

As I was soon to find out, this view was strictly in accord with the thinking of Elizabeth Taylor. Coming from her, it made sense. She had always stuck to the view that sex on its own was utterly meaningless. But from Rich? Who could blame Kenneth Tynan for not believing his ears. He posed the obvious follow up. How could Rich square his philosophy of marriage in general with his own in particular?

"Speaking for myself," said Rich, "I couldn't be unfaithful to my wife without feeling a profound sense of guilt."

Well, that was good to know. But what about Elizabeth? Presumably he felt guilty about her.

"Absolutely not. I'm not unfaithful to my wife. I never have been, not for a moment."

Tynan gave him a way out.

"Physically or spiritually?"

Rich spurned the offer.

"Neither. It's wrong to assume I've been unfaithful simply because I happen to live in the same hotel as another woman." He went on, "What I have done is to move outside the accepted idea of monogamy without investing the other person with anything that makes me feel guilty. So that I remain inviolate, untouched."

There was more nonsense of this sort before Tynan mercifully let his victim off the hook. In reply to the last question, Rich confessed that he was "a mass of contradictions". To which we could all respond, "You can say that again."

I have quoted at length from this interview without the intention of showing that my brother was capable of making a fool of himself. That he did appear foolish was undeniable, but there was more to it than that. Rich was a deeply troubled man, possibly close to breakdown. The pressures were too many and too heavy for him to take.

Soon after he and Elizabeth departed Rome, the rumour went round that *Cleopatra* was, to put it mildly, an unmanageable film. Before its release, two hours had to be cut from the original running time. Even so, the

200

story line was tediously protracted. Awesome spectacle there was in plenty but it could not compensate for lack of pace.

Depression settled on Twentieth Century-Fox. For weeks, it was said, the only sound to be heard at the studio was of senior staff clearing their desks. After the first shock of failure came the witch hunt. Who was to blame? The prime candidates were Richard Burton and Elizabeth Taylor. However competent as performers, their personal shenanigans had distracted producer and director from their professional responsibilities. Another version of the charge sheet held that while the film was good, if not brilliant, family entertainment, the stars' behaviour destroyed its appeal at the box office. At least four major US distributors took this view. So strongly did they feel about it they sued Fox for eight million dollars as compensation for loss of revenue.

Because of bad reviews and all the recriminations, it is usually assumed that *Cleopatra* was a financial disaster. I am not sure that anyone outside the boardroom of Fox has ever seen the true figures but from what Elizabeth has told me about her earnings from the picture (she was on a share of the gross) it must, in the end, have broken even. Certainly Rich emerged with a much healthier bank balance. It was his professional esteem that was on the sick list.

Despite all the traumas of *Cleopatra*, Rich and Elizabeth immediately decided to do another film together. From Rich's point of view it was a way of putting off the time when he would have to make a clearcut decision about his marriage. For Elizabeth, it was a step in the right direction. But making the film was torment for both.

Written by Terence Rattigan, *The VIPs* was an attempt to cash in on the glamour of the jet set. Various important persons gathered at Heathrow for a New York flight. Among them was an enormously wealthy businessman (Rich), his glamorous jewel-decked wife (Elizabeth) and her lover (Louis Jourdan) who was plotting to steal her away. Stranded at the airport by fog these and other characters who were in no way connected except by the coincidence of their flight bookings, were able to act out their little dramas in and around the VIP lounge.

What should have been a modest production was elevated far above its station by producer Anatole de Grunwald, whose idea it was to hire Burton and Taylor for roles that were perilously close to recent experience. Having produced several of Rich's earlier films he had a direct line to the now infamous actor. His backers urged him to make use of it.

I worked alongside Rich for several weeks on the making of *The VIPs*. As his near double, except for about an inch in height, I was the natural choice for stand in. There was some difficulty in getting away from my regular job but by combining back leave with that year's entitlement I managed to achieve the equation. Hilary, my wife, was not best pleased at losing her holiday but we agreed the extra money would come in useful.

Long periods of waiting around gave me the rare opportunity of observing my brother, the film star, at close range. Part of what I saw distressed me enormously and made me think he had shrugged off any chance of returning to the heights of his profession. Hard drinking started with breakfast as Rich knocked back a tomato juice heavily laced with vodka, followed by another, followed by another.

If still the hard liquor had no obvious effect on his performance, it was, I concluded, more than a lucky chance that he had to play a morose, introspective character who spent much of his time contemplating a wasted life. But there was a happier, more open and naturally relaxed side to Rich. It showed itself when he was off the set, in the company of Elizabeth.

I had decided not to like Elizabeth Taylor. But the resolution went by the board almost as soon as I met her. She was, more than I could ever have imagined, a natural woman. That she was naturally beautiful any fool could see though, for me, she was less the pin-up model than I expected. There was none of the passive, laidback "look at me, aren't I the greatest" manner about her. Hers was a personality and a strong intelligence which demanded attention and respect. Twice in a week we went out to dinner together. (It was a sign of the times that on both occasions Rich was too drunk to accompany us.)

The conversation took the inevitable turn.

"Will you marry Richard?"

"What do you think?"

"I think he's a troubled man."

"He needs someone to look after him."

"Isn't Sybil supposed to do that?"

She laughed. "Sybil was yesterday."

Later, I was asked, "Should I go to Wales?"

For a moment I was lost for a reply.

"It'll be difficult."

This brought a snapped response.

"I never imagined it would be easy."

"You really want to meet the family?"

"I have to, don't I? It might as well be soon."

What could I say? I just shrugged.

"I suppose so."

I realised then I was just a little frightened of Elizabeth. To stand in her way was to risk being hit by an avalanche. At the same time I could see very clearly how she captivated Rich. If Sybil stood for security, Elizabeth was excitement. She made you feel that life was interesting because it was unpredictable and dangerous. More than anyone I have ever known she could lift Rich out of his deep moods of depression. That was her great gift to him. What she could not do was to manage his life. That was one of the penalties of losing Sybil.

Before Elizabeth's visit to Wales (who could doubt it would happen?) Rich made his own exploratory trip. It was when filming on *The VIPs* was mainly long shots. For these I was indistinguishable from my brother. So, while I played Rich, he went off to give a more penetrating performance as the celebrated lover at odds with himself. I anticipated a huge row but the occasion passed off without a single cross word.

"How could we be angry with him?" Cis told me. "He looked so sad."

Tom put it another way.

"His coming home. It was like a cry for help."

Elizabeth was not mentioned until the last day when Rich was saying goodbye to Cis.

"Do you want to meet Elizabeth?" he asked her.

"You must do what you think best," said Cis in a tone of voice which implied, yes.

"I know you'll like her," said Rich.

This line, "I know you'll like her," was used to good

effect on friends and relatives alike. Elizabeth never let him down.

When Rich got on the phone to one of his closest friends, the response was cautious. Tim Hardy could scarcely reject an evening with Elizabeth Taylor but he felt a loyalty towards Sybil. A few days earlier she had called by for a long and tearful session of times remembered. Driving her back to Hampstead in his battered shooting brake, they chuntered up Park Lane, past the Dorchester. Sybil had a quiet sob.

"Do you still want him back?" asked Tim.

"I do," wailed Sybil.

"Then you shall have him."

Tim pulled hard down on the steering wheel, roared into the forecourt of the hotel and braked outside the revolving door. Then, made brave by good wine, he stomped up to the reception and demanded to speak to Richard Burton.

The desk clerk was understandably nervous. He was not used to paging important guests in the middle of the night to tell them a visitor had just walked in off the street. He summoned the duty manager, a tall, dignified figure, Tim recalls, resplendent in white tie and tails. Tim's confidence was fast ebbing but he repeated his demand.

The manager spoke as to a small child, explaining with great care why Mr Burton could not be disturbed. As he talked, Tim was made aware that his dog, a playful labrador who had followed him in from the car, was taking a more than passing interest in a large potted plant. Mumbling apologies he backed away leaving the Dorchester night staff to contemplate a lengthening trickle across the parquet floor.

The evening with Elizabeth Taylor was less traumatic.

"She was natural and charming and interested; not at all the big star straining to make an impression. When we said goodbye, she gave me a huge kiss. I was captivated."

Other of Rich's friends were quick to agree. Elizabeth was rather special.

It was the same in Wales. When the couple turned up in a pale grey Daimler with Elizabeth looking like a million dollars, the gasp of wonder could be heard the length of the valley. But she was not seeking reverence. She wanted friends and she went all out to win them by launching what I can only describe as an electioneering campaign. When anyone wanted to shake hands, she shook hands; when anyone asked a question, she answered them. She asked quite a few questions of her own but none so simple as to suggest she had not done her homework.

Where Rich led, she followed, apparently happy to defer to the social pattern we had known since childhood but which must, to her, have seemed very strange indeed. The tiny houses and narrow streets; the pubs with their back room talk of victories on the rugby field; the family reunion with too many relatives arguing against each other.

They stayed with Hilda and slept in the small, spare room. It was a long trek down to the lavatory. Elizabeth asked for, and got, the only luxury of the week — a chamber pot under the bed.

The contrast with life at the Dorchester could not have been greater. There they occupied two roof-garden suites — the Harlequin Suite for Elizabeth and the Terrace Suite for Richard, and another corridor of rooms for Elizabeth's children, nannies, secretaries and personal assistants. Heading the administration, a full time job and no mistake, was Elizabeth's chief of staff, Dick Hanley, a gentle, unruffled character who started his career as secretary to Louis B. Mayer, the legendary boss of Metro-Goldwyn-Mayer. At that time, Elizabeth had been an MGM child star, one of the Mayer front runners in his unashamed pursuit of wholesome, escapist family entertainment.

When Elizabeth was on her travels, Dick Hanley led the advance party. At the Dorchester his first point of contact was Marjorie Lee, head of public relations, who knew all the celebrities. Then he would gladhand a procession of porters, waiters and barmen. While Dick was in town, a table close to the bar was put on permanent reserve. It was here, at what was known as The Office, that he entertained journalists, producers, directors and actors — a tightly controlled selection process which determined the lucky few who would eventually be summoned to the presence.

Rich was not too fussy about decorations or furniture. If it was comfortable, that was fine by him. If it was sumptuous, as at the Dorchester, even better. But familiarity with the good life made Elizabeth choosy. Chairs and tables had to be shifted about or replaced to suit her mood. During the filming of *The VIPs* she turned up at the Dorchester with a Van Gogh landscape which she had spotted in an auctioneer's catalogue. An interior designer was summoned to advise on the hanging of this latest acquisition.

Then there was the jewellery. Lots of it. Security demanded that it should be kept in a safe to which Dick Hanley alone had access. Each morning Elizabeth made a selection of the baubles she needed for the studio (she always wore her own jewellery on set) and each night they went back under lock and key.

Rich quickly got into the habit of adding to the collection. One Saturday morning Dick Hanley was summoned by telephone to meet Rich in a pub just off Piccadilly.

"And I want you to bring some cash."

"How much?"

"Five thousand should do it."

It was a lot of money to raise when the banks were closed but Dick Hanley had the best connections. Within an hour he was back; mission accomplished. Now he had to cope with Elizabeth.

"Where is he? What's he doing? Why does he want the money? Who's he with?"

Dick Hanley made soothing noises. "There's no one with him. I met him in a bar. I gave him the money. He asked me if I wanted a beer and I said, no thanks."

Elizabeth would not be pacified. For some reason she was terrified that Rich was up to no good. Not for the first time I wondered who was the dominant partner.

Just before lunch the errant lover returned, apparently unaware that he had caused any upset. He greeted a tight-lipped Elizabeth, gave her an enthusiastic kiss, turned her round and fastened a string of rubies round her neck.

It was more than a gift. It was a declaration.

"I often wondered if they would take ready money in the Burlington Arcade," he said. "Well, today I found out. And what's more, for cash, they give a discount."

The life that Rich and Elizabeth started together was nothing if not stylish. In a party thank-you note, Tim

Hardy remarked that the Burton-Taylor assemblage in full swing made him think of a minor court of Imperial Germany. Back came the reply: "Bugger 'minor' ".

But this idol of the screen never lost his fondness for the simpler pleasures. Once, after a hard week's filming, he contemplated the perfect relaxation.

"Do you know what I really want to do? I want to see the Welsh-Scottish match, tomorrow. Can you get tickets?"

I thought it might be arranged. We took the morning train to Cardiff and the early train back. The conversation flowed but not as fast as the drink. On the return journey the bar was packed with London-based Welsh supporters, everyone wanting to tell his pals that he had clicked glasses with Richard Burton. As we fell off the train at Paddington, the call went out for a last round to cement lasting friendships. A cheerful pub across the road looked ideal for the purpose.

But once in we realised our mistake. The place was packed with young toughs who looked as if they might have a cruel idea of fun. The appearance of a glamorous film actor fuelled what was already an aggressive mood. Rich did not seem to notice at first or chose to ignore the comments. But then they started in on Elizabeth. Rich was leaning against the bar facing me. I saw his face redden and I could guess what he had heard behind his back. Abruptly, he straightened, turned and hit the man full in the mouth.

After that, the pace of life accelerated alarmingly. The man with a swollen lip fell back over a three-legged stool. Grabbing at the bar for support but not quite making it, he took with him on his descent several glasses and assorted drinks. Rich stepped back clenching his fists as if to make ready for a return match. I grabbed him by the shoulder.

"Let's get out of here."

Rich tried to shake me off.

"Don't be stupid," I shouted. "This could be real trouble."

I pushed him into the crowd of spectators who were pressing forward to see the fun. I was not quite fast enough. The yob who had pulled himself up from the floor, was propelled forward by his friends. He butted Rich in the small of the back. Both of them stumbled forward and collapsed, Rich catching his head on the side of a table. I gripped his arm and made one last heave for the door.

There was a taxi parked just down the road. We made a run for it. If I had been the driver I would have set off in a hurry to look for a more respectable fare. But he was evidently unshockable because he took us on board, Rich spilling blood from his face, and did not even turn a hair when we told him to make for the Dorchester.

As we turned into Park Lane, the cabbie spoke for the first time.

"Are you Richard Burton?"

Rich admitted that he was. The driver glanced in the mirror to observe the two of us nursing our wounds.

"Is this for real?"

"How do you mean?" I asked.

"Well, I just wondered. Are we in a film?"

"No, no," said Rich. "This is for real."

We stopped at the Dorchester and got out. I searched my pocket for change.

Rich bent down to talk to the cabbie through the driver's window.

"Now you know," he said. "Truth is stranger than fiction."

"That's as maybe," said the cabbie. "It's cheaper as well. If you had been filming, I'd have charged you double."

We were left standing on the pavement. With the excitement wearing off, Rich was contrite.

"I can't go in like this."

I could see what he meant. With his torn jacket, a gash on his cheek and ripening black eye, the lobby of the Dorchester was the last place he wanted to be seen.

"Isn't there a side entrance?"

Rich was suitably grateful. "Of course there is. Come on."

We ran out into Park Lane and along to the far end of the hotel. "This is it," said Rich. He pushed into the revolving door, stepped smartly across a small foyer, through another set of doors and into — the ballroom. At least two hundred people were gathered for a formal dinner dance. Nobody called for the police but we did attract some shocked stares as, heads held high, we made the long march to our exit.

The following morning, the story of the pub fight was reported, more or less accurately, in all the popular Sunday papers. Rich was philosophical.

"It could have been worse," he said, "I might have spilled my drink."

If *The VIPs* added nothing to the reputation of either of its leading actors, it did get them through an agonising period of indecision. Five weeks into shooting Rich told me he had asked Elizabeth to marry him. I knew she had said yes when she appeared on set sporting her engagement present — a large emerald and diamond brooch.

Sybil was invited to start divorce proceedings, on the understanding that Rich would not contest a generous financial settlement.

When Sybil recognised there was no going back, she rediscovered her energy for living. A lady of independent means (she could expect at least one million dollars from Rich) she wanted a fresh start. In April 1963 she set up home in New York. She knew and liked the city and after the year of *Camelot* she had more friends there than in London. But there was something else about New York. It had an infectious enthusiasm. Ideas were welcome; all things were possible.

"I knew if I came here, I'd be all right," Sybil told a journalist. "If New York had failed, I'd have been in real trouble."

Making best use of her talents — wit, an ability to get on and a first hand knowledge of the entertainment business, she bought a partnership in a production company. A year later she took over the Strollers Club, renamed it Arthur's and turned it into one of New York's most fashionable discos.

Among those who played at Arthur's was a twenty-four-year-old rock musician, Jordan Christopher, one of a group called The Wild Ones. The gossip writers reported that he and Sybil, who was twelve years older, spent a lot of time with each other. Will they; won't they? asked the prurient who were eventually answered by the glimpse of a wedding ring. Sybil was happy again.

We all sent our love while speculating how long it would last. It was brother Tom who settled our doubts.

"You don't have to worry about Sybil," he said. "She's not a girl to make the same mistake twice."

More than twenty years on it looks as if he was right.

Rich, meanwhile, was enjoying, if that is quite the word, his own full measure of excitement. The trauma of *The VIPs* was followed by two good films which did wonders for the Burton reputation and self confidence. In *Becket,* a straight reworking of the Jean Anouilh play, Rich played the title role against Peter O'Toole as Henry II. The project worried him for a whole number of reasons.

"Can you imagine me as a saint? The critics will die laughing."

I told him he would be mad to reject the part.

"I'd be better as the king," he insisted.

What I think he meant was that it would be easier to play the king. Between Becket the saint and Becket the insufferable prig was a narrow line. Rich was not sure he could tread it without too many steps on the wrong side.

Another fear was the inevitable comparison with Peter O'Toole. Seven years younger than Rich and an international star by virtue of *Lawrence of Arabia,* Peter too was blessed with that promise of greatness. For both actors to share the screen was for Rich to risk being toppled by the newcomer. But it was not like Rich to think in this way. His normal attitude was to welcome talent in others.

"To work with clever people," he used to say, "is not only a pleasure; it's a necessity. You can't win against fools."

That he started *Becket* wishing that Peter O'Toole was

just a little less gifted was a measure of his confused thinking, the self-inflicted turmoil.

Another cause of nervousness was the director. Rich still recalled the spot of difficulty when Peter Glanville disposed of his services to the West End production of *Adventure Story*. Was there more conflict in store? Altogether it was a fraught time.

To hold back the panic, Rich drank more. It is usually said that my brother did not surrender to alcoholism for another five years. But if an alcoholic is one who cannot do without his daily booze then, in 1963, Rich was an alcoholic.

Beer was no longer the staple diet. After the breakfast vodka came the whisky pick-me-up for lunch and great quantities of wine followed by more whiskies in the afternoon and on, late on, into the evening.

To be in his company during these marathon sessions was to play life dangerously. When he was feeling good he could engulf you in a marvellous sensation of well-being. I loved him then and felt as close to him as any brother could be. But the fun times were interrupted by terrifying bouts of depression and ill temper when he became a stranger to us all. No one could tell when the storm would break.

At Rich's invitation, I turned up at Shepperton one day with a painter friend. When Rich came off the set we went to the King's Head, a genuine English oak-beamed pub in the heart of the village from which the film studio took its name. The small talk was about the skill, and cost, of recreating history for the screen. We had just seen Rich as Becket filmed against a façade of Canterbury Cathedral. What looked as imposing and solid as the real thing was, in fact, constructed entirely of papier-mâché over a steel scaffold. When told this, I was suitably amazed.

"You could have fooled me," I said, "I thought it was there for good."

It was a lead in for Rich to tell one of his stories about falling through the scenery. Instead he just grunted.

"Don't be a bloody fool, Gray. You know better than that."

I should have realised then we were in for trouble but for my friend's sake, I persevered. We had a few drinks chatting about this and that with Rich throwing in the occasional sour comment. Suddenly, he cut across the conversation.

"Well, let's get on with it. What do you want?"

The question was to my friend who was understandably lost for an answer. Stupidly, I tried to joke.

"Another drink," I suggested.

Rich gave me a black look.

"Don't muck about," he growled. I could almost hear the anger mounting. "You're here," (he pointed to my friend) "and you want something. What is it?"

My friend cracked out a denial.

"I wanted nothing from you," he said, "except the pleasure of your company. It seems I'm to be disappointed."

He put down his glass and walked out. Now I was furious.

"What the hell are you on about?"

Rich sneered, "Don't tell me he wasn't trying to sell me a picture."

"I don't think the idea even crossed his mind."

"So you say."

He turned away and I left him to sink deeper into his

own foul mood. For a week afterwards I felt angry and depressed.

In fairness to Rich and to be honest about myself there were occasions (this last was not one of them) when an over-trusting nature led me into bad company. Shortly before the release of *Becket* I was telephoned by a journalist who asked if I could help with an article on Rich for a woman's magazine. We met over lunch and got on well together. I agreed to an interview. I was even to be paid for my trouble; not much, it was true, but the thought was welcome.

A week or two later, I had a call from Rich.

"Have you been talking to the papers?"

I told him about the magazine article.

"I don't know anything about that," he said. "But you might just go out and buy a copy of the *News of the World*. Then ring me back and we'll decide what to do."

I did not have to open the paper to know I was in trouble. There, slapped across the centre spread was the Richard Burton story as told by Graham Jenkins. It was not greatly sensational but more was promised for the following week and the week after that. I started worrying about how much I had said or hinted at. It took me a little time to pluck up courage to get back to Rich. After a tirade which did not allow for interruptions, he asked, "Did they pay you?"

I admitted to receiving two hundred pounds.

"Is that all?" he shouted. "I can just about understand you wanting to sell your brother. What I can't forgive is selling me off so cheaply." And he slammed down the phone.

This can only get worse, I thought, as I waited on tenterhooks for the next edition of the *News of the World*.

216

But when it appeared there was no mention of Richard Burton. The lawyers had been at work, particularly my own lawyer and good friend Dai Morris.

When, some time later, I dared to ask Rich how he had managed to blow the whistle, he was reticent. All he would say was, "It cost me more to get them to stop writing than it cost them to start you talking."

Becket was greeted respectfully in Britain and enthusiastically in the United States. There was some reservation here as to the accuracy of the setting. It was all too clean, neat and tidy, like the story book portrayal of Merrie England. This did not worry the Americans who were less concerned with the historical niceties than with the quality of the acting. In this respect, Rich emerged with honour. He gave a sensitive and entirely convincing performance as the cynical, self-seeking courtier turned turbulent priest. The mantle of holiness was not the awkward fit he had anticipated.

In fact, all Rich's fears about taking on *Becket* proved to be unwarranted. His relationship with Peter O'Toole was close and convivial. Rivalry over the bottle appeared to be of greater moment than rivalry for the attention of the camera. Gleefully, they played up to their proud boast to be the only drinkers left standing at the last round. When Paramount trouble shooters flew in to assess the chances of ever getting their money back, the stars put on a convincing display of helpless inebriation. While they were rolling about the set acting drunk (in reality both were stone cold sober) one of the grey suits was heard to come up with an idea for a salvage operation.

"Maybe we can turn it into a comedy. Those two get more laughs than Laurel and Hardy."

Throughout the filming of *Becket*, Elizabeth stayed on at the Dorchester. I have no doubt she turned down lucrative offers to be with Rich though she did manage to fill in time and make some money narrating a CBS documentary on London. She continued to play second fiddle in Rich's next film, a steamy drama filmed in Mexico called *Night of the Iguana*. Rich played a disgraced priest clapped out by booze who scraped a living as a tour guide.

Director John Huston described the character as "a broken man, drinking heavily, and at the end of his tether," adding, "Ray Stark (the producer) and I agreed that Richard Burton was ideal for this role." A few years later we might have called it typecasting.

Rich's co-stars were Ava Gardner, Deborah Kerr and the nubile Sue Lyon. Unkind gossips claimed that Elizabeth tagged along to keep a watch on her future husband, as the proximity of so many attractive women was thought to put too much of a strain on his fidelity. I believe that to be nonsense. Elizabeth went to Mexico for two reasons. She wanted to be with Rich but also by showing that his career came first, she hoped to overcome his sense of inferiority. Elizabeth knew well enough how Rich smarted at the cheap jibes. In public he joked about his junior status in the partnership.

"My sole ambition is to earn as much as Elizabeth and her only ambition is to play Hamlet."

But in private his anger at journalists who called him Mr Cleopatra was terrible to behold. Elizabeth did not escape the lash. When he wanted to prove his superiority, usually after heavy drinking had made him rancorous, he baited her on her lack of formal education.

218

"Give me a line from Shakespeare, any line you can think of. I'll tell you the rest of the speech."

"To be or not to be."

"That's too easy. Come on, think of another one."

Knowing what was coming, Elizabeth tried to divert the attack.

"This is silly. Let's talk about something else."

But Rich stayed dead on course.

"Oh yes," he sneered, "I forgot. You don't know any Shakespeare, do you? Not one bloody word that doesn't come out of the dictionary of clichés."

"Well, love. We can't all be geniuses."

Elizabeth was at her best when she kept calm. As a shouter and furniture thrower she just added fuel to Rich's temper. But she had a way of delivering a gentle rebuke which could stifle an argument and turn Rich from anger to remorse.

Once, after listening impassively to a long, loud diatribe she got up and went to the door. Rich was about to start again when she said, very softly, "You should be careful, love. One day you might harm more than yourself."

When she left the room, Rich was close to tears.

In sober state he welcomed Elizabeth's knack for diffusing an argument. "She makes me less volatile," he told friends. But Elizabeth was closer to the truth when she responded, "He's not less volatile. He just chooses when and where to be volatile with more discrimination."

One of the bonuses of filming in Mexico was the discovery of Puerto Vallarta, a small fishing village on the Bay of Banderas. Rich and Elizabeth fell in love with the long and, in those days, empty beaches, warm and snug in the arms of a green mountain. It was here that they made their first home together, a tiled villa straddling two sides of a narrow street by way of a Bridge of Sighs, an exact replica of the original in Venice. For the next ten years it was to be their refuge, a place where they could be themselves. They called it Casa Kimberley.

Filming *Night of the Iguana* was in itself an escape. Though not exactly alone in Mexico — even when they were off the set they were always followed by a small crowd of staff and hangers-on — the couple did enjoy each other's company without the constant pressure of having to behave like stars.

In letters home, Rich talked openly for the first time of his love for Elizabeth. Long afterwards, when I could see their lives in some sort of perspective, I came to the view that it was in Mexico that Rich discovered how much he really needed her. Up to then he had worried incessantly about his own capacity for easy infatuation. What made Elizabeth different from any of the others? Was it just that she was a big star, a princess of the cinema? Or was there more to it? In Mexico he finally decided there *was* more, much more to it. His surrender to Elizabeth was total. Once he had come to terms with this, the sheer joy of knowing spilled over into every other part of his life. There were still rows, of course. With two such mercurial people, it could not have been otherwise. But taking a wider view, I could see that in his love for Elizabeth, Rich was at last beginning to understand his own character which in turn gave him a sense of contentment he had never known before. Where I was wrong was in believing it would last.

CHAPTER
ELEVEN

More evidence of the changed Richard Burton came in a short book called *A Christmas Story*. It was a journey down memory lane to his early boyhood in Wales; days remembered with affection and gratitude. The style owed much to Dylan Thomas but the characters were true to the life of Richard Jenkins with, of course, Cis in pride of place.

"She was naive to the point of saintliness, and wept a lot at the misery of others. She felt all tragedies except her own . . . I knew that I had a bounden duty to protect her above all other creatures. It wasn't until thirty years later, when I saw her in another woman, that I realised I had been searching for her all my life."

I found it hard to believe that Elizabeth had such a great need of protection but the sentiment was happily in tune with childhood fantasy.

I was one of the many who read *A Christmas Story* in manuscript and who urged him to get it published. His reluctance was less to do with false modesty than with the desire to be taken seriously as a writer. He knew that the book would sell on his name, but popularity alone was not his objective.

"It's just a first effort" he told me. "I know I can do much better than this."

Privately I agreed but I could see no reason why he should not have the encouragement of seeing his first book in print. It would stimulate him to try again which is really what he wanted to do. This came across very clearly in a note to his one-time tutor, Nevill Coghill. It accompanied one of the first copies of *A Christmas Story* to arrive from the printers.

"If I can persuade Elizabeth to keep me free for three months," he said, "I'll write a book of bulk and prove, I hope, that actors can be literate."

This was the period (the mid-sixties) when, more and more, Rich seriously contemplated a move away from films back to the theatre but, more particularly, to writing and teaching. He knew he had talents which were not stretched even in the best movies and with youth turning to middle age (he was forty in 1965) he felt a genuine desire to use his time, that most valuable commodity, to better advantage. Without knowing it, I suspect, Elizabeth encouraged his deliberations. Confident in his love for her, he found the strength to think beyond tomorrow. Elizabeth's influence was not always for the good, as we shall see, but in the early years of their relationship she above all others helped him to make sense of what was churning around in his mind.

Another important influence for good was Nevill Coghill whom Rich called his "wise counsel". They met infrequently but in correspondence Nevill was always ready to advise his protege and to help him achieve his ambitions. In many ways he was the natural successor to Phil Burton who, in Rich's view, lost his claim to offer objective guidance when he started inflating his reputation as a talent spotter ("I discovered Richard Burton") to boost his own flagging career.

As early as 1961 when Rich was in *Camelot*, Nevill was writing to urge his return to Shakespearian theatre. A specific project, a new production of *The Winter's*

Tale, was mentioned. But Rich was already mesmerised by the prospect of donning a toga in *Cleopatra*. He sent his regrets.

"I'm afraid that with modern actors, especially if they combine film work with the stage, the idea of accepting an attractive offer spontaneously is dead. My commitments loom for years. In fact, the only free time I shall have in the next couple of years will come about only if the next play I do on Broadway fails quickly."

Three years on, having emerged from his trial by media to discover some peace of mind, Rich was more disposed to listen to Nevill and to think about renewing his links with Oxford. One much discussed idea was for Rich to play Dr Faustus, a role he had always coveted.

Meanwhile, on the strength of the critical and financial success of *Becket* and *The Night of the Iguana*, Rich was buoyed up for one of the greatest theatrical challenges of his career. He was to play Hamlet on Broadway. This daunting prospect originated with a between-scenes chat with John Gielgud on the set of *Becket* in which John played the King of France. It was coming up to the year of Shakespeare's quarter-centenary and both agreed they had to do something to mark the occasion. To miss out was the equivalent of resigning from the best club in town. With both of them, though for critically different reasons, feeling that Rich had not quite mastered Hamlet at the Old Vic, John struck a chord when he suggested a second attempt. The thought had already occurred to Rich a few weeks earlier but such then was his lack of confidence that when Peter O'Toole said he was lobbying to play Hamlet at the National, Rich had quickly backed off. Now with encouragement from Gielgud his interest revived. But the problem of the O'Toole Hamlet remained.

"We can't run in tandem," said Rich.

Gielgud waved a delicate hand. "You could if you played Broadway."

Rich was dubious. After the *Cleopatra* debacle he was not quite sure how he would be received in the United States. In any case, Shakespeare on Broadway was a rarity; profitable Shakespeare even more so.

Again, John Gielgud was reassuring. He had just returned from a successful New York run of his "solo Shakespeare recital", *Ages of Man*.

"Do remember, dear boy," he purred, "the Americans are the most dreadful snobs. They only appreciate Shakespeare when it is spoken in pure English."

The dragon bristled.

"John, you may have forgotten. I am Welsh."

Gielgud was unabashed. "Oh very well," he responded sweetly, "it is *almost* the same thing."

They shifted to less sensitive matters. The producer for *Ages of Man* had been Alexander Cohen who was well versed in presenting the classics to American audiences. It was left that Rich would sound him out on the prospect of a Burton Hamlet.

But Rich was still not sure of himself. So instead of contacting Alex Cohen direct he asked his friend John Heyman, a young British film producer who worked on both sides of the Atlantic, to get a reaction.

It did not take long to come through. Cohen was enthusiastic and wanted a meeting. Now, Rich felt he was on secure ground. Soon he was telling everyone that after *Night of the Iguana*, he was Broadway bound. But by the time Cohen arrived in London, several other producers were trying to get in on the act while Rich was happily raising the stakes.

At their first meeting, over dinner, Rich told Alex Cohen that he wanted John Gielgud to direct him. "Do you think he'll agree?"

Cohen was sure he would though privately he felt that the two greats were not an ideal match. Gielgud's style was to let the poetry carry the plot, to create what a critic described as "vocalised word music". The younger actor was more interested in discovering meaning, in putting across a convincing story even when this meant occasionally sacrificing the lyrical splendour of Shakespeare's verse.

But Gielgud himself did not seem to anticipate any difficulty — even though Rich's earlier version of Hamlet had wounded his poetical sensitivity. He told Cohen he had a notion to stage *Hamlet* in modern dress. Would Rich go along with that? Since my brother's concept of heaven was never again to be asked to put on costume, his acceptance was immediate. The show was on the road.

And what a show! Even before casting, media interest was vigorous, bordering on the frantic. After the sojourn in Mexico when the Burton-Taylor affair lost a little of its novelty value, Rich looked forward to publicity tempered by discretion. No chance.

With two divorces imminent and the certainty of a marriage to follow to make all come right (at least in the eyes of the popular press) his Hamlet became a sideshow to the continuing marital drama. The effect on Rich was to bring on a severe attack of the jitters. Though polite and outwardly cheerful in rehearsals he easily lost his concentration and had trouble remembering his lines, a problem which was still in evidence when the play opened its pre-Broadway tour at the O'Keefe Center in Toronto.

It was not the only fault with the production. There was a feeling among the critics that director and star were somehow at odds with each other, the Burton energy and passion trying to escape from the restraints of Gielgud's agonising, introspective version of *Hamlet* — and not quite making it. There is no doubt they had trouble in agreeing an interpretation of *Hamlet*. Though he took guidance from the director when it suited him, Rich was determined to go his own way. Sadly it was in a direction where Gielgud was unable to help him. The result was an undisciplined and unpredictable Hamlet who, at times, had the rest of the cast running round in circles.

The other curiosity of the production was the use of modern dress. It was an interesting if not entirely original idea to give the play a contemporary feel but Gielgud decided he could best do this by having his actors appear in rehearsal clothes. He told everyone to go out shopping for the sort of casual clothes they would wear for a cold day in Toronto or New York. Naturally, when they reappeared they looked ready not so much for rehearsal (a comfortable, rather shabby look) as for a smart weekend in the country. A fancy dress weekend, perhaps, what with those swords and scabbards and long flowing capes.

The audience was not quite sure how to take it and those who were unfamiliar with *Hamlet* were thoroughly confused when actors doubled on some parts. But then, as David Dillon Evans who played Osric and Reynaldo

226

was heard to point out, Gielgud assumed that everybody knew *Hamlet*, line by line.

Whatever the faults on stage at that first night at the O'Keefe Center, they were obliterated from the public memory by the performance at the King Edward Sheraton where a crowd gathered at the elevators to see "Liz and Dick" leave for the theatre and in the O'Keefe auditorium where the audience concentrated its attention on the seat in the front stalls reserved for Elizabeth. When the curtain rose and she had still not appeared, some of those to the rear kept standing up in the hope of spotting her. When she did slip in, soon after the beginning of the second act (for once, the delayed entrance was scheduled) there was a buzz of appreciation which, on stage, must have sounded like the warning of an earthquake. In a sense, I suppose it was.

Despite several hostile reviews, advance sales on a three-week run were at such a level as to justify an extra week. But Rich had no illusions as to the reason for the box office bonanza. After a party in which he and Elizabeth spent most of the time surrounded by security guards, he complained bitterly, "People just stare at us as if we're prize animals."

Interest in the Burton affair climbed again when it was announced that divorce proceedings on both sides were finalised and that the couple were free to marry. In fact, it was not as easy as that. Elizabeth's divorce from Eddie Fisher was hedged by legal niceties which advisers thought best not to challenge by remarrying within American jurisdiction. The answer was to take advantage of the more liberal Mexican marriage law which Alex Cohen, in his capacity as producer and father confessor contrived to do by arranging for a ceremony in the grounds of the Mexican embassy in Montreal. It took place on Sunday 15 March, 1964. Bob Wilson was best man. Hume Cronyn (Polonius), one of the best of actors and kindliest of men, was there as a witness. Less than an hour later there was a repeat performance conducted by a Unitarian minister on the eighth floor of the Ritz Carlton hotel. After which, the party flew back to Toronto to find a dressing room full of useful kitchen utensils — presents from the cast. Among sundry pots and pans the bride noticed, with appreciation, two rolling pins.

After the final curtain call at Monday's performance, Rich presented his wife "for the first time on any stage". As Elizabeth joined him to receive tumultuous applause, Rich spoke Hamlet's line to Ophelia in the nunnery scene, "I say we will have no more marriages." In response to our cable of congratulations he wired back, "And they said it wouldn't last."

Chaos in Toronto was followed by hysteria in Boston where the play was booked for a two-week run at the Schubert Theater immediately prior to its Broadway opening. When their plane touched down a crowd of some five thousand was waiting at Logan airport. It did not wait for long. As the pilot taxied towards the reception area, the fans broke through the police barriers and rushed on to the tarmac, bringing the aircraft to an abrupt halt. Very sensibly, the pilot refused to budge until his way was cleared. This took an hour at least by which time airport control had figured the best way of having their visitors disembark without causing a riot was to tug the aircraft into one of the maintenance hangers. There, a limousine was waiting to ferry the Burtons via the freight terminal to their hotel. But the excitement was not over yet. Another crowd, mostly fans but with a heavy contingent of press photographers, refused to clear a way through the lobby. In the melée Elizabeth was pushed up hard against a wall and hurt her back. Rich had his jacket torn and lost some hair to a maniac souvenir hunter.

Knowing what it was to be like for the rest of the run, Alex Cohen took over all the rooms on the Burton floor. It was the only way of retaining a little privacy.

Boston audiences enjoyed a Burton who had come to terms with his role. Or perhaps the role had come to terms with him because what we saw on stage was Richard Burton playing Richard Burton playing Hamlet. It was a commanding performance which delighted audiences and most of the critics for its power and excitement.

By now, Rich had settled into a routine. Maybe the life of a super celebrity was not so bad after all. He was friends once more with the press who clearly had decided that his rightful place was on the front page. He enjoyed the crowd of convivial acquaintances who gathered every time he showed his face, though afterwards when the bar-room haze had cleared he was hard put to it to remember anyone's name.

And then there was the money to be made — lots of it. When *Hamlet* finished its record-breaking run on Broadway (four more performances than Gielgud had achieved when he was the prince), the gross was close to two million dollars. A dreadful film version made with the new "electronic-optical process of Electronominium Theatrofilm" and inadequate lighting (Rich, dressed in black, seemed to disappear for large parts of his performance) brought in almost as much again before it was consigned to the archives. No wonder thoughts of retiring to Oxford were temporarily forgotten.

Elizabeth too was content to jolly along for a while — in her own laidback style. Opening night in Boston found her in her hotel enjoying a TV re-run of *How Green Was My Valley*, the 1941 Welsh weepie in which her friend Roddy McDowell played the juvenile lead. When Alex Cohen called for her at 6.45, fifteen minutes before curtain up, she was still glued to the set and had not even changed out of her bath robe.

Alex tried the gentle touch. "Elizabeth, please, it's time to go. Do you think you might dress?"

Elizabeth glanced up. "Not before the movie's over," she declared firmly.

They arrived an hour late.

Rich was surprisingly tolerant of his wife's inadequate time-keeping. He saw it as all part of her act which he treated as a huge joke. He told friends, "Elizabeth is one of those women who thinks if she's fifteen minutes late she's half an hour early." Or, "Elizabeth will be late for the Last Judgement — without an excuse."

The build-up for New York was stupendous. The play was on the way to a sell-out a month before the critics came in and by opening night tickets were changing hands at four or five times their face value.

In the event, the reviews justified the euphoria. Rich was praised for his "thinking man's Hamlet", more heroic than tragic, while John Gielgud was congratulated for "pitching the performance to match Mr Burton's range and intensity". In other words, the critics did not resent the play being adapted to suit the Burton style though *Time* pointed out that Hamlet portrayed as a hero "can scarcely evoke the torment of a man who is to be overmastered by fortune and by fate". I fancy London critics, ever the purists, might have made the same point, but much more forcefully.

With all the signals out for an extended run, the publicity machine went into overdrive. Every night crowds of sightseers blocked Forty-Sixth Street in front of the Lunt-Fontanne Theater. At about nine the police turned up with barriers to create a path from the stage door to the limousine parked in the road. At nine-thirty Elizabeth arrived to collect Rich who by then was well into his last act. An hour or so later, the couple appeared at the stage door. To make sure everybody got a good view they stood for a few moments in a spotlight beamed from an opposite building. They then hurried to the car which had to edge its way through the screaming multitude into Eighth Avenue.

None of this was strictly necessary. As someone on the production side said to me, it would have been a simple matter to avoid the mob by taking the fire exit and flagging down a passing taxi. But this was just too boring. Rich was not prepared to miss out on the chance to be the centre of attention. No longer Mr Cleopatra, he was Mr Burton in the company of Mrs Burton. For the first time in their marriage he was seen to be more newsworthy than his wife.

His drinking capacity continued to amaze. When I was with him he always managed three or four powerful martinis before going on stage and these were just a top-up on the day's intake. Alex Cohen remembers the evening Rich finished a bottle of bourbon — a half at each interval. Yet despite some stresses in the company, occasioned by inadequate playing by one of the principals, Rich was the model of consideration and good humour. And always, he was strictly the professional. He was there, on time, for every performance.

Only once did he show any signs of nervousness. It was when a party from a German adoption society turned up to meet Rich and Elizabeth. Their visit was to check out Eddie Fisher's successor as a suitable father for Maria, a four-year-old German girl whom Elizabeth planned to adopt. On his best behaviour, Rich ended a lengthy meeting with the delegation by offering them tickets for that night's performance. But he felt something more was needed to impress. It was not until he was on stage that he realised how he might pay a very special compliment. This is how Rich told the story.

"It suddenly came to me. Why not do a speech in German? Of course, if I'd have had any sense I would have chosen one of the lesser speeches but then — who would have noticed? So I roared into 'To be or not to be' in my best Teutonic. The audience was a bit uneasy, nothing more, and the Germans were pleased. But all hell broke loose behind the clothesrack stage left where Polonius and Claudius were eavesdropping on Hamlet. "Sein oder nicht sein: das ist die Frage' was the last thing they expected to hear at the Lunt-Fontanne."

The adoption order for Maria was confirmed soon afterwards. A pretty little four-year-old, she had a deformed leg which Elizabeth was determined to correct. A series of operations performed by the best surgeons justified her faith. Before she was much older Maria was able to walk normally.

After playing Hamlet for 136 performances in succession, Rich departed for Paris, taking Elizabeth, the children (Michael Wilding, aged eleven, Christoper Wilding, aged nine, Liza Todd, aged six and Maria) and sundry attendants and court jesters including Brook Williams, Bob Wilson and Ivor. The exodus was signalled by Aaron Frosch who warned that dallying on Broadway, or anywhere else in the States, could soon attract a hefty demand for back taxes.

The attraction of Paris was the opportunity for Elizabeth to get back into movies. For over a year she had limited herself to playing Mrs Burton, a part she enjoyed but one which did not make any money. Moreover, there was the risk that a longer absence from the set could adversely affect her earning power. So when an offer came from MGM with the customary one-million-dollar fee attached, Elizabeth was hooked. The touchy problem of what Rich would do for three months was solved, to Elizabeth's satisfaction, by inviting him to co-star, albeit at half her rate for the job.

That a Californian setting was recreated in France was one of the least bizarre features of the movie. If Rich and Elizabeth were keen to escape the grip of the taxman, MGM was happy to take advantage of lower operating costs. Given a highly favourable exchange rate there was plenty of scope in the budget for the stars to enjoy a majestic lifestyle.

All this was on the plus side. The minus was the story line and the script which were, to put it mildly, banal to the point of incredulity. *The Sandpiper* was the story of an affair between a bohemian artist and a lapsed Episcopalian minister.

"It was," said Rich, "pure soap opera but without the subtlety."

Elizabeth was more circumspect. "We never thought it would be an artistic masterpiece."

Allowed a free choice I believe Rich would have turned

down *The Sandpiper*. He told me more than once he was worried about the script which reminded him uncomfortably of the potboilers of his earlier career. But as he told me when he rang to suggest a visit to Paris, "It is Elizabeth's turn, you know. She's done a lot for me. She can't just go on following me around."

They both kept alive the hope that dross would turn to gold. They were disappointed. Rich comforted himself that, at least, they had done their best.

"There's not much you can do with a bad film. With a play you can tickle it, coax it into life. But when a film is dead, it stays dead."

The compensation was the scale of creature comforts — more lavish than anything he had previously encountered. At the studios in Boulogne-sur-Seine he and Elizabeth shared a caravan about the size of a small hotel. They were ferried around in a Rolls-Royce which had a little red dragon engraved on the nearside door. The booze flowed as from a ruptured brewery and the parties were open-ended.

I sampled the VIP treatment at first hand when Rich asked me to go to Los Angeles to collect Elizabeth's mother and bring her to Paris. Normally such a task would have been totally unnecessary. Mrs Taylor was quite capable of looking after herself. But not long before Elizabeth's father had suffered a stroke from which he never recovered. The shock of his death was still very much in all our minds and Elizabeth spared no effort in trying to make life tolerable for her mother. In this latest instance, the best service was on offer at every stage of the journey. I felt guilty for those who were travelling economy.

Though he never made a show of planning ahead Rich

234

must have been giving thought to his future because early on in the filming of *The Sandpiper* I saw a pile of well thumbed scripts in his hotel suite. I can't imagine when he found the time to read them.

On a weekend trip to Wales he talked enthusiastically of John Le Carré whose excursion into the seamier aspects of cold war espionage were judged by Rich to be a healthy antidote to the whizz bang heroics of the Bond movies. He had seen a treatment for the third and most cleverly constructed of the Le Carré novels, *The Spy Who Came in from the Cold*. I read the book and wondered how he could possibly make it work for him. The part of Leamas, the weary and expendable agent who engages blindly in one last game of double double dealing behind the Iron Curtain, called for low-key acting of a style that was certainly foreign to Rich. Hitherto when he had played the victim he went down bellowing defiance. Yet Leamas, the bewildered innocent who discovered too late how he had been manipulated, made his exit on a feeble whisper.

Maybe Rich imagined that he could keep up the part. Or perhaps he really did want to try something new although he gave no hint he was about to show us an unexpected side to his talent. My belief is that the director, Martin Ritt, who had taught at the Actors Studio and was known for his ability to extract strong performances from his actors, persuaded Rich that his character had great inner strength which, to be credible, must be kept below the surface.

The result was the best Burton film to date and probably the best he ever made. Disobeying all the rules for contemporary spy drama, Ritt filmed in black and white creating images said by Le Carré to be as "factual and clinical as a street accident".

The Spy Who Came in from the Cold was given a rapturous send-off by the critics. Leonard Mosley of the *Daily Express*, who had had some harsh things to say about Rich in the past, thought that Leamas compensated "for every bad part he has ever played and every indiscretion he has ever committed off the screen or on". He added, "If he doesn't win an Oscar for it this year, there is not only no justice left in Hollywood but no judgement either."

Mosley might have tempered his view if he had known what the competition was to be. Rich was indeed nominated for an Oscar but then so was Laurence Olivier for *Othello*, Rod Steiger for *The Pawnbroker* and Oscar Werner (who was also in *The Spy Who Came in from the Cold*) for *Ship of Fools*. In the event, they all lost out to Lee Marvin for his marvellously comic portrayal of the inebriated gunslinger in *Cat Ballou*.

Rich took his defeat in good part though on his fourth Oscar nomination, his expectations had been high.

"What do you think they are trying to tell me?" he asked rhetorically. "That Lee Marvin is a better class of drunk?"

Filming *The Spy* was a pleasure and a profit. Rich set himself a new market value with his three-quarter-million-dollar fee from Paramount. At the same time he was working with people he respected and whose company he enjoyed, including old friends like Tim, alias Robert Hardy, and Warren Mitchell. At his best, he was warm and expansive. With Claire Bloom, cast as his girlfriend, he was edgy and nervous. Thoughts about what might have been disturbed him. He tried to keep his mind on the present.

"I know just the part for you," he announced to Tim Hardy when they were talking about another film just about to go into production. "It'll only take you a few days. I'll talk to the director."

Tim was grateful but felt bound to decline. "I'm off on holiday. I promised my wife months ago we would have this break. If I went back on my word, she'd never forgive me."

Rich had the answer. "Don't worry. You can follow on in our plane."

Elizabeth thought this an excellent idea. "It just sits there at Geneva. It's about time it paid its way."

But Tim was adamant. "All right," said Rich, "use the plane anyway." And he went off to pour another drink. When he came back, Elizabeth was showing signs of impatience.

"Well, go on, love. Get on the phone. Tim wants to leave tomorrow." Which is how Tim Hardy and his wife came to travel to the sun in real style.

There was a memorable weekend when, on an impulse, Rich and Elizabeth flew in from location in Dublin for the last occasion to date that England beat Wales at Cardiff Arms Park. In case there was any doubt as to her loyalty, Elizabeth wore a red bowler which, in moments of elation, she waved above her head, shouting and singing with the most raucous of our party. After the match we went to the Queen's Hotel along with several thousand other Welsh supporters.

Elizabeth seemed to be taking it all in good part, though filtered through the roar of the crowd I doubt she understood most of what was said to her. I worried more about the risk of her being trampled underfoot.

I leaned close to Rich. "Let's find a way out of here."

"Any ideas?" he shouted back.

We were squashed against the bar. I looked over to the door where thirsty fans trying to get in were holding back those who were trying to get out. There was no escape that way.

"It looks like the back door for us," I roared.

We took hold of Elizabeth, one on each arm, and hoisted her up and over the bar. As we scrambled after her there was a moment when Elizabeth, red bowler still in place, stood in magnificent isolation behind the beer pumps. A customer surveyed her with interest.

"About time too," he slurred. "I want two Guinnesses, a gin and tonic and a pint of bitter." He looked at her more closely. "Here, haven't I seen you somewhere before?"

Rich grabbed Elizabeth and pushed her towards the kitchens.

"Hang on, hang on," pleaded the customer, as we made our exit, "what about my drinks."

But making *The Spy* was perhaps more of a struggle for the Burtons than any of us realised at the time. To play Leamas convincingly Rich had to look bloated and tired and to feel despair, a mood from which it was not easy to break out, particularly when there were two bottles of vodka inside him. He drank heavily, he joked, because it was one of the terms of his contract. Leamas had to be convincing as a downhill boozer.

"Why act it," asked Rich, "when I can do it for real?"

Elizabeth, I suspect, was not entirely at home in her

238

role as the Good Samaritan. She travelled around more on her own, always with a good reason (a visit to her mother in Los Angeles, a trip to Paris to console one of her staff whose teenage son had been killed in a shooting accident) but partly to escape the claustrophobia of someone else's film set.

The tensions surfaced easily. When *The Sandpiper* was released to a universal panning Elizabeth had to endure a chorus of "I told you so," from Rich. She got her own back a few months later when the box office returns showed an indecent profit.

Meanwhile, Maria went down with a bad attack of measles, valuable jewellery disappeared from Elizabeth's hotel suite in Dublin and Sybil remarried. This last item overlapped bad and good news. The first reaction from her former husband was "Good luck to her, she deserves it." But then, in his cups, he could be vicious about the younger man who had replaced him. Rich was just forty and was feeling his age. He did not like to be reminded of the competition close behind him.

After *The Spy* it was time for another joint effort. Both realised the financial clout they could muster when they appeared together. At the same time, neither wanted to gamble on another *Sandpiper*.

"It was our notoriety that sold that film," Rich declared. "It's a trick you can play only once."

There was no shortage of offers. One that looked interesting but impracticable was a screen treatment of an Edward Albee play, *Who's Afraid of Virginia Woolf?* Among the most exciting of the younger playwrights, Albee had hit the jackpot with *Virginia Woolf*. A withering exposure of a certain type of middle class family, recognisable on both sides of the Atlantic, the play caught the popular mood of rebellion against domestic hypocrisy. But the storyline seemed ill-suited to the screen. There was not much the camera could do with a savage verbal punch-up except record it straight which meant putting an awful trust in the quality of dialogue and acting. A cynical producer might have asked, "How many punters will pay good money to be depressed?"

Albee was fortunate in attracting a producer who could see the possibilities. Ernest Lehman was better known as a script writer and in this capacity had a number of successful social dramas to his credit such as *Executive Suite* and *Sweet Smell of Success*. But while both these were unconventional for their time, they depended on all-star casts to start them on their way. The same was needed for *Virginia Woolf* which was why the script turned up in Elizabeth's mail.

Legend has it that when Elizabeth was asked if she wanted to play Martha no one had any idea of suggesting Rich for the opposing role. I suppose it is just possible but Rich himself never believed it for a moment. It was standard practice to send a script to one of them in the hope that they might, of their own volition, come up with a joint proposal. That way it was likely to be cheaper for the studio.

The theory was, catch Elizabeth first and Richard Burton will not be far behind. But with *Virginia Woolf*, it almost didn't work. Elizabeth, who had seen rehearsals of the play in Paris, took an abiding dislike to Martha. And who could blame her? Elizabeth was thirty-five, very attractive and best known for her sympathetic roles. Martha was fifty-three, fat, loud-mouthed and a slut. The part, she decided, was not for her.

Rich was less hasty. He was attracted by the dialogue, some of the finest he had ever seen.

"You've only to read the first lines and you know this is a great play."

So what if Elizabeth had to play against type. Wasn't that what acting was all about? "I've just proved it with *The Spy*, haven't I?" he argued.

"Okay, so why don't you play George?" Elizabeth demanded to know.

The other part of the equation was filled in when Mike Nichols, whose Broadway reputation endeared him to Rich, signed as director. Warner Bros. had themselves a deal.

Who's Afraid of Virginia Woolf? was a professional commitment to a three month slanging match in front of the cameras. It took its toll on Rich and Elizabeth as it did on George Segal and Sandy Dennis, the other pair of fine actors who were the butt of George and Martha's cruel games. But they did not have to live together.

Professionally, the film was a triumph. Rich turned in the second best performance of his career and Elizabeth, by far the best of her career. The prize was an Oscar for Elizabeth, her second, and yet another near miss for Rich who lost out to his old rival Paul Scofield for his Thomas More in a worthy rendering of *A Man for All Seasons*.

Virginia Woolf shocked many including the puritan diehards in our family who thought that husband and wife behaving in such a way on screen was too degrading for words. But if a play or film is supposed to make you sit up and take notice then *Virginia Woolf* achieved its objective ten times over.

The cost, to Rich and Elizabeth, was the illusion that they could fight without getting hurt.

CHAPTER
TWELVE

Over-running on *Virginia Woolf* and the subsequent cancellation of another film allowed Rich to fulfil his promise to Nevill Coghill to perform at Oxford on behalf of the appeal to build a new theatre in Oxford. One hundred thousand pounds was needed. Rich determined to raise every penny.

So it was that in February 1966, just over twenty-one years after his departure from Oxford for the RAF, Rich made his pilgrimage back to academia. It could so easily have been a disaster. A different type of actor might have lorded it over the students, expecting obeisance when vigorous debate on equal terms was more in order. But whatever his faults, the need for unmerited devotion, least of all from the young, was not among them. Rich threw himself in at the deep end, accepting every invitation to talk and argue about the business of acting. His audience, mostly of the university dramatic society (OUDS), were enthralled. However long the seminar and however late the hour, they wanted more. Nevill Coghill suggested half jokingly, that Rich should set aside a few weeks each year to lecture at the university.

"You are a natural teacher," he told his former student. "We could do with you here."

Rich said he would think about it.

The rehearsal period for *Dr Faustus* was dangerously short. Rich had just ten days to fashion a complex role. Nevill, who directed, assumed that his star knew his lines before he set foot on stage. He was wrong. Rich could recite the big speeches but for the rest of the play he wandered like a lost man, groping for Marlowe's words and, when they would not come, throwing in a few of his own. The supporting actors, OUDS members who had mugged up on their parts weeks earlier, were understandably confused. Not experienced enough to be spontaneous on stage, they were easily thrown by a missed or mistimed cue. They had my sympathy. I recalled the sheer terror Rich engendered in the cast of *Hamlet* when in the first previews in Toronto he was clearly floundering. True professionals, masters of their craft, were made as fearful as a first night understudy who learns that the star has a sore throat. *Hamlet* was a Broadway triumph. But the transformation took weeks to achieve. For *Dr Faustus*, there were only hours for Rich to bring off the trick.

He did not make it. The first night was a classic of theatrical confusion. What should have been treated as a dress rehearsal or, at best, a cheap price preview, was mounted as a full scale charity premiere. Welcoming all the pre-publicity he could get for what, after all, was a money raising event, Nevill rather naively assumed that the critics would be tolerant of the imperfections. Instead they, and their editors, accepted the Burton hype at its face value. They anticipated great things and when they suffered disappointment, they let it show.

The evening started badly with a misallocation of tickets which had some eminent critics walking up and down the side aisles looking for spare seats. The confusion was made worse by the late arrival of a section of the audience who appeared to be misinformed on the time of curtain up. That they saw the entire play was thanks, if that is the word, to the technical difficulties backstage and a subsequent delayed start. The inadequacy of behind-the-scenes support showed throughout the production but most obviously when Elizabeth made her entrance in the non-speaking role of Helen of Troy (her first part in a stage play). The billow of dry ice from which she was intended to emerge was so thick as to mask her from the first dozen rows of the stalls. For some minutes those who had paid most for their tickets saw nothing except Elizabeth's feet. With their attention thus directed they could hardly fail to notice that below her period robes, she was wearing Gucci shoes.

Rich looked nervous and distressed. The more charitable observers pointed out that for much of the play Dr Faustus is nervous and distressed. Furthermore, it was a largely amateur production for which the Burtons had given their valuable time. It was not as if either of them were aiming at a top award.

But the London critics were not easily swayed by sentiment. They found the direction fussy, the humour misplaced and the acting lamentable. Leading the attack, *The Times* declared *Faustus* "a sad example of university drama at its worst". The other papers were hardly less vitriolic.

The pity of it was that after two or three nights, Rich settled into the role while the other actors took strength from his gain in confidence. By the end of the week, he was turning in a performance which satisfied him and pleased his audience. Those who enjoyed the final product, as it were, fought back against the critics and their hasty denunciations. Francis Warner, a fellow of St Peter's College, and an enthusiastic friend of the Burtons, told readers of the *Western Mail* that Faustus was "the greatest performance" of Rich's career. "As the last words faded ... we were aware not only that this Faustus was Everyman but that the rendering was that of a great actor at the full, majestic stretch of his powers."

Other defenders of OUDS leapt into that familiar battleground of literary discourse, the letters column of *The Times*. Praising Rich's "electrifying performance", the writer Wolf Mankowitz accused the theatre reviewers of missing the real significance of the production. "It is, surely, that by contributing his superb talent and incredibly valuable and highly sought after time to a student production, Mr Burton has made it possible for several generations of young theatrical talent to work with greater freedom and in better circumstances. By the gift to the Oxford University Dramatic Society of not only his services in the live theatre, but also of the total ownership of the projected film which he and Miss Taylor are to make with Mr Nevill Coghill, the Burtons' contribution to this Oxford nursery of the theatrical future is likely to be in the neighbourhood of £250,000 to £500,000."

Unfortunately the appeal income from *Dr Faustus* was far below expectations. The stage production made just £3,000 while the film, financed by Rich to the tune of over £300,000, was a disaster at the box office and returned a loss.

As Elizabeth was heard to comment, "We might as well have played Hollywood and let the profs have whatever we earned."

But Rich did not see it in such cut and dried terms. His willingness to appear in *Faustus* and, with Nevill Coghill, to co-direct the film had less to do with the theatre appeal than with his perception of how his career should be developing. With the exception of *The Sand-piper* he had enjoyed a fair run of good work which had re-established him as an actor to rank with the best. He had also made money which suggested that it was not only the junk which could command record fees. It was now that he began to think that maybe his highly bankable name could be used to best purpose by participating in film reconstructions of the classics. *Dr Faustus*, which came at the end of 1966, fell well short of every target — artistic and financial. But between the stage and the screen versions of *Dr Faustus*, he scored a palpable hit with the filming of *The Taming of the Shrew*.

The idea sprang from the fertile imagination of Franco Zeffirelli, the cosmopolitan Italian-born director who was best known for his operatic extravaganzas and, in Britain, as the instigator of two Old Vic productions, a joyously memorable *Romeo and Juliet* and a totally misconceived *Othello* with John Gielgud.

Having made up his mind to break into films, it was natural for Zeffirelli to choose a story which lent itself to colour and excitement. *The Taming of the Shrew* was ideal. It had been filmed only once before, with Douglas Fairbanks and Mary Pickford in 1928. That version had not been a success but it had opened up one or two interesting ideas, such as livening up the domestic conflict with an infusion of slapstick and of casting a husband and wife team as Petruchio and Katherine. (The earlier film had seen out the last years of the Fairbanks-Pickford marriage.)

Rich had first met Zeffirelli in Paris when he and Elizabeth were going through the torture of filming *The Sandpiper* while the director was enjoying the triumph of his stage version of *Who's Afraid of Virginia Woolf?*

Zeffirelli came back into their lives when Rich was filming *The Spy Who Came in from the Cold*. By then Rich and Elizabeth had decided on a team effort to translate *Virginia Woolf* to the screen though Elizabeth was still uncertain about her role and what it might do to her fan mail. The thought of another rough edged part was, for the moment, more than she dared contemplate. While Rich enthused at the prospect of working with Zeffirelli to popularise Shakespeare, Elizabeth stonewalled.

"Why can't we take one death defying risk at a time?"

But when they were into *Virginia Woolf*, knowing they had a winner, and Columbia had come up with a generous budget which was to gross the couple close on four million dollars, Elizabeth surrendered.

"Hell, why not? After this lot, it could even be fun."

The location for *Taming of the Shrew* was Rome, a city which brought back not entirely happy memories for Rich and Elizabeth.

The paparazzi was out in force. Setting up camp outside the Burtons' villa, Ivan Kroscenko, the self-styled leader of the pack, threatened a battle royal.

"You'll notice I'm wearing my leather combat jacket," he told a television interviewer.

At first, there was little to report. Though it was Zeffirelli's first major film, his experience in coping with temperamental opera singers made him a perfect master of ceremonies. The only serious problem was trying to match the work patterns of the two stars. Rich liked to start early in the morning to dispose of the main business of the day before settling down to a long, liquid lunch. If he reappeared at all in the afternoon, Zeffirelli could count himself lucky. Elizabeth on the other hand needed the hours before noon for dressing and make-up. It was, after all, a lavish costume production — a contrast to *Virginia Woolf* where she could just slip into something slovenly.

The logistics would have been simpler had Elizabeth and Rich not shared so many scenes. But unless there was to be a wholly original interpretation of *The Shrew* with Petruchio and Katherine barely meeting, the film depended on one of the stars accepting a radical change of lifestyle.

It was Elizabeth who gave way. She did not like it but she came on set every morning without complaint. Her conversion said a lot for Zeffirelli's powers of persuasion.

The only disaster was when the paparazzi, deprived for too long of sour gossip, staged a horrendous spectacle. Rich and Elizabeth were in the hotel lobby with Maria when they were confronted with a strange couple who wanted to pose with them for pictures. As the camera bulbs flashed, Rich was suddenly aware of what was happening. They were standing side by side with Maria's real parents who had been flown in from Germany by courtesy of the gutter press. Maria screamed, Rich lashed out and the photographers went away complaining that the Burtons were so uncooperative.

Aside from this unpleasant memory *The Taming of the Shrew* was a joyous romp. Some of the London critics were a bit sniffy about the play, seeing it as substandard Shakespeare out of tune with modern feminist ideas, and were dismissive of the Zeffirelli treatment which played up the comedy to the hysteria of knockabout farce. But where reviewers were able to cut themselves free from conventions, the praise was ecstatic. Picking up on the

Zeffirelli sense of fun, the American press vied with each other to create the most outrageous puns.

Acclaiming the Burton Petruchio as "the lusty, magisterial master Shakespeare meant him to be," *Time* magazine depicted the film as "a perfectly matched battle of the sexes in which the male of the species proves deadlier than the moll." *Newsweek* countered with praise for Elizabeth as the "sharp tongued tigress" who "makes Kate seem the ideal bawd of Avon".

For my money, Elizabeth pulled off the extraordinary trick of making attractive an otherwise irritating woman. Her Kate was a tough cookie, but she never lost her spark of femininity. A wonderful cast which boasted Michael York, Michael Hordern, Cyril Cusack and Victor Spinetti caught the mood perfectly and stopped just short of playing over the top.

I loved the film and so did everyone in my circle. Of great pride to Rich was the knowledge that he was reaching a public not otherwise attracted to Shakespeare. Success here spurred his ambition to film more of the classics.

The London premiere was a rollicking West End beano with the added glitter of a royal guest. Princess Margaret was in attendance with her husband, Lord Snowdon, formerly Anthony Armstrong-Jones. This allowed Rich to make jokes about "keeping up with the Joneses" a feat he achieved with masterly ease by taking twenty rooms at the Dorchester and inviting his entire family to spend a long weekend in London.

We arrived Friday evening, a party of three dozen or more, to a sumptuous dinner hosted by Rich and Elizabeth. The next day, after a late start, the men departed to Twickenham to see England play Scotland in the Calcutta Cup while their wives bought up Harrods. Another splendid feast was followed on Sunday by a party which went on for most of the night. And none of us had yet seen the film.

That was on Monday. To accommodate his personal guests at the Odeon, Leicester Square, the flagship of the Rank circuit (it really did have the look and style of a cruise liner) Rich paid charity prices for 150 seats. When the first of our convoy of chauffeur driven Daimlers pulled up alongside the red carpet, the last car still had not left the Dorchester.

Arriving early, I readily admit to the pleasure of vicarious fame when, as a Richard Burton lookalike, I caught the attention of onlookers. Autograph books were pushed under my nose. I tried to wave them away but this did not go down too well and since easy explanations were not in order (just try shouting against a concert of admiring fans) I signed anything and everything with an indecipherable scrawl. I like to think there are still a few ageing romantics who hold dear the memory of Graham Jenkins masquerading as his brother.

The evident pleasure of the audience — laughter, applause and loud cheers — put us in fine mood for the big party, star night at the Dorchester's Terrace Room which was booked through until ten the next morning.

I had no idea I knew so many famous people though here again, the Burton looks made for easy identification.

"Who was that you were talking to?" asked Hilda.

"Sophia Loren," I said, firmly.

"Don't be silly," said Dai, "that was Gina Lollobrigida."

I was on safer ground with long standing friends of Rich such as Stanley Baker and Emlyn Williams though

I did have some trouble remembering Laurence Harvey. Evidently, Princess Margaret had the same problem because when she asked what he was doing and he said he was working in dockland (where he happened to be filming) she must have assumed the worst.

"I see," she murmured sweetly. "Well, never mind. I do hear there are some divine little places down there."

By the early hours the Jenkins family was in the ascendancy. There was plenty to celebrate — the film, Elizabeth's thirty-fifth birthday, our togetherness. We all did our party pieces.

Verdun told a couple of exaggerated stories abut our early childhood which Rich loved to hear over and over again. Hilda sang. I did my special solo which was to sing "Sorrento" in three languages, accompanied at the piano by a rather tipsy Christopher Plummer. We finished up with the whole family ensemble performing as a massed choir. That included Cis, who had a superb soprano voice, her children, Marian and Rhianon, Verdun and Hilda and their children, Megan and Sian, and the rest of the clan. Rich and Elizabeth joined in, and we made music until the first shafts of light filtered through the curtains.

The sad moment was when we sang for Edie, the youngest of our sisters, who had died a few months earlier. Only forty-two, she was the first of our generation to go. And because it was so sudden, the loss was all the more traumatic. I could not help falling back on the old banality, "It's later than we think."

At breakfast we were all still in formal dress; a trifle jaded except for Elizabeth who sat there, radiant as ever, carrying enough jewellery to open a branch of Tiffanys.

Hilda leaned over towards me.

"What do you think that little lot is worth?" she asked.

Elizabeth must have overheard.

"Do you mean me or the trinkets?" she wanted to know.

Richard interrupted. "It's the jewels she's talking about," he said. "She knows you're priceless."

Elizabeth threw a bread roll at his head. He threw one back.

Judging by that day's papers a lot more than bread rolls was exchanged between Rich and Elizabeth. But I must say if there were any rows they passed me by. Could it have been that our friends in the press wanted to keep alive the titillating notion of real life copying fiction? In writing up *The Taming of the Shrew*, Donald Zec of the *Daily Mirror* gave as his subtitle, A Day in the Life of the Burtons. From this time it was a favourite with show business writers to relay every incident in the Burton relationship which seemed to re-enact scenes from *Virginia Woolf* or *The Shrew*.

Before returning home I went to see the latest acquisition — an ocean-going gin palace called *Kalizma* after three top girls, Kate, Liza and Maria. I did not have far to go. The yacht was moored on the Thames Embankment, just below Tower Bridge. But why, you might ask? Was there not enough room at the Dorchester? For humans, yes, but there was a problem with animals which were restricted from entering the country on short visits by the quarantine regulations. Since Elizabeth would not go anywhere without a small zoo, the yacht was there to accommodate her four-legged friends. In her absence two French poodles, O'Fie and E'en So, were left in charge. There was also a captain and crew of nine, but they did as they were told. No wonder the *Kalizma* was known alternatively as Noah's Ark without the flood or, less respectfully, as the most expensive dog kennel in the world.

It was, in fact, a fine craft; 147 feet of best oak fashioned at the turn of the century. Rich and Elizabeth bought it for £80,000 and spent more than twice that sum on a refitting. The stereo equipment alone cost more than my house. Among the little extras that make the lives of the super rich worth living was a "mini moke", a vehicle designed like a jeep, which could be taken ashore to visit the sights wherever the yacht was berthed.

Mine was a fleeting visit, conducted in the glazed aftermath of a gargantuan party. I saw little. More observant, by nature and circumstances, was a friend of my younger days, Gladys Williams, who encountered the *Kalizma* a few weeks later when she was leading a group of fifty or more on a tour of the Italian lakes. Having lived most of her married life in the south of England, she had achieved a certain notoriety as the girl who went to school with Richard Burton. So, when the coach pulled into Portofino and the Italian guide announced that the splendid craft in the harbour belonged to the Burtons, the cry went up for Gladys to renew acquaintanceship with her old classmate.

"Come on love, now's your chance!"

Gladys was understandably nervous.

"Oh, I don't think I could. Anyway, they're probably not there."

But the guide made sure she would not get away as easily as that.

"The whole town knows they are on board. I have seen them."

By now the coach was on the jetty, just a few yards from the *Kalizma*. Gladys had no choice. She edged along the gangplank and spoke to the bearded Sicilian who stood on deck barring her way.

That Rich and Elizabeth were not keen on uninvited guests was made plain by the sight of a gun slung over his shoulder.

"Can I speak to Mr Burton, please?"

"Who wants him?"

She said her name but the guard did not seem inclined to move. Then an unmistakable voice boomed out from the lower deck.

"Is that Gladys then?"

Rich appeared and threw his arms round his visitor. It was a great reunion, performed under the appreciative gaze of all the coach passengers who crowded against the nearside windows.

"Stay to lunch," commanded Rich.

"I can't do that," said Gladys. "I've got all this lot to look after."

Rich surveyed the crowd scene.

"Everybody stays for lunch," he decided.

It was an afternoon to remember — four hours of champagne and caviar. Thereafter, fifty-three holiday-makers associated the *Kalizma* with three stars — Rich, Elizabeth and Gladys.

One of the best holidays of my life was enjoyed on the *Kalizma*. With Hilary, our two boys Richard and Alun, and Hilda, we spent two weeks cruising the Mediterranean. I remember having to persuade Hilda that it was not just tomato juice Rich was imbibing by serving her an equivalent drink. It laid her out for two hours.

The last I heard of the *Kalizma* it was owned by the financier, Peter de Savary. He had it redecorated but I am pleased to think he left in place the little brass plaque marking the spot where Rich presented Elizabeth with one of the biggest cut diamonds in the world. Elizabeth had bid for the Cartier diamond when it was put up for auction in New York but had dropped out at one million dollars. Rich tried harder and bought the elusive jewel in a private transaction.

I am told it costs £4,000 a day to hire the *Kalizma*. Cheap at the price, I would say.

CHAPTER
THIRTEEN

If *Taming of the Shrew* was a high point in the Burton career, the film of *Dr Faustus* touched the depths. From the outset, Rich knew that it could not be a world beater. Everything about it was too modest. But he did hope for a quality picture which would enhance his reputation as a serious artist. Instead, he created a mess, with more special effects, as a technician pointed out, than fifty average films. And this time the responsibility was his alone. Rich put up the money, got in formidable talents such as Gabor Pogany as director of photography and John de Cuir as production designer, and co-directed.

But though the disappointment was chastening, it did not deter him from working again with Nevill Coghill. Among the ideas mooted was a film of *'Tis a Pity She's a Whore* — thought eminently suitable by Rich and Nevill because, like them, John Ford was an Exeter man. *The Duchess of Malfi* was also a lead candidate for adaptation to the screen. But the plan which travelled furthest was a film version of *The Tempest* for which Nevill hoped to re-enact the partnership of Richard Burton and John Gielgud.

For almost six months the triumvirate debated the question of a suitable location. The decision was critical because most of the scenes were exteriors of an unusual nature.

"We need," wrote Gielgud, "landscape that is remote, dreamy. Sometimes sand beach, sometimes rocks, with

257

strange tracts of deserted scrub inland, with shadowy woods and jungles, changing to marshes and dangerous pools — strange animals and insects."

The Coghill vote was for Tobago.

"It is a fantastic island, with rockiness as well as yellow sands and tropical, wooded vegetation; it is not heavily populated like parts of Jamaica, so it should not be hard to pick places where there is no sign of habitation."

But this was not quite what Gielgud had in mind.

"My fear is that it is too conventionally tropical for *The Tempest*. Palm trees and lushness are all right for certain scenes. But I also crave for mists, silver birches and pools." He thought Japan might suit. "I do wish you could visit that country and see for yourself. Their films have such a unique and original quality, so much more poetic than the Bahamas."

Rich gradually distanced himself from this esoteric discussion. The shock of a nearly complete write-off on *Dr Faustus* brought home the perils of independent production. Critical rejection was one thing, but a big financial loss was more difficult to take. Around this time, the easiest way to get on the wrong side of Rich was to point out that his *Faustus* was tax deductible.

"I've spent all these years trying not to pay tax," he growled. "Now you tell me I should have stayed at home and made nothing."

Like others from a poor background, Rich was frightened of losing everything. Possessions were important to him. He gave away a lot of money, to family, friends and to causes that stirred his interest. But straight gifts were containable, while investment in high risk film production was open ended, and liable to be horribly expensive if plans did not work out.

In April 1967, a further missive from Nevill on the charms of Tobago brought back a cable, "*Tempest* could not possibly begin for at least a year and a half or two years because of other commitments."

These other commitments amounted to a succession of lacklustre movies, starting with *The Comedians*, in which Elizabeth also starred. Rich has often been criticised for the rubbish he turned out over the next few years but while he never shirked his portion of the blame, it is crassly unfair to suggest that he wilfully sought mediocrity. *The Comedians*, for example, had the hallmarks of a quality product. Based on a Graham Greene novel, it dealt with a topical subject of wide interest, the tyrannical and corrupt dictatorship of Haiti in the days of Papa Doc. A strong cast of supporting actors was led by Alec Guinness and Peter Ustinov, both of whom turned in magnificent performances.

But somehow the film did not hang together as a convincing story. Part of the trouble was the mismatch of Rich and Elizabeth. This might seem unlikely after the success of *Virginia Woolf* and *The Shrew* but in both these earlier films they were playing on equal terms. In *The Comedians* there was a huge difference in style between the down-at-heel owner of an empty hotel and his mistress, the glamorous wife of a German diplomat. Try as they might, they did not even begin to look as if they were made for each other. While Rich was believable in his now familiar guise as a noble washout, Elizabeth was too strong for her role, too obviously in control of events which should have been beyond her comprehension.

But if Elizabeth was miscast in *The Comedians*, it was Rich who was sadly out of place in *Boom*, a film adaptation of the Tennessee Williams' play, *The Milk Train Doesn't Stop Here Any More*. As the mysterious young stranger who creates emotional havoc in the community, everything, including his age, was against him. Even a director as brilliant as Joseph Losey could do nothing to save him. The film was a write-off — hardly suitable nowadays for off-peak television.

If these films proved anything it was that Rich and Elizabeth were straining too hard after shared credits. They were equally responsible. For *The Comedians* it was Rich who insisted on casting his wife (she accepted at half her usual fee — an offer the producers could not refuse); for *Boom*, Elizabeth was the power broker. They recognised the error of their ways — neither was too proud to admit mistakes — but still they refused to work at a distance.

The compromise was to sign for different pictures on the same location. This is what happened when Rich made *Where Eagles Dare* at Elstree. Elizabeth was just down the road making *Secret Ceremony*.

Where Eagles Dare was the brainchild of an independent producer, Elliot Kastner, whose great skill was to put together an alluring package — scripts, stars, director — and then sell it on to one of the big studios. When he first made his approach to Rich, all he had was a draft script, based on Alistair MacLean's bestselling novel and a formula which was to earn a huge amount of money. On top of a one-million-pound fee (at last, the barrier was broken), Rich was on ten per cent of the gross — a deal which was to relegate all his earlier films into the league of minor earners.

It was a film without pretensions. But then, so much else of what he had been doing of late had ended up that way. If he was destined to be stuck with the mediocre, he reasoned, he might as well take the biggest reward for his time.

Five years on, I was with him when he received a financial update on *Where Eagles Dare*. He glanced at the paper then pushed it over to me with his finger pointing to the bottom line. His earnings were in excess of eight million pounds.

Nobody, least of all Elliot Kastner, suggested that this *Boys' Own* adventure was likely to win prizes for originality, but thought was given to developing a convincing storyline. The three double agents who were central to the convoluted plot but were also the weakest link were made plausible by showing how they were brainwashed with fanatical ideology. All this was eventually cut to make way for more death-defying hand-to-hand combat, a decision which explains why such cerebral actors as Peter Barkworth, Donald Houston and William Squire were to be seen hanging off mountains and fighting for their lives on runaway cable cars.

When I saw the rough cut I was sitting behind Clint Eastwood who was watching himself in what must have been his last supporting role before he achieved superstardom. As the lights went up, he turned to me. "They've got the wrong title for this movie," he drawled. "They should have called it, 'Where Doubles Dare'."

For the snowy mountain sequences, the location moved to Switzerland, home ground for Rich and Elizabeth who used their connections to get the best of everything. As the partner who was not working, Elizabeth put herself in charge of the good things in life —

like champagne picnics brought up the slopes by a procession of hotel waiters.

"Isn't she beautiful?" murmured Rich when he caught sight of his wife, wrapped in a sable fur at the head of one of these processions. "Isn't she just the most beautiful thing in the world?"

There was no one to disagree.

Where Eagles Dare was an old fashioned adventure — Bond without the sex and fast cars — which met the ever present demand for escapist entertainment. It satisfied the fantasy we all share of battling successfully against overwhelming odds. The critics hated it but, for once, their view was irrelevant.

Rich was on top form throughout the making of *Where Eagles Dare*. He was, to use his own phrase, "supremely famous" and living life to the full. In London, it was one party after another, either at the Dorchester which the Burtons now regarded as a second home or on the yacht somewhere on the Thames. When the *Kalizma* had to go off for a refit, a slightly smaller vessel called the *Beatrice* (it slept only ten) was hired as a substitute. It cost a thousand pounds a week for fifteen weeks. Animals collected along the way — and Elizabeth was forever gathering to her small cuddly creatures in search of a home — stayed at the hotel until it was time to leave town when they were incorporated into the sailing menagerie. Elizabeth was extraordinarily tolerant of her pets. One interviewer who spent hours waiting to meet his dream heroine complained afterwards that his only lasting impression was of a squeaky little dog that pee'd on the carpet.

While Elizabeth fussed over her extended family, Rich brooded on the future. When their preoccupations clashed, usually over some domestic crisis, Rich would back away, if necessary locking himself in the bedroom. This is precisely what happened when we met for a brotherly chinwag at the Dorchester at the time when Elizabeth was proudly displaying her latest gift from an admirer — a pearl grey kitten with, as it turned out, an advanced sense of the ridiculous.

Lunch came up on two trolleys — one for the smoked salmon, the other for wine and beer. Rich started drinking and talking, leaving me to the eating.

"How do you see me as Simon Bolivar?" Rich wanted to know.

"Who?"

He was incredulous.

"You don't know Bolivar? One of the great South American heroes?"

I had to confirm my ignorance.

"It's just the part for me. It has everything . . ."

I settled down for a short history lecture but Rich was suddenly interrupted by a squeal from Elizabeth. He turned to where she was standing by the window.

"What's the matter, luv?"

"It's the little kitten," she screamed, "it's out on the terrace."

As we were six floors up with a drop straight down to Park Lane, this was not good news. But there was worse to come. Understandably terrified by the sight of three grim-faced humans slowly advancing on it with hands outstretched ("Here, kitty," Rich boomed, "come to daddy you little bugger before I tear you apart") the feline sought the only refuge to hand. It shot across to the far side of the terrace, climbed into the spout of a lead drainpipe and disappeared.

"Thank you," said Elizabeth bitterly. "Thank you so much for your help. Now, what the hell am I supposed to do?"

Rich was not in the least perturbed.

"Only one thing for it," he said. "Tell the engineer." Then to me, "Come on Gray, let's find somewhere quiet to talk."

I followed him into the bedroom leaving Elizabeth shouting into the phone. Five minutes later, when Rich went back for the drinks trolley, the Dorchester rescue service had already swung into action. Two men in blue overalls were out in the terrace carefully dismantling the drainpipe.

"Best leave them to it," said Rich as he came back to the bedroom and closed the door. "They seem to know what they're doing."

I don't know what happened to the Bolivar project except that it never got further than the talking stage. Presumably, the studio bosses did not share my brother's enthusiasm for rebel causes.

But there was no scarcity of options. Even the filming of *The Tempest* came back into the realm of practicalities. In May 1968 Nevill Coghill wrote, "in great excitement" to announce that he had found a Prospero's island which would meet all the possible demands of Burton and Gielgud. The idyllic spot was Garnish Island off the Irish coast in Bantry Bay.

"It has everything. Cliffs, rocks, bogs, mountains in the near neighbourhood of incredible romantic beauty and wildness. Many sweeping landscapes with no sign of habitation. Marvellous lights and cloud effects, due to Atlantic weather conditions. The island itself is a paradise of flowers, the most gorgeous garden in Ireland;

every sort of rhododendron, from white to crimson, and brilliant azaleas in wild effect, all sorts of trees, some flowering just now. Grassy glades, abundance of flowers; the whole planted so as to seem growing wild, and yet with the feeling of some overall magical control. Believe it or not, there is also a rustic Italianate palace at the centre of the island (habitable) which is just what I imagine Prospero would have conjured up for himself and described as 'my poor cell'. There would be no need to build a single set. It's all there already, flights of steps, a tower or two, a lily-pool, lawns, crags, groves. I can hardly wait to show it to you."

The suggestion was for Richard and Elizabeth to take time off in the summer to sail the *Kalizma* to Bantry Bay. A week was duly set aside in August.

Meanwhile, Nevill had other excitements to occupy him. His translation of *The Canterbury Tales* into modern English, an unexpected bestseller which brought Chaucerian verse into popular currency, was now ready for what surely was its final manifestation — as a musical. When *The Canterbury Tales* opened at the Phoenix in London's West End, Rich and Elizabeth were in attendance. Everybody was nervous, except for Elizabeth who went about giving words of comfort and encouragement for all the world like Florence Nightingale at the front. Otherwise mature men wilted before her and afterwards, in proud recollection, fell to disputing her allocation of favours.

"My fondest love to Elizabeth," wrote Nevill. "I think of her always with happy memories, especially the memory of her presence and hands holding mine on the terrible night of the opening of *Canterbury Tales*." He added, "Eric Starkie [the director] claims she held his hands too, but I put that down to jealousy."

This was the night on which Nevill made peace with the critics — or rather, they made peace with him. With a pocketful of ecstatic reviews and the assurance of a long run, later to be repeated on Broadway, he had finally made the leap to professional theatre. It is curious that in this transition, the relationship between Nevill and Rich underwent a sea change. Hitherto, the student had paid homage to the professor. Now the role of mentor shifted to the younger man, just as it had with Phil Burton. Nevill paid tribute to Rich for pushing him towards the full enjoyment of creative enterprises. It was a compliment Rich was unwilling to accept. He believed his own debt had still to be paid. For him, Phil Burton had started the ball rolling, Nevill had given it a powerful kick and Rich had simply kept it moving along. His gratitude to Nevill was such that when *Dr Faustus* brought disappointment he sent his friend a cheque for £15,000, a tidy sum in those days, in recognition of all that he had done to nurture young talent. Later, much larger sums were subscribed by Rich to the Oxford theatre appeal.

If helping Oxford was a pleasure worth savouring, so too was the opportunity to promote the culture of his beloved Wales. At the behest of many friends but notably John Morgan, a broadcaster Rich much admired, he and Elizabeth put £100,000 into Harlech, a consortium of business and the arts which aimed to secure the commercial television franchise for Wales and the West Country.

Rich was suspicious of television. He thought of it as an intrusive art form.

"If I made a bad film, people don't have to come to

see it. But if I'm bad on television, people will still watch because it's so easy to switch on and so hard to switch off!''

His decision to back Harlech was made with the genuine hope that the new talent coming in to television would raise standards.

With the help of the Burton name, Harlech won its bid and was a great financial success. But Rich was never entirely happy with his investment. It did not achieve what he and, he assumed, his fellow directors had hoped for. The failure was all the more frustrating because, as we shall see, his own involvement did nothing to help his cause.

In mid-1968 Rich went to Celigny for the first time in more than two years. It was not a happy occasion. The caretaker at Pays de Galles, one of the longest serving members of the Burton household, had killed himself. Rich decided to go to the funeral. There was nothing directly he could do to help but he felt badly that he so rarely visited the home he had shared with Sybil. This was chiefly in deference to Elizabeth who naturally had an emotive objection to the place but who also preferred her own home at Gstaad, a magnificent chalet perched on the mountainside overlooking the famous ski slopes. It was the more impressive residence in every way though, perversely, Rich could never be persuaded to recognise its virtues.

Elizabeth was not pleased when Rich told her of his plans. She was booked to go into hospital for a few days and while it was nothing serious she felt the least he could do was to be close at hand. She knew also that his motives for travelling were not entirely altruistic. Rich had just finished a short and entirely satisfying piece of work (a recording of *The Rhyme of the Ancient Mariner* which, against all expectations, was to break into the charts with sales of over half a million copies) and was now at a loose end. A trip down memory lane appealed to his sentimental nature. He was supported by Ivor and Gwen who had their own fond recollections of Pays de Galles and indeed went back there periodically as part of their domestic round. Rich suggested they should accompany him.

So it was agreed, though Elizabeth remained unhappy. She acceded only on condition that they stayed at Gstaad, driving from there to Celigny for the funeral.

The story of the next three days has to be pieced together from snippets of information from many sources. No one knows the whole truth. What is beyond question is that events in Celigny that July left their mark on Rich for the rest of his life.

After the funeral, Rich and Ivor went to the Café de la Gare for a simple meal and a few drinks. Gwen said she would follow on; she wanted to visit some friends. When eventually she called by, the two brothers were well away, swopping old stories over large glasses of lager. Ivor complained that if he drank much more he would not be able to drive but Rich was in a talking mood and showed no signs of letting up. Leaving them to it, Gwen went off to find the wife of the proprietor, who, she knew, would keep her busy with a feast of village gossip.

It was late evening when Ivor rose unsteadily to announce that he was fetching the car. Rich pushed him back into his seat.

"We're not driving anywhere. We'll stay here. In my home."

Gwen was secretly relieved though she knew that if Elizabeth found out they would all be in trouble. There was another problem. Pays de Galles had been empty for a long time. Obeying the instinct of a professional housewife, Gwen declared that the place needed a thorough airing before it was fit for habitation. She would go on ahead, she told them, to open up the house.

It was at least another two hours before Rich and Ivor decided to call it a day. By then it was dusk but they saw, as they trudged their way up the road to Pays de Galles, there were no lights on in any of the rooms.

Gwen met them at the door. "The electricity is off," she said, "and I can't find the main switch."

Still merry on beer and, Gwen guessed, a more than generous quota of chasers, the men held each other in uproarious laughter at the thought of Gwen scrabbling around in the darkness. She was not amused.

"You're such children," she complained. "Just get those lights turned on, will you?"

Ivor stepped back. "Oh, very well; very well."

He held a finger to his lips. "I am the only one who knows the secret of the lost switch."

And still laughing he moved off towards the garage. Gwen went back into the house and Rich followed her. A few minutes later, the lights came on.

A few minutes after that, Rich announced he was going to bed.

"But where's Ivor?" Gwen wanted to know.

"Probably walking off a hangover," said Rich. "Sensible man. I'll join him."

Gwen went on pottering for a while until she was

ready for bed. As she came out of the kitchen she heard the front door bang and caught a glimpse of Rich hurrying towards the phone. As she came up to him he was lifting the receiver and dialling furiously. He was breathing heavily.

"Ivor's hurt. But don't worry. I'm getting an ambulance. Don't worry."

It was two days before I knew there was something badly wrong. The news came to me by a circuitous route. Hilda's daughter Sian, who was in London, had a chance meeting with Jim Benton, one of Rich's many assistants, who was then staying at 11 Squires Mount. In casual conversation Sian asked after Ivor.

"How is he these days? I haven't seen him in ages."

Jim went into his conspiratorial pose.

"Well, he's ill, very ill. But you're not supposed to know. So don't tell Gwen I said anything."

Sian could understand that news like this was not to be bandied about but she did take for granted that her mother had been told. Yet, when she rang home that evening, Hilda was mystified.

"Maybe Graham knows."

I was just as much in the dark but I knew what to do to find out what was going on. Or I thought I knew.

I rang Pays de Galles. No answer. I rang again and again and again. Still no answer. Finally, I got through to someone who announced herself as "Mr Burton's secretary". I asked for Rich but was told he was not available; likewise Gwen. When she asked if there was anything she could do to help, I put the question bluntly.

"Has my brother had an accident?"

There was a short pause. Then she said, "It's true. He has been hurt. He's in hospital at Geneva. We think he has a broken neck. But the doctors will know more in a day or two. Please be patient. He is well looked after."

A few days later Gwen rang.

"We're flying home," she said. "Ivor needs specialist treatment. He'll be in Stoke Mandeville hospital and I'll stay in a hotel."

"Can he have visitors?"

"Yes, but I'm not sure he wants to see anyone. Not yet."

I took a chance and drove to Stoke Mandeville a day after Ivor was brought in. When I arrived at the hospital I was told that Gwen was with him. I was shown to a waiting room. I read all the magazines without taking in a single word.

Gwen came in and I gave her a hug. Her eyes were red but otherwise she was her old self; capable and in control.

"He won't see you," she said. "I did warn you. Most of the time he just wants to be alone."

I sat her down.

"I don't understand. Why does he want to keep me away? Is there something I haven't been told? What sort of shape is he in?"

She looked surprised. "I thought you knew. Ivor is paralysed from the neck down. He'll never walk again."

I said nothing for a while. I could only think of my elder brother as the tough guy, the fitness freak who had lived by muscle power. The idea of him bound to a bed or to a wheelchair was beyond comprehension.

"What happened?"

"He tripped on a grid. One of those things you use to

scrape mud off your boots. He must have fallen badly. When Rich found him, he couldn't move."

The next morning Gwen rang me in my hotel room.

"Ivor will see you. Just for a few minutes. Can you come over now?"

I sat by his bed for twenty minutes and exchanged as many words.

As I got up to leave he said, "You shouldn't have come."

"I wanted to," I said.

He was tight-lipped but there were tears in his eyes. Never before in my entire life had I seen my brother cry. I took hold of his hand.

"You'll be all right. Up and about in no time, eh?"

He gripped me hard.

"Oh yes, boyo. You wait. I'll be up and about."

We both knew we were lying.

On the way home I stopped off to see Elizabeth. I had assumed she was still in the London Clinic but she was already back at the Dorchester, fighting fit and spoiling for a row. She knew about Ivor, that much was clear. Also, that she held Rich responsible for what had happened.

"Hell, I told him not to go to Celigny. Why does he always have to do such damn fool things?"

I considered the question.

"Where is Rich?" I asked. "I thought he might be here."

Elizabeth's voice sharpened.

"Don't ask me where he is. How should I know? He's not in Celigny. He's not in Gstaad. Maybe he's run away from home."

It was a week before I heard from Rich. We had a

brief telephone conversation during which he steadfastly refused to discuss the accident. And he never did talk about it in any logical way, at least not to me, or to anyone else in the family.

But the tragedy stayed with him. More than that it came to dominate his waking hours. For the rest of his life he was preoccupied with a sense of guilt which could be relieved only by heavier and heavier doses of alcohol. On many a drunken evening when I helped him to bed he would talk to me as if I was Ivor. When I stayed with him in Rome, sharing a room, he woke in the middle of the night calling out for Ivor. Yet he stayed away from the hospital. He hated sickness and, as I came to discover, he feared death — not as much his own as the death of others. He had a deep horror of annihilation.

Why did he feel responsibility for what happened at Celigny so keenly? The clue is 'if only'.

If only they had stayed away from the funeral. If only Rich had not encouraged Ivor to drink. If only they had driven back to Gstaad instead of lodging overnight at Pays de Galles.

But there is something more. Rich and Ivor were both in drunken, boisterous mood. If they behaved to pattern, and from what Gwen told me, I have no doubt they did, it is quite easy to imagine them in horseplay, pushing and shoving each other about, throwing punches, wrestling, running and tripping. If the accident was not a simple fall but part of a silly game which went terribly wrong — an explanation which rings true for me — I can quite understand why Rich saddled himself with the blame and suffered the remorse.

When Rich talked about the family he was always open about his favourites. "After Cis," he told me, "I loved Ivor the best. He was the nearest to a father to me."

In the years ahead Rich and I were not always on the best of terms. Once or twice we had rows which got near to violence. After one of these bouts, by way of explanation, he invoked Oscar Wilde:

> "Yet each man kills the thing he loves,
> By each let this be heard,
> Some do it with a bitter look,
> Some with a flattering word,
> The coward does it with a kiss,
> The brave man with a sword."

The note was addressed to me but I remember thinking it could more suitably have gone to Ivor.

When it was plain that Ivor was not responding to treatment, he and Gwen went back to Switzerland to live at Gstaad. Two nurses joined the staff so that Ivor had whatever he needed, day or night. Cassie too had devoted herself to nursing him with loving care. The last time I saw him was in February 1972, less than a month before he died. I sat by his bed and we talked. We must have said more to each other in those three days than in the previous thirty years. For the first time I felt close to Ivor, realising that what I had always believed to be an unfeeling nature was in reality a barrier against genuine emotion which he feared as weakness. And living as he had as a young man when, against the odds, he had kept us together as a family, weakness was a luxury he felt he could never afford.

On the last night, he refused to let me go to bed. We talked on right the way through to breakfast when I drank a pint of coffee to keep me awake for the drive to

Cherbourg. It was a stupid thing to do but for some reason, vital at the time but now long forgotten, I had to be on the Channel ferry by evening. I nearly did not make it. Driving on the wrong side of the road round a steep corner I was saved by a French truck driver who was doing the same in the opposite direction.

When at last I was allowed to sleep, my last waking thought was of Ivor. How curious it was. He had revealed so much of himself, but not once in our long exorcising sessions had he said a single word about the accident that was to be the death of him.

CHAPTER
FOURTEEN

The turn of fortune for Rich showed first in his dealing with Woodfall Films, the company which had produced *Look Back in Anger*. The director from that film, Tony Richardson, offered him the lead in *Laughter in the Dark*, a thriller of sorts in which a wealthy art dealer, blinded in a car crash, takes revenge on his persecutors.

But after a few days' work or rather lack of work, Rich was thrown off the set. The statement put out by the company, that he was "unpunctual and unprofessional", wounded him greatly but he could hardly deny that his initial enthusiasm for a tight budget film had waned considerably when he was told he had to put in an appearance on Sunday and after lunch.

A young Nicol Williamson took over his role (the competition was coming up fast) leaving Rich free to go off on a three-day binge. Elizabeth was furious. There was an angry exchange in the bar at the Dorchester which ended up with Elizabeth tipping her Jack Daniels over Richard's head. Rich took it in good part.

"Imagine what she could have done with a Bloody Mary."

In his less endearing moods he was capable of goading Elizabeth into a terrible anger. If he was bored he would pitch in an unprovoked and outrageous opinion, just to get a reaction. Like,

"There can be too many Jews."

"There can be too many Welsh."

"There are more Jews than Welsh."

"But it feels like there are more Welsh. They make so much noise. Talk, talk, talk."

"They have a lot to talk about."

"Oh no. They just take longer saying it!"

"I don't!"

"Sshmuck!"

It was a game for children and like all children's games it could end in tears, even when or especially when there was no serious content to the argument. The racial insult was a case in point. Of all people, Rich had an abiding detestation of racial prejudice and would jump to defend anyone he thought was the victim of discrimination. Bob Wilson, one of his closest companions, was unmistakably black.

Yet on a visit to Africa he caused a major upset with a response to a simple question. He was asked to name his favourite confectionery.

"Niggerheads," he declared.

There was an awful silence. Rich was unperturbed.

"They're marshmallows with chocolate topping," he explained innocently. "They're called niggerheads."

Suddenly, everybody was talking to change the conversation. Days later, Rich was at a dinner party hosted by a black politician. As the coffee was handed round, a delectable sight appeared centre table. In a voice that could always be heard above the competition, Rich boomed his appreciation: "Niggerheads."

There is no point in my arguing that it was all harmless fun. Rich could be thoroughly offensive, even when relatively sober. What I would say in his defence is that in his frequent verbal assaults on pretentious fools, he did us all a favour. I recall an awful meal when a well-

277

known show business writer (one who had it in his power to do Rich and Elizabeth a lot of harm) bored us rigid with a diatribe of misinformed Hollywood gossip. When he could take no more, Rich leaned towards the speaker.

"I want you to know," he declared, "you really are the most disgusting little shit."

Then, to an accompanying murmur of "Hear, hear," he got up from the table and weaved his way out of the room.

If in this first phase of the downturn of his career, Rich upset a lot of people, not least his wife, he always tried to keep on good terms with the children. They in turn gave him unstinting love. Not that Rich was what you might call an active father. It was Elizabeth who suggested things to do and places to go and who involved herself with the children.

Rich was just there. If the children wanted him he gave himself freely. And if he was not in the mood, Elizabeth was usually on hand to take the strain. As she described the relationship: "The children have fun with Richard. As a family we have a sense of the ridiculous — way out ridiculous. We laugh at the same things and it's Richard who makes us laugh — by being himself — great, charming, rough with the kids as with everyone else. He may say to them, 'Get a bloody move on' when they're wasting time or late and they'll accept it. But if he's in a really black mood, one of those melancholy Welsh moods, the word gets around, 'Cool it'. The children will warn me, 'Watch it, Mom', or I'll give them the nod."

To spend time with the family Rich and Elizabeth tried to adapt their work schedules to suit the school vacations of England, where Michael and Christopher were at Millfield, and Switzerland where Liza and Maria were at school. (Kate was at school in America and for most of the year lived with her mother.)

The holiday logistics were formidable. Gathering everyone at Puerto Vallarta, that most attractive hideaway, often entailed loss of school time for one or more of the children. This disturbed Rich who kept a close watch on educational standards. Tutors were employed to supplement what the regular teachers were able to provide. When Christopher had problems at Millfield, Rich promptly withdrew him from the school and turned to Nevill Coghill for advice.

"Do you, by any chance, know an able chap who would like to do a little globe-trotting for six or eight months and keep the boy up to the mark for entrance into school next autumn . . .? Be sure that I do not want a crammer but somebody who will keep his mind working . . . I would like his mind to be ticking over at this terribly important time of his life and not atrophying in this land of comic-cuts."

Nevill duly came up with a suitable candidate to instil an element of stability in the erratic world of the Burtons. John David Morley adapted easily to his curious job though registered with surprise the quantity of liquor Rich could take on without losing his senses and equally the unpredictable moments when his employer could slip from apparently sober conversation to an incomprehensible slur — "as if he had fallen off a cliff".

After the false start with Woodfall Films, Rich chose to wait for an offer that would attract Elizabeth. He was confident that the work would come in, despite the shaky fortunes of the film industry.

Twentieth Century-Fox was the first to put together

an attractive package. For Elizabeth there was *The Only Girl in Town* with Warren Beatty. For Rich, an extraordinary caper called *Staircase*.

In this he was called upon to camp it up as a gay hairdresser trying to come to terms with middle age and a deteriorating relationship with his partner, played by Rex Harrison. The story goes that both actors thought the idea so outrageous they just had to say yes. But Rich at least took it all very earnestly. It was, he said, an important film about the pain of loneliness made more acute by a defiance of convention. The association of Burton and Harrison, both obviously, some might say notoriously, heterosexual in real life, would, it was hoped, command respect for the story and its message.

The plan misfired. Critics and public alike failed to detect the underlying seriousness of what looked curiously like a burlesque. Audiences either laughed in the wrong places or cringed with embarrassment as the two stars cavorted through every cliché known to gay life.

Rich was for ever loyal to the film claiming that it was one of his best efforts which would eventually be reassessed in a more favourable light. "This is a great love story," he wrote. And later, "It is a kick against the system."

If that was true, he might have thought of his next film as the system kicking back. *Anne of a Thousand Days* gave Rich the opportunity to show what he could do with Henry VIII. The answer, given the banality of the script, was not much, though the film was quite well received in America. Incredibly Rich landed an Oscar nomination, his sixth, but was not in the least surprised that it did not lead to the actual award. The fact was the film bored him out of his mind. He agreed with a London reviewer who described it as "a plod through Tudor history" which should be retitled *Anne of a Thousand Hours*.

Warned that his reputation for boozing was beginning to worry producers, he made a resolution to cut back. But it did not last. Given the dreadful scripts that were for ever being thrown his way, he could not bring himself to believe that his drinking made any difference one way or the other. It was the easy way out. What he should have been asking himself was why the good scripts were going elsewhere.

The best moments for Rich in the making of *Anne of a Thousand Days* were in his caravan talking with old friends who remembered the great days — Anthony Quayle, Michael Hordern, William Squire. One afternoon, when I called to see him, I was told to approach warily because the order had been posted, Mr Burton is not to be disturbed. I feared the worst. But when at last I was ushered in I found my brother surrounded by a group of distinguished character actors, all in Tudor costume, engaged in a heavy discussion on the mysteries of county cricket. Interestingly, there was not a drink in sight.

The natural, spontaneous side to Rich showed up again when he heard from a classmate he had last seen when they were together at Port Talbot Grammar. Thirty years on, Trevor George was a headmaster in the West Country. He wrote asking if Rich would mind if he brought a party of children to the studios. The reply was by return.

"Mind? Why should I mind? Bring them all."

He laid on a guided tour which ended up with Rich leading a debate on the art of film making. Then there was tea on the lawn and a group photograph with Rich at centre in his Henry VIII costume.

A week later each of his guests received a signed picture. It was a small gesture but the children loved him for it.

After his excursion into sanitised history, Elizabeth suggested a break. Rich agreed. It was time to take stock. The movie industry was in poor shape. In the days when television was still the enemy and before video had come along to give home viewing a boost, the studios could think only of trying to hold audiences by appealing to the lowest common denominator. The Burtons followed the trend, hoping it was a short run.

"I've done the most awful rubbish," Rich admitted to a journalist, "just for somewhere to go in the morning."

But it was not simply that bad movies predominated. There had been times like that before. What was worrying was the clearly perceptible slide in the popularity of the Taylor-Burton partnership. Younger audiences, on whom the industry increasingly depended, were no longer transfixed by the *Cleopatra* love story. It was so tame by the standards of the swinging sixties. What place was there for the Burtons in the age of the Beatles?

As always, Elizabeth took the knocks more easily than Rich. It was not that she was less sensitive, simply more realistic. Having experienced the vagaries of public opinion she knew how to work events in her favour. And if she failed? Well, there was a strong impression that Elizabeth didn't give a damn. With Rich, it was quite different. His insecurity surfaced very quickly and the future troubled him.

A little time on when arguments with Rich were commonplace, he told me, "I drink to drown fear." I could understand that. Depression was a pervasive enemy which had gathered strength from Ivor's tragedy and the guilt Rich carried with him. Now he was haunted by the prospect of a career trailing away into mediocrity. He needed somewhere he could feel safe. And when the real world had nothing to offer he sought refuge in fantasy.

For six months in 1969 and the early part of 1970 Rich and Elizabeth drifted from Switzerland to Mexico to Botswana in Southern Africa. This last trip started with a children's hospital appeal and ended with Elizabeth satisfying a long felt wish to go on safari. It was a nerve-racking time for their guides who failed conspicuously in their efforts to persuade Elizabeth that some animals could be dangerous.

Having made friends with a young leopard, described by Rich as her feline psychopath, she declared her intention of studying at close hand a dangerous breed of wild monkeys. Tales of severed limbs and blood all over the floor did nothing to deter her. She set out a trail of nuts and fruit from the trees where the monkeys lived right up and onto her veranda. There she placed a large bowl filled to the brim with the sort of goodies monkeys appreciate. In no time at all she had these apparently savage beasts climbing over the furniture and generally behaving as if they were part of the family.

"The one thing you must not do," warned an attendant who spoke to Elizabeth from the far side of the room, "is to let them eat from your hand. A false move and . . ." He clawed the air in a way that left no room for misunderstanding.

The next day the same attendant nervously amended his advice. "Okay, if you *must* let them feed out of your hand, try to keep very still." Elizabeth turned her head sharply.

"What's that you say?"

The man fled.

For Rich the holiday was cut short by a severe bout of malaria. Apart from occasional back pains this was the first sign that his much abused constitution was not, as he loved to believe, invincible. His frailty angered him and he was not the easiest patient. But, at least, for seven weeks he was off the drink.

His nurse for all this time was Chen Sam, a remarkable young lady whose unabbreviated name confounded the assumption that she must be Chinese. In fact, her early years were spent in the Middle East, the child of an Egyptian father and an Italian mother who was sent to Britain as a teenager. A failed marriage later she was in Africa making a living as a pharmacist. She had a son in Paris.

It was not just her knowledge of pills and injections that qualified Chen for the job of restoring my brother. It was her refusal to be overawed by a loud voice and a dictatorial tone which really tipped the balance. An unconventional upbringing had made Chen self-reliant. She did not expect anything from the Burtons and so was not afraid to say what she thought. She told Rich plainly that if he wanted to recover he had to come off alcohol.

"For how long?" he demanded to know.

"For as long as it takes."

As the fever mounted Rich gave away more of himself than at any other time in his life. Delirium stripped him of his actor's disguise. In the middle of the night, in a half sleep he talked of Ivor as the father he had always wanted. It had been such fun with Ivor, the straight talking, hard drinking man who was never afraid of trouble and who always gave straight advice. And where was he now, this father of his dreams? In a terrible half-life from which all the money in the world could not release him. Just like Jessica, the daughter he had loved. When he had last seen her she had screamed at him as a stranger to be feared. He had never gone back to the hospital. He would never see her again. But the memory of an eleven-year-old girl, locked away in an institution, stayed with him. And always there was the question. Am I to blame?

Recovery left Rich with a powerful awareness of time passing. If there was also a tinge of self pity — "if only, if only" — it was wiped out by an event on the flight back from Botswana. It concerned Chen Sam who, recognised as a valued friend by Rich and Elizabeth, had been persuaded to join the Butron staff. This had not been achieved without some argument. More than once she had asked Rich, "But what am I supposed to do?" and more than once Rich had responded, "We'll think of something. Eventually." His only insistence was on a change of name. The Welsh intonation of Chen Sam was not to his liking. As he emerged from convalescence he came up with an alternative.

"I will call you Zen Bhudda."

So it was that Zen Bhudda alias Chen Sam was on the private jet with Rich and Elizabeth for their journey home. On landing, they were met by the usual bevy of photographers and reporters who caught everyone by surprise by making straight for Chen. Over the glare of the flashbulbs they shouted questions she could barely interpret. What was it they were trying to say? Something about her son? Had she heard about her son? Her son had pneumonia? Her son was dead?

The nightmare of coming to terms was for Chen a private matter. She did not want intruders, however well meaning. Elizabeth knew this and after the first awkward attempt to give comfort allowed Chen the freedom of her own thoughts. But Rich had difficulty in understanding the need to be alone. Grief had to be shared to be bearable. Always, Rich sought company. When Chen told him gently he could not help, he reverted to his own sadness.

"Right, then. I'm off for a drink."

In the weeks following Rich turned again to Oxford, the perfect refuge even if made so by nostalgia posing as reality.

After *Dr Faustus* the Oxford fund had suffered a relapse. Where Burton had failed others refrained from trying their luck. Rich decided to mount a rescue operation with an outright gift of one hundred thousand pounds.

"Obviously it will not be enough," he wrote to Nevill Coghill, "but with a certain amount of brainwashing we will, hopefully, be able to get a lot more from the Gettys and Onassises of this world. The latter is a warm friend of ours and I'm sure that if he were given the right kind of publicity (which he loves) he might write us a splendid little cheque. On the other side of the Atlantic Aaron is in touch with all kinds of people whose wealth is awesome. So one way or another we might be able to multiply the original £100,000."

In his letter of thanks ("it is a dream of a lifetime

286

made real'') Nevill returned to the idea of Rich spending a year's sabbatical at Oxford.

"I am excited to hear you are already finding an idea on which to ground your lectures. I am confident you could give us a great series if you can steadily explore this idea in the light of your experience and imagination. You have so many approaches that no one else has."

To Aaron Frosch, Nevill wrote, "I look forward to Richard making a big hit in the world of university teaching, as Granville Barker did a generation or so ago."

Why did it not happen? It is too easy to suggest that Rich was tied to a style of living which precluded Oxford. He and Elizabeth had enough money to live how they wanted and where they wanted for the rest of their lives. But while it was quite possible to think of Rich bumbling round the cloisters, matching every eccentricity known to academic life, it was not so easy to imagine how Elizabeth might adapt. On brief acquaintance, she found Oxford amusing, but not compelling. To give it a year was asking a lot of a child of Hollywood, as Rich knew perfectly well.

The other difficulty for Rich was matching performance with promise. However much he told himself he wanted to write and to lecture, he found it hard to sustain a theme. He would start well only to be distracted by irrelevant and disconnected arguments. He was best at delivering ideas when he spoke other people's words or when he spoke his own spontaneously, as in a free-for-all debate.

At Puerto Vallarta or on board the *Kalizma*, Rich methodically set aside two or three hours a day for writing but rarely turned out anything substantial. He was only forty-four and had achieved more than most artists could claim for an entire career, yet he was burdened by the fear that somehow life had passed him by. Maybe it was too late for Oxford; maybe it was too late for anything except what he knew he could do — with one hand tied behind his back.

It was no surprise to me when, after months of introspection, the offer that tempted a return to work was top billing in a second-rate war movie. That *Raid on Rommel* ever got beyond the first planning meeting was entirely thanks to a cost-saving idea for recycling action footage from *Tobruk*, a Rock Hudson adventure yarn, made four years earlier. The fee was modest by Burton standards but it was only three weeks' work and the Mexican location was within easy reach of Puerto Vallarta. Rich excused the inevitably poor reviews by saying it was his way of getting back into the swing of things. There was one encouraging sign. He stayed on the wagon for the duration.

Towards the end of 1970 Rich came back to London to make another film for Elliot Kastner. But this was quite different from *Where Eagles Dare*. In *Villain*, Rich was, for the first time, the out-and-out nasty, a sadistic East End gang leader who murdered for fun. He had always wanted to play the master criminal, to let himself go in a role that was as outrageously evil as anything in Elizabethan drama. He had tried for it two years earlier when his own production company had put together a treatment for *The Greatest Train Robbery in the World*. But it was not just the title that was altogether too grandiose. In the end, the project and the part Rich fancied for himself went to his friend, Stanley Baker, who was practised at turning out workable films on a tight budget.

Not that there was anything excessive about *Villain*, except perhaps the acting. Rich went way over the top with a performance that was pure ham. But it was a conscious decision, reflecting with unnerving accuracy the public image of any number of London heavies who made their mark on police files in the late sixties. Grotesque to the point of hilarity they could choke laughter with a vicious twist.

Villain upset some of the older generation of fans who refused to accept a Burton without any redeeming features. Possibly for this reason the film came in for more flack than it deserved. Even today it is sadly underrated. I still believe it was a chilling commentary on its time with a stronger regard for authenticity than most of its kind.

Rich was hurt in two ways; financially, because he waived his fee in return for a percentage on gross which turned out to be very modest; and professionally because instead of giving his career a lift, as he had intended, *Villain* left producers with the impression that he was desperate for parts, however inapt.

The consolation was a visit to Buckingham Palace to receive the CBE. This was his only public honour and I often wondered if he was a little envious of those actor luminaries who were able to put "Sir' before their names.

In conversation, he affected not to be worried by such trifles but he was too ready with excuses to make me believe he was entirely unconcerned.

"The Inland Revenue won't have it," he confided. "How can they give a knighthood to someone who doesn't pay taxes?"

"What about Noel Coward?"

Rich thought for a moment.

"True. But then he's much older. Maybe they have an amnesty for septuagenarians."

He chose not to take into account, or at least to talk about, his failure to come to terms with respectability. To appear high up on the honours' list it was necessary either to be pure (a rarity) or to sin discreetly. Rich was disqualified on the first rule and congenitally incapable of obeying the second. I don't think he ever did anything discreetly in his entire life.

Still, he made great show of his CBE — Commander of the Most Excellent Order of the British Empire. He went to the Palace with the two women who meant most to him — Elizabeth and Cis. The pictures of the three of them, all smiling proudly, are among the happiest in the family album.

Before returning to Mexico (partly for a rest, mostly to avoid the attentions of the taxman) there was just time to fulfil a long standing ambition to film *Under Milk Wood*, a lasting homage to the memory of Dylan Thomas. Financed by Rich, it was a superior home movie put together without the help of a director by an extraordinary cast who did it for love. Elizabeth was there, so were Peter O'Toole, Glynis Johns, Vivien Merchant, Sian Phillips, Victor Spinetti and Ryan Davies. If the film proved anything it was the difficulty of translating poetry into pictures. But the words came across beautifully. As Rich commented after the press show, "You can always close your eyes and think of Dylan."

By now he was back on the drink. Interminable sessions of boozy reminiscences were interspersed by bouts of foul temper which Elizabeth alone was able to contain. Considering her own run of ill health, I wondered at her capacity for taking so much.

Elizabeth was good for Rich in every way, domestically. Professionally, I was not so sure. When it came to choosing scripts she nearly always deferred to Rich. Sometimes he was right; more often he was wrong. In the confusion of his middle years (a familiar crisis even to those outside the movie industry) he needed someone close to him who could say where he was going wrong. Elizabeth was unable to oblige because she did not know the answer.

With Hollywood in the doldrums and the British studios virtually out of business, offers of work popped up from the unlikeliest sources. After the disappointment of *Villain*, Rich was open to any suggestion as long as it was made to sound big and exciting.

"I can add up the money. The rest is luck."

He knew it was not so but lacked the will to argue on matters that were central to his life. He went on with films which appalled him for the same reason that he went on drinking — to hold off the day when he had to make critical decisions.

His biggest fear was ending up on television — "the little box" as he called it. Though a major shareholder in Harlech television he seldom put in an appearance or responded to calls for ideas. His only suggestion for a drama series, an adaptation of Richard Llewellyn's novel *How Green Was My Valley*, was received politely but, as he might have expected, it did not appeal to the young turks who rejected the cosy, sentimental interpretation of Welsh culture.

Lord Harlech, chairman of the company, admitted his frustration to a journalist.

"The truth is, whenever we approach Richard to do something specific he is never available. His approach to everything is wholly emotional, so that, although he appears willing, whenever we try to get down to details we run into a complete fog."

Ah, little did the noble gentleman realise how frightened Rich was of compromising himself. Olivier, Richardson, Gielgud — what need had they of television? Mitchum, Lancaster, Grant, Douglas — when were they seen on the small screen except on chat shows or in reruns of old movies? Television was for the fading stars. That was how Rich saw himself when at last, he agreed to perform for the audience in the living room. He anticipated disaster. And, for once, he was right.

CHAPTER
FIFTEEN

Meanwhile he had a quartet of embarrassing films to complete. The first, *Hammersmith is Out*, was financed by J. Cornelius Crean, a wealthy building contractor in search of glitter. What he found was an easy way of losing money. Rich was called upon to play a certified lunatic who escapes from an asylum to roam across America in lustful pursuit of wealth and power. Along the way he teams up with Elizabeth, cast as a fast-food waitress (can you believe this?) who falls for his psychotic charms.

There was a hope that, as director, Peter Ustinov might use his undoubted talents to lift the stars above their material. But miracles were not in his line. Came the day when Rich could say to David Blewitt, editor on the film, "Well, we blew it, Blewitt." It was not a very good joke but it afforded one of the few laughs of the month.

Soon after the wrap on *Hammersmith* the Burton entourage migrated to Yugoslavia where Rich was under contract to the Ministry of Culture. This improbable alliance came about with an offer to play the country's president, Marshal Tito, in a reconstruction of his days as a freedom fighter against the German invaders. It was inspired casting. Rich assumed an uncanny resemblance to the young Tito, a leader for whom he professed a great admiration. But everything else about the film spelt disaster. A bad script was rejuvenated by Wolf

Mankowitz (brought in at Rich's insistence) who then had to stand by while every semblance of originality was squeezed out by the official guardians of ideological purity.

It was impossible to be angry. Rich and Elizabeth were treated with great ceremony, enjoying a level of hospitality reserved for visiting world leaders. While the personal staff (now over thirty strong including the aircrew for the private jet) were installed in a plush hotel, Rich and Elizabeth stayed at the presidential palace. There they enjoyed a standard of luxury which put their own trappings of wealth into the minor league.

"Whatever Marx said about egalitarianism," observed Rich, "it certainly didn't extend to politicians."

Summoned to Belgrade for a family discussion, I looked forward to sampling Yugoslavian largesse. But the palace was denied to me. Security forbade me or anyone else not of the elect to step beyond the stout iron gates which separated ordinary mortals from the president.

My first sight of Rich after an interval of several weeks disturbed me profoundly. He looked tired and sounded exhausted. The drinking was steady and relentless. By lunch he had put back more than I could take in a week. It did nothing to improve his mood which veered from the sullen to the brutally argumentative.

I took it as a blessing when work on the film was postponed while the Yugoslavian exchequer tried to grapple with an inflated budget. It took them three years to sort out the mess and to summon the nerve to finish the job.

Meanwhile, the Burtons and company proceeded on their Cook's tour of Europe. Next stop was Rome, the location for the reconstruction of *The Assassination of Trotsky*. Rich perked up a little at the prospect of a second chance for getting it right with the legendary Joseph Losey. Even the script looked good.

"For one thing, the lines I have to speak are Trotsky's own. That is a decided advantage."

But it was one of those films put together by an international consortium with an international cast (Alain Delon was the assassin) which foundered on mutual misunderstanding. Rich remained outwardly confident that Trotsky was a cut above his other recent portrayals. But the tension was missing. It was almost as if the story was being played as a documentary — worthy but uninspiring. When in the weeks ahead Rich spoke hopefully of *Trotsky* he was praying for a miracle in the cutting room. It did not happen and the film was panned. One critic suggested it should be sold as a cure for insomnia.

The fourth shot at giving new meaning to the phrase "disaster movie" centred on Budapest. Hungarian and Italian money was solicited to make *Bluebeard*, the sort of film Rich always swore he would never get into. In this blatant attempt to cash in on the soft porn market, Rich was the nutty Baron von Sapper who compensated for impotence by murdering a succession of beautiful wives. His acting in bed was convincing enough to cause Elizabeth some irritation but to those who lacked a personal interest the sequence of attempted couplings was hilarious. The last pretence of any seriousness of purpose was abandoned when Raquel Welch appeared as a nun. In real life, her cleavage would have threatened another dissolution of the monasteries.

Rich liked to think he was immune to press jibes but

the rush of stories accompanying *Bluebeard* hurt him greatly. For the first time he felt the world was treating him like a fool — and a pathetic one at that. He needed to show he still had fight in him, that he was a force to be reckoned with.

There are no prizes for guessing what he did to proclaim his comeback. He threw a party — the wildest, most extravagant party of his career. The excuse was Elizabeth's fortieth birthday but, from the day the news broke, no one doubted that the celebration had an ulterior motive. The message was clear: We're still around, we're still on top and we're still in command of the headlines.

The invitations went out by cable — the Burtons' favourite means of communication and, given the antiquated postal service in Hungary, the one most likely to get through.

COME TO BUDAPEST FOR THE WEEKEND OF FEBRUARY 26 AND 27 TO HELP ELIZABETH CELEBRATE HER BIG 40 STOP YOU WILL BE OUR GUESTS FROM ARRIVAL TO DEPARTURE STOP THE HOTEL IS VERY HILTON BUT THERE ARE FUN PLACES TO GO STOP DRESS INFORMAL FOR SATURDAY NIGHT IN SOME DARK CELLAR STOP DARK SUIT OR DINNER JACKET FOR SUNDAY STOP DARK GLASSES FOR HANGOVER

Who could resist?

Replies from the British contingent were channelled through Marjorie Lee at the Dorchester. As a guest herself, her assumption of the work of chief organiser was a noble act of self-sacrifice.

The family was well represented — seven of us with

partners travelling together to London. Our holiday weekend started on Thursday at the Dorchester where we had our own private party. The following morning we were shepherded by Marjorie to Heathrow where Rich had chartered a 150-seater Trident to ferry his pleasure seekers into central Europe. Among those linking up with us from the States were Elizabeth's brother Howard, who could be relied upon to keep his head whatever the circumstances, his wife Mara and their children.

Budapest was not the most cheerful of cities in those days but we did our best to liven it up. The welcome laid on for us by Rich and Elizabeth gave us a flying start. We were installed at the Intercontinental, better known as the Duna Hotel, where our hosts had the penthouse suite. To give us all a good view of the Danube, Rich booked the entire top floor. In each room we found a huge bouquet of out of season blooms, champagne on ice and a bar stocked with best wine and spirits. Cards identifying us as belonging to the Burton party entitled holders to free access to all the hotel services. Elizabeth even arranged for the hairdresser to stay open on Sunday so that the ladies could look their best for the big night.

The first of what turned out to be a succession of lavish celebrations was held in the hotel's wine cellars, the only surviving part of the old Duna which had thrived in the days of the Empire. To recreate what it must have been like when dress-suited flunkies sought out the finest vintages, Rich insisted on candlelight and cobwebs, the latter ingeniously created by the designers from the film studios. Their cleverness did not impress Cis whose housewifely instincts reacted against dirt of any kind. She was seen flitting about with a pocket handkerchief dusting away the offending draperies.

"Do you mind?" said Rich coming up to her. "Those cobwebs cost a dollar a time to put up."

The guests were a curious mix of friends and colleagues from both sides of the Burton partnership, representing an extraordinary range of interest. I listened in on a lively conversation between an international pop artist (Ringo Starr) and a man of letters (Stephen Spender) in the full knowledge that neither had any idea of the other's identity. Nevill Coghill talked to Frankie Howerd, a favourite comedian since 1955 when Rich had seen him as Charley's Aunt — one of the funniest performances, Rich claimed, on any stage at any time. As a young actor, not yet a star, Rich had sought and achieved a guest appearance on Frankie Howerd's radio show.

"I wasn't much of a comedian," Rich admitted, "but I learned one hell of a lot about timing."

The press corps was not specifically invited but neither was it discouraged from looking in. The publicity, Rich calculated, was bound to have a sharp edge (it always did when the Burtons were involved) but there was nothing outrageous to be heard or photographed and so no point in trying to impose restrictions. He reckoned without Alun Williams, the older son of Emlyn who was there with his father and Brook Williams. Why Alun bothered to come I cannot imagine because in the course of the evening he made it abundantly clear that he strongly disapproved of all this junketing. In a voice which could be overheard the other side of the Danube he demanded to know why so much money should be wasted in idle frivolity when, out there, ordinary, decent

Hungarians were wondering where to find their next crust?

There were several good answers to this question. For a start, party-giving was a perfectly legitimate feature of the star system. If you've got it, flaunt it, was the first rule for getting to the top in Hollywood. No doubt there were better ways of managing an industry but the Burtons could hardly be blamed for following custom. For them to have stopped giving parties would have been the equivalent of a resignation from the league of top earners.

Then again, the fifty thousand pounds it cost to set up the Budapest jamboree was money earned and spent in Hungary, with obvious benefits to local employment on both sides of the equation. It would have been easier for Rich to take the money and run though what good this would have achieved (except for easing Alun Williams' conscience) I found it difficult to imagine. Needless to say, the press was not too interested in the subtler arguments. The following day, the papers reported Alun's outburst as the central attraction of the party. Rich was pressed for a response. What did he intend doing about it?

Fighting down the urge to deliver some apposite comments on the abuse of hospitality, Rich stopped the affair in its tracks and saved the weekend by announcing that whatever the cost of the party, a corresponding sum would be donated to charity. Subsequently, a cheque was handed over to the United Nations' Children's Fund.

Weekend sightseeing took us to the old part of the city (really two cities, Buda and Pest, separated by the Danube). The museums and art galleries were less fun than wandering the streets which, to our amazement, were a happy release from the formality of state-organised leisure. People stared at us as if we were prize exhibits but once we made the effort to start conversation we were beset by friendly strangers eager to try out their halting English.

On the Saturday afternoon the men divided between those who wanted to enjoy the sweaty pleasures of the Turkish baths (there was a wide choice of establishments on the banks of the river) and the rest who were happier watching others sweat on the rugby field. Rich had asked me to bring a video of the British Lions triumphant tour of New Zealand. An appreciative audience joined him in his suite to watch the re-run on television. There followed a small dinner party, mostly family but with one or two special guests. Verdun found himself next to Princess Grace of Monaco, an opportunity he relished but one which he thought he would have to forgo when his new shirt threatened to strangle him.

"I can't understand it," he apologised when his attempts to release the pressure on his windpipe became too obvious to ignore. "I know I asked for the right size."

The princess was understanding. "You must change. You can't sit there all evening looking as if you're about to have a seizure."

With many apologies, Verdun departed the table. Ten minutes later he was back, looking much happier but with the same shirt.

"There was nothing wrong with the size," he confessed sheepishly. "It was just that I'd forgotten to take out the cardboard stiffeners."

He expected and got a ribbing from us all but his

humiliation was short-lived. Within hours the target for jokes had shifted from Verdun to Tom who was found by Rich contemplating a mound of Beluga caviar.

"What is it? What does it taste like?" he wanted to know.

Thinking carefully for a comparison that would make sense, Rich fastened on the Welsh delicacy made from seaweed.

"It's a bit like lava bread," he told his brother. Tom relaxed. "Oh, that's all right, then." And taking hold of a piece of bread, he ladled on enough caviar to satisfy a royal banquet. At about thirty pounds a bite it was, thought Rich, a sandwich so expensive as to qualify for the *Guinness Book of Records*.

The big party was on the Sunday evening. For this we went up in the world, from the cellars of the Duna to the rooftop nightclub which was specially decorated with thousands of gold balloons and masses of white lilacs and red tulips.

"Madam's done it quite well, hasn't she?" observed Frankie Howerd.

Everything about the evening was magnificently and extravagantly grand including the thirty-piece orchestra, a distinct improvement on the Hungarian pop group from the Friday session, whose favourite number, "I Left My Heart In San Francisco", was repeated to the point of insanity.

Since this was the birthday party proper, Elizabeth wore her present from Rich, a heart-shaped pendant that once belonged to Shah Jehan who built the Taj Mahal. Valued then at over one hundred thousand dollars it was inscribed "Eternal love till death". Obviously, we could not match such largesse but I think we acquitted ourselves handsomely with a presentation of an engraved plate crafted from finest Welsh steel.

The journey home was one long delicious round of anecdotes. How, on encountering Raquel Welch with her arm in plaster, one of my brothers, who must be nameless to protect him from his wife, asked if he could help put on her bra. How we all danced with Princess Grace and how Rich, in a delightful impromptu speech, nominated her Princess of Gwalia (an old name for Wales). And how Hilda on meeting Michael Caine told him how much she enjoyed *The Man Between*, only realising afterwards that she had been thinking of James Mason.

Staying overnight at the Dorchester we were invited to the BBC Lime Grove studios for a group interview. I was asked about Elizabeth's presents and mentioned that she had been given yet another dog, a large Hungarian hound of indeterminate breed. What I did not know then was that the beast had turned out to be a fast worker with the ladies. Left alone for a few minutes with the treasured Shih Tzu, he had worked his wicked way on the innocent poodle. Well, not so innocent according to Rich, who thereafter called her the French tart.

Back home we suffered the inevitable anticlimax. Brother-in-law Dai spoke for us all when, resuming work as a carpenter on the new M4 motorway, he told a friend, "I feel like a multi-millionaire who's just gone bust."

Thinking back on the Budapest party my only sadness was in noticing the change in Rich from the rock-like hero I had known most of my life to the tired, middle-aged celebrity who was feeling the days getting shorter. Caught off guard he looked in poor health. His back was playing him up (an inherited problem shared by all the Jenkins children) but more serious, or so it seemed then, were the after-effects of his bout of malaria. Elizabeth told me of at least two seizures, almost like epileptic fits, which had come upon Rich with terrifying suddenness. On the second of these, but for the presence of Chen Sam who turned in some nifty first aid, he might easily have choked on his own tongue.

For someone who needed to take better care of himself, Rich showed no sign of letting up on the harmful pleasures. The drinking bouts were sporadic but they still added up to a formidable consumption. And because the drinking was so obviously a problem it was easy to forget smoking — at least a hundred cigarettes a day — and the inadequacy of his diet. Fried chips were still his staple food. It was almost as if he was defying the fates to do their worst.

I checked with friends that it was not just my imagination. The consensus held that Rich was playing a dangerous game, putting himself and his marriage at risk. An actor who had worked with Rich on and off for over a decade told me that Elizabeth, who was no mean drinker herself, found it difficult to understand the total loss of control which could turn a loving husband into a raging brute. Maybe, it was suggested, she might decide to take it personally. If Rich was indeed fighting against something she did not have to look very far for an obvious target.

In seeking out opinions I tried to distinguish between sympathetic concern and malicious, often wishful, gossip. But it was not that easy. There was no denying that Rich had troubles; what was less obvious was the extent to which Elizabeth and Rich himself, thought of the troubles as self created. Who, in all this, was the real victim?

The opportunity to find out more came later in the year with an invitation to Munich where Rich was filming. He was coming up for his forty-seventh birthday and he wanted one member of the family to be with him on 10 November. He was fitter than when I had seen him in Budapest and when I said how well he looked, Elizabeth chimed in with the proud boast that he had been on the wagon for six months.

"But tonight," declared Rich expansively, "we celebrate." Elizabeth was understandably cautious.

"I wouldn't have too much if I were you, love. Why don't we order a beer each to give you a toast?"

The drinks were brought up; good German lagers, ice cold. While I sipped mine I watched Rich fill his glass. With an almost malicious grin of satisfaction, he contemplated the light froth. Then he put the glass to his lips, tipped it back and swallowed the contents in one long gulp. Elizabeth looked on in near despair.

"That was a bit silly, wasn't it, love?"

A still playful Rich answered. "It's my birthday, isn't it? Surely I can do something special on my birthday."

A little later he cut across a conversation I was having with Elizabeth. "I am mindful of another drink," he bellowed. "And why am I drinking beer when I can afford champagne?"

The waiter came in so fast he might have been listening at the keyhole.

"If it's champagne," said Elizabeth grimly, "you two are on your own." She got up.

"You stay where you are," Rich shouted but without another word she turned and left the room.

Rich transferred his attention to the waiter who was standing by.

"Champagne! Champagne! Champagne!" he roared, banging his fist on a small table like a child demanding a toy.

The waiter hurried away. I sat tight, not quite knowing what to say or do. Rich had his head down, his elbows on his knees. He showed no inclination to talk and did not even look my way until there was an open bottle of Dom Perignon and a glass by his side. Then he started in on me.

"Well, young Gray. What are we going to do with you?"

His question surprised me. "I don't think you have to do anything."

"So you're happy. Contented with your lot. Is that it?"

"I wouldn't say so."

"No, I didn't think you would. It can't be much of a life. Measuring out your days in a council office. With your intelligence you could be something better than, what do you call yourself? A chief clerk?"

The sneer in his voice was unmistakable. I bridled.

"I don't know what you're trying to say. It's not like that and you know it."

But Rich had touched a sensitive nerve. By most standards I had done reasonably well. I had gone into local government as a late teenager and had risen through the ranks to become manager of the Afan Lido in Port Talbot, the biggest sports and entertainment complex in Britain. My other job, as a rugby reporter on Welsh radio, was essentially part time but it gave me huge pleasure. I had a lovely wife who knew me better than

I knew myself and two fine youngsters. Not much to complain about there.

And yet. And yet. I was in the sod of job where the pressure to conform led to petty jealousies and vindictive backbiting. I was sick to death of having to justify any success I enjoyed by arguing my own merits against the implied advantages of starting as Richard Burton's brother. At forty-five I was thinking seriously of a change.

Rich interrupted my thoughts by slapping me hard on the knee.

"It's obvious. There's only one answer. You've got to work for me."

The suggestion came as such a surprise, my response must have sounded ungracious.

"Oh no. You've got me wrong. That's not what I want at all."

Now it was Rich's turn to bridle.

"And what the hell's wrong with working for me?"

I pointed to the now empty champagne bottle and to the replacement he had put on ice.

"It's not my sort of life."

"You enjoy it when you're here."

"But I'm only here for a while. Full time would kill me. Anyway, I wouldn't want to watch you destroying yourself."

Rich stood up. He was shaking, though from anger or alcohol, I could not tell.

"You little bastard," he shouted. "How dare you tell me how to behave. Who do you think you are?"

There was a lot more of this. The two of us standing face to face, trading insults, mostly in Welsh, until we were too tired to go on.

306

The next morning at breakfast no one talked. After his second coffee Rich got up and went into his bedroom. We heard the soft tap of his portable typewriter.

"What are you writing?" Elizabeth called out.

"A letter," said Rich.

"Who to?"

"My brother."

After a few minutes he came out and handed me an envelope.

"Don't open it until you're on the plane," he ordered.

Fastened into my seat with the air hostess hovering with a drink, I stared at the envelope a long time before lifting the flap. The letter read:

The first day of my forty-eighth year.
Dearest Graham,
Thank you for tolerating my blown mind yesterday. There is an element of schizophrenia in everybody's make-up (not done by Ron Berkeley) and peculiarly so in our family's and fine honed to a razor's edge in mine. My chief and most vicious faculty when I lose my balance on the tightrope is to attack with malicious venom the people I love most. Towards the apathetic, I am apathetic. I don't bother to attack Harry John Doe Jones because he is not worth my attention, but show me a loved one and the bludgeon and sabre and épée and foil are out with lips curled the wrong way and my name is "fang".

Anyway, you are a fine and splendid man and I am proud to tell people so and the job and the jobs you have done are truly remarkable. With very few of my advantages you succeeded beyond the dreams of envy. Keep it up and — here comes the pot advising the kettle — watch the booze.

The letter confused me. It was a handsome apology; more, perhaps, than I deserved. But was it reasonable to see in it any hint of redemption? I was sufficiently encouraged to put the row behind me and not to talk about it with the family.

Good news followed in a day or two when I heard of a move forward in Rich's long promised intention to do more at Oxford. His election as an honorary fellow of St Peter's College required him to appear for the occasional lecture or seminar but not to live in Oxford for any length of time. It was, I thought, the perfect compromise. But contrary to the impression given by the papers, the honour was not entirely unsolicited. Engineered by Francis Warner, his lobbying was undoubtedly helped by Rich's promise to raise his contributions to the theatre appeal.

Nevill Coghill was delighted. Now well into his seventies he knew that time was short to achieve his ambition of a fine new theatre for Oxford. His sense of urgency heightened a few months later when he suffered a stroke. He wrote with typical lack of self-pity of his slow recovery and of his wish to get plans underway, "before my time runs out".

The problem seemed to be a lack of communication between Rich and those who looked after his affairs. Nevill tried to spell out what was wrong. On the plus side was a letter from Aaron Frosch: 'I am informed by telephone that Mr and Mrs Burton have indeed stated they are prepared to increase their gift and that the plans presented by Professor Coghill are acceptable to them . . . I note that the plan is to commence building next March. We are scheduling a substantial payment on account of the said gift prior to that time."

But March came and went without any transfer of funds. Nevill appealed directly to Rich.

308

"Do you think Aaron could be authorised by you to let us have the payments he mentions?"

As far as I know he never received a satisfactory response. Consequently building was postponed indefinitely. Rich, meanwhile, was still bubbling on about how he was planning to take Oxford by storm. He told a friend of his meeting the economist Kenneth Galbraith.

"I asked him the secrets of being a successful lecturer and he said, 'You have to mumble so they can't hear anything you say and be as obscure as possible so they'll go out and buy the books.'"

He reassured a journalist who asked him if he was really made out to be a teacher. "Oh yes. I'll wear a rotting cap and a rugger scarf and say, 'Good morning, Jones Minor. Never mind your tutorial. Send your sister up with the essay.'"

I could not help wondering if Oxford was truly ready for him. Perhaps it was just as well we never found out. Still, my sympathy went out to Nevill Coghill and his friends who were victims of the very peculiar circumstances of the Burtons' lifestyle. These arose because there were too many self-interested people involved in their affairs. Letters did not get to Rich, telephone calls were not put through and meetings were cancelled at the last moment. All this was done, so it was said, to protect him from unnecessary pressures. But I suspect other motives, not least the desire by some of his employees to monopolise a valuable property. Aaron Frosch most definitely did not fall within this category. But he was made frail by the mounting torment of muscular sclerosis and was beginning to lose out to less scrupulous members of the household.

The position was made more complex by the changes

in Rich's character which made him altogether less predictable and by the deteriorating relationship with Elizabeth.

I realised all this at first hand when, after the Munich incident, I was encouraged by Rich to think again about a change of job. I made it clear that under no circumstances could I join the Burton staff. "All right," said Rich, "what do you want to do?"

"If I was to resign my job and if we could afford it, we'd live in the Channel Islands, Guernsey probably. It's what we've always wanted to do."

"Then what's the problem? Just do it. I've got some money there. You could look after it for me. You wouldn't make a fortune but with commissions and such you could bring in twenty or thirty thousand a year."

It sounded like a fortune to me.

"Are you serious?"

"Never more so. Have you ever heard me joke about money?"

Well, that was true at least. After talking it over with Hilary, I decided on a break for freedom. But, sadly, like Nevill Coghill, I pitched my expectations too high. After the first flush of excitement at handing in my resignation accompanied by a few choice words on my reasons for leaving, I spent some anxious weeks trying to persuade Rich to advance beyond vague promises. By the time we came to move to Guernsey, there was still nothing in writing though Aaron assured me he could work out some sort of deal. It didn't happen. Instead we made our own way, me in property development, Hilary in the hotel business.

Looking back, I am profoundly grateful to Rich for giving me the push towards a new life. Returning from

Guernsey I landed a job doing what I always wanted to do — sports organiser for the BBC. But for Rich telling me to get off my backside, it would never have happened. And if, along the way, I voiced my resentment at what I believed to be his lack of consideration or decent regard for business courtesies, I must now temper my views with the knowledge that he had more than enough problems of his own to occupy him.

CHAPTER
SIXTEEN

After Budapest came the time for Rich and Elizabeth to fulfil their long-standing promise to do something for Harlech Television. Dozens of scripts were considered and pushed aside before one was found to satisfy the stars, the company and the money men who spoke for American interests. The writer was John Hopkins whose pedigree led with *Talking to a Stranger*, one of the most powerful domestic dramas ever to appear on British television. In this quartet of plays he looked at a family crisis from the point of view of four of the participants. Now he was called upon to try a similar technique with *Divorce His, Divorce Hers*, a study of a marriage break-up as seen by both partners.

But the idea was horribly misconceived. In trying for a re-run of *Who's Afraid of Virginia Woolf?*, Rich and Elizabeth were playing dangerously close to home. The rows they were having on set were so overlapping the rows they had in private, there were times when they hardly knew whose lives they were talking about. Professionally this might have worked, if the stars had been forced to submit to a higher discipline — an Edward Albee dialogue, for instance, or a Mike Nichols direction. But neither the writer nor director had that sort of power. In *Divorce His, Divorce Hers*, whatever Burton and Taylor wanted, Burton and Taylor got. And since they were in such turmoil they could not even begin to impose a sense of unity on what turned out to be a long-winded discourse of marital platitudes.

By now, Rich was well on the way to an emotional collapse brought on by excessive alcoholism. Elizabeth too, was hitting the Jack Daniels. What angered me so much was that no one, not even Elizabeth, seemed capable of spelling out to him the terrible dangers he was running. It took Rich himself to prove to me that you can't just tell an alcoholic to give up or die. He knows the choice is not so stark. He will tell you of a half world he has shaped from his own fantasies, somewhere between life and death. It is here that he can come to terms with his own troubled nature, where all questions are answered and all responsibilities lifted. But this half world has no permanence. It has to be recreated day after day while the fear of being left alone in the real world grows ever more painful.

Poor Rich. The passer-by would have said he had everything. If contentment was not his, then contentment was not to be had. To which my brother would reply,

"To have everything is to lose everything. The dread of losing is the greatest dread of all."

And Rich was losing. He had already lost Ivor who had died three weeks after the Budapest party. He was losing his career to the inanities of the film industry, he was losing his mind to the mediocre film opportunities offered him and he was losing his wife to the anger of his failure. It was full circle.

Early in 1973 he admitted to me for the first time that he was an alcoholic. Confession frightened him. He made me promise not to say a word to Cis. He said she would worry more than was good for her but while this was true, he was really more concerned to sidestep her disapproval.

"I need all the help I can get," he told me. "I'm talking to doctors who know about this sort of thing. They say I can pull round."

A few weeks later he submitted to a rigorous diet which excluded hard spirits and permitted only occasional glasses of wine.

The experience was terrifying.

"You shake, you sweat, you can't read. You can't pick anything up because your hands shake so much."

But no sooner was he over the first horror than he went back on drink. A mutual friend said of him, "He sees too many others who need their daily fix."

In mid 1973 the Burton circus was back in Rome — Rich to play a Gestapo officer in a Carlo Ponti production, *Massacre in Rome*, and Elizabeth to play the older woman in a mawkish love story called *Ash Wednesday*.

They raved about their films (each thought the other was in a degrading role), about the people they worked for and about the people who worked for them. Of the joint staff only Chen Sam, Bob Wilson and Ron Berkeley inspired the trust of both employers. For the rest there were accusations of plotting and double dealing which, if half true, would have done credit to the Borgias.

Rich looked dreadful — his face loose and puffy, his arms hanging loosely, he shuffled about like a tired old man. Elizabeth hid weary eyes behind dark glasses. Billowing dresses could not disguise her excess weight. Though more obviously in command of herself than Rich, she was not easy to talk to. Quick to misinterpret, she could turn a kind word with a stinging rebuke.

The press reported every angry exchange, every traded insult, real or rumoured. Those of us who loved them both went through agonies of frustrating inactivity. What could we do to help? Telephone calls were refused, letters unanswered (I suspect Rich never even saw most of them). One letter was actually returned unopened.

In over a month there was just one communication, a cable to brother Tom. It read, "Worry not. All is well between us."

A few days later, Elizabeth flew to California. Officially it was put out that having finished work on *Ash Wednesday* she was travelling ahead of Rich who would join her when he was free to do so. Unofficially, it was an open secret that Elizabeth wanted to get away.

Recalling this time, she told me, "We were killing each other. And for why? I couldn't just sit there and let it happen."

Rich was befuddled, not knowing what to do next. After a week he was mooching about his hotel suite when he found his daughter Maria, now aged twelve, packing a suitcase.

"What are you up to, love?"

"I'm going to New York to be with Mommy."

"Are you packing for me too?"

"No."

They said goodbye and Maria left with her nanny.

From Elizabeth he heard not a word. When there was nothing else to do, Rich joined the trek to America. In New York he went to the Long Island home of Aaron Frosch and from there he rang Elizabeth in California, asking her to join him. Contrary to the usual story he did not rant or rave. According to Elizabeth he was almost plaintive, begging her to come back. She agreed as long as he would keep sober. He promised.

They met at Kennedy Airport. Rich was waiting for her in the back of a chauffeur-driven limousine. Elizabeth knew immediately he had been drinking. She sat tight-lipped as Rich embraced her and as they drove away her head drooped.

There followed the inevitable row. Rich tried to pre-empt his wife's justifiable anger by accusing her of being unfaithful. Harsh words were said of businessman Henry Wynberg who had been seen with Elizabeth; "that second-hand car salesman", as Rich contemptuously described him. It was an epithet which stuck even though cars were only a small part of his business interests.

The shouting lasted all of two hours and at the end of it Elizabeth ordered the car for the drive back to Kennedy.

The formal announcement of a separation came from John Springer, Elizabeth's press secretary. By way of explanation Elizabeth spoke of "loving each other too much" and of having "been in each other's pockets constantly". The statement ended a trifle dramatically. "Pray for us."

Aaron was told to work out the financial arrangement.

"It'll be very complex," he warned.

"Just do whatever she wants," said Rich.

Sensibly, Aaron went about his business cautiously. Like everyone else he hoped for a reconciliation. The signs were not entirely unhopeful.

Self-disgust and the shock of knowing Elizabeth was no longer in thrall to him sent Rich back to his booze-free diet. He hired a doctor and a nurse to make sure he stuck to it.

In August, he returned to Rome for another Carlo Ponti production, *The Voyage*, for which his co-star was Ponti's wife, Sophia Loren. These two were incredibly kind to Rich. Carlo Ponti believed in his talent and Sophia Loren in his humanity and though both had their faith strained to breaking point, they remained loyal. To stay on the wagon he needed someone near him who was witty, diverting and extremely patient. It had to be a woman, and a beautiful woman at that. Sophia Loren, unpaid and unthanked, accepted the role.

I spent several weekends with them. The call from Rich would come late in the week. "Can you get over here, I want to talk?" It was always about Elizabeth; how life was joyless without her, how he wanted so much to recapture her love.

We slept in the same room, the conversation, often disjointed and always circuitous, going on late into the night. His last words before he went to sleep were ever the same, delivered in a deep growl.

"Another day, yr uffern, you hell; another day, drink, you devil. I've beaten you."

I was intrigued to find that women still flocked round him. If they were seeking some advantage, financial or professional, I could understand but if they wanted more, I seriously doubted that Rich could deliver. One of them certainly had intimations of bliss. I was fast asleep one night when I felt a tug at my arm. I came round, hearing a whispered plea close to my ear.

"Reechard, Reechard. I am here. I love you. Take me. Take me."

"Sorry love," I said, lifting my head, "the man you want is in the next bed."

I was in Palermo with Rich when word came through

that Elizabeth had been rushed to hospital. It sounded bad. Whoever rang from Los Angeles mentioned the probability of cancer. Rich went immediately to Carlo Ponti who gave him time off to fly to California. Before leaving Rich asked me to go to Naples in the *Kalizma*. I sailed in lonely state wondering how much more drama could be packed into two lives.

On arriving I was told to expect to see Rich before the end of the day. And not only Rich. Elizabeth was with him. It appeared she was not desperately ill, after all. Maybe, just desperately in love. When they came aboard the *Kalizma* I had never seen them look happier. We had a wonderful meal together, joking and laughing about old times. Hardly able to believe what I was witnessing, I wished them all the joy in the world.

"Tell them at home," said Rich. "The bad times are over."

The good times lasted until Christmas when "just to celebrate" Rich had a little drink. They were in Gstaad. There had been some thought of a family reunion in Wales but when nothing further was heard from Rich, we assumed he and Elizabeth wanted to be alone. In fact, Elizabeth was not even there. On the first appearance of a bottle she had packed her bags. When the bottle was replaced she, booked a flight. And when the third bottle was emptied, she left.

They met up again briefly in Puerto Vallarta and in Oroville in northern California where, in March 1974, Rich went to co-star with Lee Marvin in *The Klansman*. A more inappropriate alliance it was difficult to imagine. If Rich was the reformed drinker who had lapsed, Lee Marvin was the unrepentant drinker who was still far short of his limit. The two got on famously but brought everyone else on the film to the edge of a nervous breakdown. More than once, the director, Terence Young, thought of abandoning the project.

Elizabeth came and went. She was on set just long enough to know there was nothing she could say to bring Rich to his senses. Just before leaving she urged Valerie Douglas, who now handled Rich's domestic affairs, to book him into St John's Hospital in Santa Monica.

"Either that," she said, "or he's a dead man."

By all accounts it was a close run thing. The doctors told him if he continued to drink, he had less than a month to live. He submitted to treatment and suffered the torture. One of his lines from *The Comedians* came back to me: "I've always wanted to know the worst about myself; to feel the bottom of the gutter with my toes." Now he knew. He could hardly walk without someone holding him up; he could hardly talk without someone finishing his sentences and he could not sleep without someone handing him the glass and the tablets.

The tumbril moved on. Rich was in hospital for about ten weeks. When he came out, divorce papers had been filed. The formalities took another six months to complete.

"I wonder," mused Emlyn Williams, "who will get custody of Brook?"

The first of many Burton comebacks started promisingly. At a time when not one of the big studios would invest a penny in him, Rich had one of the best offers for many a year. The BBC wanted him to play Churchill in *A Walk with Destiny*, a ninety-minute dramatised documentary co-produced with Hallmark. Based on Churchill's memoirs, the programme was to cover the period 1934 to 1940 when Sir Winston became prime minister. The producer, Jack Le Vein, had worked with Rich on *The Valiant Years*. It all looked very promising. There was just one problem. The deal was linked to a remake of *Brief Encounter*, the Trevor Howard and Celia Johnson classic which came out in 1945.

To this second, riskier enterprise Rich made token resistance. He enjoyed being told by people who should have known better that he was not too old or too world weary for the part. Then there was the touchy question of precedence. It was no secret Rich was second choice to Robert Shaw who was held up on other film commitments. But as Rich graciously put it, when he knew that Sophia Loren was to co-star and he heard "her gently imperious voice which turns my stomach into a bag of butterflies", he was persuaded.

Now it was the turn of the BBC to need some persuading — that Rich was, indeed, fit for work. I can't say I blamed them. Superficially, he was a reformed character. He looked fitter and leaner. He dressed with care. Some of the old sparkle was back. He was able to laugh his booming laugh without sounding like a cracked bell.

But his mind was in uproar. He told me he felt as if he were coming out of a nightmare and still half asleep. He said the strangest things at the strangest times. Strolling the promenade in Nice he stopped an attractive woman, a perfect stranger, fixed her with his eyes and said, "If I should go away, beloved, do not say he has forgotten me. Forever you abide a singing rib within my dreaming side." Then he walked on. I often wonder how the story went down in some quiet French home above the town. "I met this loony today who called me beloved . . ." No doubt it was put down to the effect of the sun.

Also in Nice, in a packed bar, observing three nuns come in carrying charity boxes, Rich thunderously ordered everybody to "kneel and pray". "And do you know," he later ruminated, "some besotted bastards actually went down on the floor."

But there was not much to laugh about. He talked a lot of Elizabeth. It was almost as if she was in the next room. Further away, perhaps, when he growled, "She's better off without me."

His temper was edgy. He could be cruel without provocation. We had a lot of this; the sneering dismissal of old friends, the snide remarks to create mischief.

When he saw Valerie Douglas quizzing one of his companions he shouted at her across a crowded table.

"I know what you're trying to find out. You want to know if I've slept with her."

The assembly laughed dutifully.

Occasionally, the public was permitted a glimpse of the black side of Rich's character. A week before the American TV premiere of *A Walk With Destiny*, Rich was asked to write an article about Churchill for the arts section of the *New York Times*. They expected a laudatory piece on the great war leader. Instead, they were treated to a vitriolic assault on Churchill the right-wing politician, of whom Rich declared, "to know him is to hate him".

In other circumstances much of his argument might have been judged a useful corrective to the mythology of Churchill as the hero who could do no wrong. But having just played the man in a favourable light, after seeking extensive help from the Churchill family, his attack was in bad taste to say the least. To say the worst, it was way over the top, a catalogue of violent histrionics and gross inaccuracies. (Churchill did not order the shooting of Welsh strikers in the labour troubles of the 1920s.) The wild flights of prose indicated to some an unbalanced mind, though, in my view, allowance must always be made for Rich's lifelong desire to emulate Dylan Thomas.

The producers were appalled and made haste to disassociate themselves from the Burton thesis. Ironically, the publicity achieved a higher American rating for the play. But in Britain, the unfavourable press cut a swathe through the ranks of the Burton fan club.

Rich maintained his reputation for being accident prone in print when Stanley Baker, his friend and fellow countryman, died of cancer in 1976. The editor of the *Observer* had the bright idea of asking Rich to write an obituary. He responded with a rough, rambling piece which filled the front page of the review section. It was written with love, no one could doubt it, but graphic references to youthful indiscretions — "we fought, we smashed windows and broke trains and lusted after the same women and drove through the Continent, pustular and acne'd and angry and madly in love with the earth and all its riches" — though liable to thrill the breakfast readers of a Sunday paper did not please the Baker family or some of the actor's straight-laced admirers.

A Walk With Destiny was greeted respectfully; *Brief Encounter* was dismissed as an absurdity.

"Where else," asked Clive James in the *Observer*, "would an Italian beauty queen with a wardrobe of exotic if badly chosen clothes pretend to be the humdrum wife of a British solicitor and make goo goo eyes at a raddled Welsh thespian trying to pass himself off as a promising physician by dyeing his hair with black boot-polish?''

He did colour his hair, not with boot polish but with a dye so strong that it would not come out by washing. It took him a year to get back to his natural grey.

"There," he said when the last traces of black had disappeared. "I feel old again. But still incredibly gift-ed."

After *Brief Encounter*; nothing. Rich whiled away his time in a hotel suite waiting for a promised deal from one of those European film consortia where there are more accountants than actors. It didn't come.

Elizabeth, meanwhile, was back with Henry Wynberg who helped to keep her in the public eye. Rich too had his much publicised diversions — Princess Elizabeth of Yugoslavia, and Jeanne Bell, a striking beauty whose claim to fame was to feature as the first black girl in a *Playboy* centrefold. The rest of the household was much reduced. Bob Wilson was still there, so was Brook Williams (who kept a lower profile when Elizabeth was around) and Valerie Douglas. Otherwise there were just two secretaries and Rich's favourite pet, a one-eyed pekinese.

Much effort went into persuading the press that Rich was teetotal. But the evidence of long evenings in dark bars counted against him.

Among those who were not deluded were the members of the Council of Oxford University who, in late 1975, finally rejected the appeal of Nevill Coghill to award Rich an honorary degree.

"This is a great blow which I know you will feel as sharply as I do," wrote Nevill to Aaron Frosch. "I had secured all the support I could find, including a unanimous petition from the Curators of the University Theatre . . . However, our hopes have been dashed and there is nothing more I can do about it except to record my disappointment and disgust at this fresh example of the hostility of the University to the Drama, against which I have striven for most of my life."

But it was not the Drama that defeated Rich so much as the slightly tatty image that now accompanied him. You could imagine that common-room conversation, "This chap, Burton, not quite our sort, do you think?"

Nevill had another disappointment. His new theatre was not built. He had to make do with a rehearsal room tacked on to the existing Oxford Playhouse. It was called the Burton Beckett annexe.

To break the run of inactivity, Rich decided on a change of management. He called Robert Lantz, a top agent whose deceptive dry humour and gentle manner disguised one of the shrewdest brains in film and theatre. Rich was taking a chance. Years earlier he and Elizabeth had made a joint approach to Lantz. He agreed in principle to represent them.

"There's just one thing," concluded Rich, "we don't pay ten per cent. Five is our top."

"I quite understand," said Robby, smiling sweetly as he rose from the table. "Why don't you come back when you can afford me."

This time there was no quibbling over figures. Rich asked bluntly, "Are you interested in representing a drunken, clapped-out old actor?"

Robby said he thought he could cope. "But this must not hurt Elizabeth. I love her very much and would not do anything to upset her."

Rich answered, "Who does not love Elizabeth?"

With a career so obviously shaking on the edge, Robby decided there was no time to mount a gradual recovery. The rescue had to be bold and decisive. Another of the Lantz clients was the dramatist Peter Shaffer whose latest play, *Equus*, was enjoying a successful Broadway run. Heading the cast as the psychiatrist, Dysart, was Anthony Perkins who was on contract until the end of the year. A replacement was needed. Why not Burton?

John Dexter, who directed *Equus* in London and New York, was not immediately taken with the idea. He pointed out that Dysart is a dry-as-dust character, an unassertive middle-of-the-road professional who discovers his own emotional inadequacies through the investigation of a shocking crime. Dexter worried that Rich was too strong an actor to show Dysart's vulnerability. The counter view held that his troubles had softened up Rich. He *was* vulnerable.

It was worth a try. A meeting was fixed in London, at Squire's Mount where Gwen, Ivor's widow, had settled. The guests were to be Robby Lantz and Alex Cohen, producer of the Burton-Gielgud *Hamlet* and of several Shaffer plays on Broadway. When they arrived Gwen was bustling about preparing lunch. Rich would be down shortly, she said. After an hour, they heard a grunting outside the door. The handle was turned and in walked Rich looking as if he had lost his way. His movements were clumsy, his speech slurred. He was, quite obviously, sloshed out of his mind.

The lunch was a nightmare of social ineptitude. At one point, leaning aside for a dish, Rich fell on the floor. It took one guest on each arm to get him to his feet.

Agent and producer were appalled but not defeated.

Fortunately for Rich, they decided to try again another day. He was signed up for *Equus*.

In his dealings with friends and relatives, Rich was equally unpredictable. From being sober and sensible he could veer off on some fantastical argument which left us all gasping. He longed to see Elizabeth again. I felt that in this tumultuous period of his life she, more than anyone, represented self-control and stability — much as Sybil had done when the *Cleopatra* saga was at its peak.

He took to telephoning his ex-wife, sometimes more than once in a day. They continued to meet, I assume without the knowledge of their regular escorts. When the press stole a picture of them arm in arm it was explained away by an accidental overlap in their schedules. But when this happened twice in a month, a likelier explanation circulated. It gained currency when the two spent a short holiday at Gstaad. They looked so happy together.

It is true that Rich gloried in the rediscovered delights of a familiar partner. He was at home. This, he enthused, is how it always should be. As for Elizabeth, I am not so sure. There was, I know, a hope that Rich had, at last, taken hold of himself. But was it conceivable that she would gamble on recapturing the old magic? Evidently, yes, because two months later they were remarried. The ceremony took place in a village in northern Botswana.

On the face of it, a more unlikely setting could not be imagined. But it was remote and romantic and they loved the place. Rich said afterwards that it had all happened in a dream world. To which I could only respond that I and the rest of the family were part of it. We really believed the miracle had happened.

Elizabeth was the first to hit reality. On the very day of the wedding she found Rich so overloaded with vodka he could barely walk.

"I led the lad back to bed and suggested he tried to get a couple of hours' sleep so that his eyeballs could change from magenta to at least a pretty conjunctivitis pink."

It was a brave attempt to laugh off what she must then have known to be a terrible mistake.

"How can you get mad at anyone so utterly outrageous? I love him deeply and truly and forever but I do recognise one or two flaws in the immense personage."

Our first chance to congratulate the couple came in November. With Rich due to stay over in London for his fiftieth birthday, Elizabeth rang ahead to ask Marjorie Lee to organise a splendid party of the style only the Dorchester knows how to lay on.

Mindful of Rich's simple culinary taste, the designers chose what I can only describe as an upmarket Cockney theme. To carry the buffet of sausage and mash, tripe and onions, ham, turkey, pork and, of course, chips, the Orchid Room was occupied by a fleet of multicoloured coster barrows. These were given a suitably luxurious setting by the addition of gold hangings and tablecloths.

Rich was surprised and pleased to see so many of his friends and family gathered to celebrate his birthday. Carrying a glass of wine which he sipped rarely he kept sober on into the early hours when he led the community singing in as fine a rendering of the Welsh language as to be heard outside the valleys.

But it was a different story when Rich and Elizabeth

327

came to Pontrhydyfen to spend a few days with Hilda. Rich was in terrible shape, drawn and haggard. I asked Elizabeth what was wrong.

"It's what happens when he's been off the booze for a few days. Withdrawal symptoms. If he could stay off for a few more weeks, he'd be all right."

Just like smoking, I thought. In the first stage of giving up smoking you actually feel much worse. Not that Rich had ever had that experience. For as long as I could remember he had been a hundred a day man. And he had no intention of giving up. Not yet, anyway.

"One of these days," he used to say, "I'll stop and suffer and be killed by a falling tree while walking the dog."

This was always his excuse for not holding to his word. At the critical point he would tell himself he might as well go back to the bottle because if he didn't, something worse was just as likely to happen. Nonsense, of course, but no one has ever claimed a link between alcoholism and rational thinking.

Back in Switzerland, Elizabeth relived the indignities of living with an alcoholic. The rows were long and painful, extending from one day to the next, picking up in the morning where they had stopped, exhausted, the night before.

Rich claimed he was bored. Having restored the old routine, he now found it wanting. But he was not so much bored as nervous. In a few weeks he would be back on Broadway, after a stage absence of more than twelve years. The challenge was almost more than he could bear to contemplate.

He sought reassurance in a way that was second nature to him — by testing the strength of his personality on a new admirer, someone who could tell him he was still the best without making it sound like a cracked record. Among those favoured for this role was a twenty-seven-year-old blonde he spotted on the ski slopes. He saw her again at a party where she was scrabbling around on the floor searching for a lost contact lens. The incident amused Rich because, at first, he thought she was roaring drunk.

Dispatched to make discreet enquiries, Brook Williams reported that Susan Hunt, wife of the British racing driver, James Hunt, would be delighted to come over for drinks. No, her husband was not with her. Moreover, gossip had it that the couple were not on the best of terms.

Elizabeth was unperturbed. She was used to seeing pretty girls come and go. Just two months into marriage she did not think she had much to worry about.

In February, Rich flew to New York. Elizabeth preceded him by a few days. Susan Hunt followed. Elizabeth flew on to California; to visit her mother, it was said.

Rich's nervousness showed more obviously the closer he came to Broadway. Taking him for the first time to the Plymouth theatre where *Equus* was playing, Robby Lantz recalls him alone on the stage staring into the empty stalls.

"I stood aside and watched knowing that he was wondering if he could recapture his kingdom."

His biggest fear was the damage he had inflicted on his memory. Had drink robbed him of his capacity to absorb lines? A recent event served to give him some comfort. As he told it:

"I was with Elizabeth in Jerusalem where I said I'd speak at the University. I thought they wanted a seminar, an invigorating informal chat. But when I got there I found I was booked to deliver two hours of poetry, for charity, in front of an audience of a thousand who had paid fifteen dollars a time to hear me. I did the lot from memory including the twenty-third psalm in Hebrew. Apart from a desperate and unnoticed bit of paraphrasing in the middle of some unfamiliar medieval piece, every word fell into its allotted slot like a computer. Ninety-nine out of a hundred. Not bad, eh?''

But there was another story told to me by an actor friend.

"I was in the middle of a *Times* crossword and there was this clue which referred to a quote from *Hamlet*. Rich would know it, I thought; he's done the part hundreds of times. But when I asked him, he floundered and got very annoyed with himself for forgetting what should have been as obvious as his own name."

The rehearsals for *Equus* gave credence to the second anecdote. Rich floundered hopelessly and it was the practised cast who kept him afloat. It was in fairness, a difficult role to grasp. Peter Shaffer agrees, "*Equus* is the most private, the most deeply erotic of all my plays." The man of reason, Dysart, pitted against the primitive spirit of the boy who, against all reason, blinds six horses can, in the wrong hands, come across as the most dreadful rubbish.

Rich had to get it right. There was no margin for error. *Equus* was already judged a success and those who had played Dysart — Anthony Perkins and Anthony Hopkins in New York and Alec McCowen in London, had all earned great praise. If Rich bombed he had no one but himself to blame.

He kept up a brave front. With Hilda, who was bold enough to voice doubts, he made a wager.

"I bet you a thousand kisses to one that I will earn a standing ovation at every performance."

Making the supreme effort to stay cold sober he sought out the company of those on whom he could rely not to press him to "one little drink". He spent time with Robby Lantz and Alex Cohen whose families were the regular providers of weekend distractions.

One evening when there was a big party Rich wanted to avoid, he asked Alex, "Do you mind if I say that Susan and I have a date with you.

"Fine," said Alex. "But who's Susan?"

Rich was incredulous.

"You are naive, aren't you?"

It then dawned on Alex Cohen that the willowy blonde who happened to be staying at the same hotel as Rich was mightily important to the actor. As the couple were seen more frequently together the question came up, did Elizabeth know? And if, yes, why did she not retaliate? But in a sense she did just that by staying in California and by giving Rich the chance to repent. Nothing would have been achieved by her storming into New York to demand an explanation. Meanwhile, he was kept wondering as to what, eventually, she would do.

Came the weekend prior to Rich opening in *Equus*. As there was still no way in which he could face the critics and get away with it, John Dexter decided on a desperate remedy. He went to Rich on the Friday afternoon to tell him he was on the following day for the Saturday matinee. It was, he calculated, the shock treatment Rich needed to bring out the innate professionalism. No way, he believed, would it be a good performance but at least the critics would not see it. They had the rest of the weekend to smooth over the edges.

When John Dexter broke the news to him, Rich was quiet for a moment.

"Are you sure it's for the best?"

"Quite sure."

"Hmm. In that case I'd better go off and learn a bit more."

The matinee audience gave him a good start. After a moan of displeasure at the announcement that Anthony Perkins would not be appearing, the rider that Richard Burton would perform in his stead brought cheers loud enough to be heard in the dressing rooms. Sustained applause greeted Rich's entrance. A buzz went round the stalls: This will be worth seeing.

But it wasn't. Rich gave not so much a bad perform-ance as a non-performance, declared John Dexter. Mumbling incoherently while barely lifting his eyes from the stage, he seemed to be begging, "Don't look at me; I'm not really here at all." At the final curtain he had to make do with a smattering of reluctant clapping. The audience filed out in depressed silence.

John Dexter was the first to see Rich in his dressing room.

"Well?" asked Rich.

"It was dreadful. Absolutely bloody dreadful."

He continued in similar vein for some five minutes. When he emerged he found Robby Lantz and Peter Shaffer waiting outside.

"Now don't go in there undoing all my good work," he commanded. "He's got to know how bad he was."

The two visitors approached cautiously. They found Richard Burton, sunk deep in his chair, enduring the humiliation of defeat. Looking at him then, a deflated mound of a man, it was difficult to imagine he would ever act again.

But John Dexter knew his actor. After a while Rich summoned up that mysterious reserve of energy he kept somewhere. He went back to the Lombardy Hotel and with Susan, rearranged the furniture of his suite to make a fair semblance of the *Equus* set. Then he started work. It took him most of the hours left to him before Monday evening but by the time the critics took their seats Rich knew as much of the play as he was ever likely to know.

It was still not the performance John Dexter wanted.

"There was too much emotion; too much of the pulpit and the pub."

But it satisfied the audience and the reviewers. The leading New York critics, Walter Kerr and Clive Barnes, were impressed. "The best work of his life," enthused Kerr. An "unabashedly star performance", intoned Barnes. It was, without doubt, his star presence which carried him though. As Robby Lantz reminds us,

"He revitalised not just the play but the whole of Broadway. In what had been a lacklustre season, business picked up all round."

No wonder the Plymouth management felt justified in putting up seat prices by five dollars for the duration of the Burton run.

The triumphant return of Richard Burton to the Broadway stage afforded one mystery. Where was Elizabeth Taylor? Or rather not, where, because everybody knew she was in California, but why? The story went round that she did not wish to distract attention from the hero of the moment. She would put in an appearance a little later. Meanwhile, she had left a month-old reminder of her presence on Rich's dressing room mirror. It was a message scrawled in eyebrow pencil, "You're fantastic, love."

A week after Rich opened in *Equus*, he was telephoned by Elizabeth to be told that she planned coming to New York the following weekend. Rich, Robby Lantz and Aaron Frosch went to Kennedy to meet her. They had two limousines, one for passengers, the other for luggage. But when Elizabeth appeared with Chen Sam at the head of a procession of porters carrying thirty-five cases, not to mention two dogs and a cat, it was evident that their transport arrangements were inadequate. A truck was ordered to bring up the rear.

On the drive into the city Rich was uncharacteristically silent. Robby occupied the time urging Elizabeth not to put in an early appearance in the Plymouth auditorium. "The audience won't give the actors a chance."

He suggested instead a visit backstage. Elizabeth said she would come on Monday.

She left it until the second half to arrive at the stage door. Even so, a crowd quickly gathered. She had difficulty getting from her car. While a path was cleared for her, the cheers and shouts of greeting could be heard inside the theatre where, for a minute or so, the noise threatened to overwhelm the dialogue on stage.

Elizabeth made her way to the wings where she was given a seat with a clear view across the set. She could also see into the opposite wings. Sitting there was Susan Hunt.

Afterwards, they all went back to the Lombardy Hotel — Rich, Elizabeth, Susan and Chen Sam. They sat quietly for some time listening to Rich tapping his fingers on the table.

Eventually, Elizabeth asked, "What is wrong, love?" And Rich said, "I want a divorce."

As Elizabeth left with Chen Sam she murmured, "It's easy to say now but we should never have remarried."

Alex Cohen was one of the first to hear the news. He had arranged a party for the following evening to celebrate Elizabeth's forty-fourth birthday. She rang to say she was leaving on the midday plane. Would Alex please issue a statement explaining about the divorce.

Five months later, in Haiti, Rich and Elizabeth were parted for the second and final time. When we talked on the phone, he confessed, "I know we can't live together and we can't live apart, and I have no idea how the future will unfold except that I can't live on my own."

CHAPTER
SEVENTEEN

On 21 August 1976 in Virginia, Rich and Susan were married during a half-day break in the filming of *Exorcist II*.

In the six years they were together I met Susan on perhaps a dozen occasions, starting in Wales when Rich brought her to meet the family and ending, in traumatic circumstances, in London. She struck me as a capable and assertive young lady but one who, coming late to the Burton story, had an awful lot to learn.

She did not stop him drinking but for a time she kept the intake at a modest level. This job alone needed the application of a saint. But she attempted more. She wanted to direct her husband's career, to put him back where she, and others, thought he belonged, at the top of his profession.

The success of *Equus* encouraged her to plan ambitiously. She urged Rich to think of returning to Shakespeare, a notion supported by seasoned observers such as John Barber, of the *Daily Telegraph*. Having witnessed in *Equus* his "personal victory over his worst self", Barber appealed to Rich to come home to the National Theatre or to the Royal Shakespeare Company where he "could keep faith with his genius and crown his career".

But financial uncertainty — the unscrambling from Elizabeth's affairs was starting all over again — made Rich more inclined towards another Broadway moneyspinner. The most unlikely ideas cropped up. Among those he consulted, Frank Hauser was startled by a proposal to direct *Timon of Athens*. "I told him bluntly," he recalls, "I thought the suggestion was preposterous."

Strongest support came for a Burton assault on *Lear* — "the big one" to use Rich's epithet. This project went a long way towards realisation. Having agreed to produce, Alex Cohen persuaded Elia Kazan to come out of retirement to prepare a shortened version of the play. Rich talked enthusiastically of the challenge. "I have to play Lear as a kind of obligation," he told an interviewer. "Lear is the only Welshman of any interest that Shakespeare wrote about. Lear, when he lets off steam, when he really lets go, is utterly Welsh."

But he moved cautiously, always seeking reassurance that the role was still within his powers. I recall a dinner when, out of the blue, he insisted on reciting lengthy extracts from *Lear*. I was enormously impressed — it was always a joy listening to him. But I could not help noticing that one or two others at the table remained grim-faced. Afterwards, I asked what was wrong. "Didn't you notice? The words were all over the place. He even threw in bits from *Coriolanus*."

But Rich was not fooling himself. From other conversations I know that he was soon looking for an excuse to back away. Timing, the place, money — there was always a problem. In London the ensemble work of the National and the RSC with their retinues of contract players and directors made him nervous. Would he fit in? Indeed, would they want him? Anyway, the fees were derisory.

In New York, the excuse was the impossible economics of producing the classics on Broadway. First off, Alex

Cohen worked out his figures on the basis of eight performances a week including one matinee. Not unreasonably, Rich argued that he could not sustain the necessary level of excellence if he had to appear twice in one day. So the matinee was cut. Then Rich said he could manage only six performances a week. This brought the profit margin dangerously low but with a few economies and a rigorous control on costs, Alex Cohen thought he might just be able to work out a deal.

He brought the good news to Beverly Hills where Rich and Susan were living. He remembers the evening well because arriving late at the restaurant where they had fixed to meet he left his Cadillac on the roadside. Before rushing in he handed his keys to a man he assumed was a commissionaire leaving him with the order, "Take my car". The total stranger did just that. Alex never saw the vehicle again. But that was the least of his worries. Having revealed that *Lear* on six performances was, after all, a practical proposition, Rich said he could only do five.

"It was the night," ruminated Alex, "that I lost *Lear* and my car."

When Rich did eventually return to Broadway it was not in Shakespeare at all but in a revival of *Camelot* — a costlier product but one that was far easier to sell.

Meanwhile, there was his reputation as a movie actor to reconstruct. The prize was the role of Dysart in the screen version of *Equus* for which Universal had the rights. Rich faced strong competition of the quality of Jack Nicholson and Marlon Brando and the antipathy of the studio bosses who judged him to be unreliable and, more to the point, virtually uninsurable. Robby Lantz set out to prove otherwise. His tactic was to get

Rich into a film, any film, where he could prove he was still capable of holding the cameras. The opportunity came with *Exorcist II*, a formula horror movie guaranteed to appal the critics while bringing a decent return at the box office.

Rich did all that he was required to do. It was a modest performance (the material allowed for nothing more) but it impressed Universal and reminded them of the Burton triumph in the stage production of *Equus*. Opinion shifted strongly in his favour. The part was his.

Rich must have understood the purpose of *Exorcist II* and the strategy that Robby Lantz was pursuing. Yet, curiously, he failed to explain it to Susan who was furious that he had in her words, "humiliated himself" in such a dreadful movie. She made him promise never to do anything like it again no matter how much money was put up to tempt him. Perhaps Rich was too shamefaced to admit to her that unless he could pull a few tricks out of the bag he might not have any choice.

When *Equus* failed to translate well to the screen (too much realism shifted attention from the emotional conflict at the heart of the story) the sniping from the sidelines intensified. Robby came under attack. So too did Aaron Frosch, not for any apparent misdirection but for holding on too closely to the details of Rich's financial affairs. In what was quite clearly an attempt to take more authority to herself, Susan found a willing ally in Valerie Douglas whose unrivalled knowledge of the Burton career proved a useful source of ammunition.

As the focus of controversy Rich kept strangely quiet. The once eager participant in any verbal punch up now ran away from confrontations, avoided meetings which threatened to touch on sensitive matters and procrastinated on decisions until circumstances compelled him to say yes or no.

A crisis point came with the 1977 Academy Awards dinner. Rich was nominated for best actor for the seventh time, knowing that it was to be a close race with Richard Dreyfus (*The Goodbye Girl*). As his agent, Robby Lantz was slightly surprised not to be invited to sit at the Burtons' table but passed it off as an administrative oversight. Later in the evening he commiserated with Rich on his near miss and received a courteous response.

Early the next morning, Robby had a call.

"I want to see you," said Rich. "Now."

Robby was apologetic. "That's impossible, I'm afraid. I have a meeting in just a few minutes."

"Then I must tell you on the phone," said Rich. "You're fired."

Robby took in a deep breath. "That's entirely understandable. I get you your best part in years on Broadway, I bring you back into films as a high earner. Yes, of course, it's quite natural you should want to fire me."

Rich broke in.

"It has nothing to do with work. You insulted Bob Wilson. You made a racist remark. I can't have that."

Robby spoke very carefully.

"If you believe that I, of all people, am capable of racism, then I am sorry for you and I have nothing else to say." He put down the phone.

They met rarely after that though, ironically, Robby was soon to become agent to Elizabeth Taylor. Rich did make one hamfisted attempt at a reconciliation. When he opened in the revival of *Camelot*, he invited Robby and his wife Shirley to the first night and to dinner after the show. Robby said they would be delighted to come to the theatre but dinner was not on unless he received an apology.

"Let me think about that," said Rich.

Some time later one of his secretaries rang to tell Robby his first night tickets had been cancelled.

Aaron Frosch was the next to encounter the new regime. Though now frail and sick, Aaron had done more than anyone to provide an essential stability in Rich's otherwise chaotic life. His work was largely financial but his wise counsel went far beyond the scope of the account books. His loyalty to Rich was unquestioned and he expected the same from everyone else on the Burton payroll. He was a tough negotiator and a cautious administrator. Chen Sam remembers the contract she was expected to sign when she was first employed by Rich and Elizabeth.

"There were several pages of closely typed rules and conditions. It was as if I was handing over my entire life." She refused to comply and Aaron, recognising a kindred will, backed down. But he was not accustomed to defeat. Though ravaged by a debilitating illness the quality of his stewardship never wavered.

I found it almost impossible to believe that Aaron had been dismissed. But Chen Sam was there and saw it happen. In fact, Rich gave her the letter to deliver to Aaron. But forewarned of its contents, she refused. In the end it was taken by one of Aaron's assistants, the man who pushed his wheelchair.

The sourness and suspicion that characterised so many of Rich's affairs extended to his closest relatives. One of the sadnesses of Gwen's later life was the falling out with Rich over Ivor's will. Both the Hampstead house and cottage were in Ivor's name and so became part of his estate. He left them to Gwen with the rider that on her death one of the properties should go to Kate. It was up to her to choose which one she wanted.

But Rich, or whoever spoke for him, argued that Squire's Mount was not Ivor's to leave. The contract of possession remained in force only as long as Ivor was alive. After that the house and cottage should have reverted to the true owner — Richard Burton. It was an argument he lost, but I still wonder what it was that made him do it.

After *Equus*, Rich made a clutch of films starting with an interesting and well constructed piece called *The Medusa Touch*. With Elliott Kastner producing he felt at home with a literate script and a strong supporting cast which included Lee Remick and Harry Andrews. The theme was telekinetics, the mysterious power claimed by some, notably Uri Geller, to make objects move without touching them. Rich played a lawyer who discovers that by sheer force of concentration he can influence people and events. Called variously an intellectual or science fiction thriller in an understandable attempt to avoid the horror movie label, *The Medusa Touch* went down well with critics and audiences.

During filming at Pinewood, I saw a lot of Rich and Susan whose rented house in Windsor was not far from my London base. His back gave him pain but he overcame it, he said, by regular exercise. He claimed not to be drinking though I heard he took in what he called "an occasional glass of good Burgundy". His temper was on a yet shorter fuse, if that was possible, and while he clearly delegated a lot to Susan and usually fell in with her way of doing things, he was quick to apportion blame when things went wrong. The strain on Susan was having to watch him all the time.

"If I wasn't his wife, he'd need me as his nurse," she commented, not without a trace of bitterness.

Her worries were intensified by the fear of what could happen on Rich's next assignment. He was to appear in a big budget adventure story which revived memories of *Where Eagles Dare*. This one was called *The Wild Geese* and was about a bunch of mercenaries who pitch into African politics by rescuing a deposed moderate leader from the hands of a corrupt dictator. The location was a collection of mud huts on the northern veld of South Africa. Rich and Susan had an air-conditioned villa but when he was working he was out in one hundred degree heat.

The physical strain over three months was matched by the mental struggle of coping with the film actor's tribulation — the hours of waiting for something to happen; hours which would pass so much more congenially with the help of a little drink.

Rich's co-stars were Richard Harris, whose reputation was of an imbiber of Olympic status and Roger Moore who, having spent his youth as a teetotaller, was now making up for lost time. The producer, Euan Lloyd, was a nervous man.

Happily, Richard Harris was also under doctors' orders. The two actors called a truce for the duration. "We'll let Roger Moore do the drinking for the three of us," they agreed. Harris did have one small lapse. When Rich heard of it he sternly admonished his friend. "You broke your word," he rumbled. "Remember, if I start drinking, I'll make Africa burn."

It was a friendly and good-humoured cast of skilled

character actors most of whom knew each other from other pictures. In the capable hands of director Andrew McLaglen who, better than anyone, knew how to deliver the thrills, they threw themselves into this latest caper with all the energy of a (slightly ageing) rugger team.

But the abiding memory was of the infinitely modest Roger Moore whose self-effacing style made him unique among film stars. There was the scene in which Burton, Harris and Moore started with some ten lines each. After the first runthrough, Roger asked for a cut, in his own lines, an almost unheard-of request from any actor. Another runthrough and another suggested cut. A third try and Roger thought it best if he lost all his lines.

"But why?" asked the director. Roger puffed on his long cigar. "Do you think I want to act against these guys? I'll just sit here and watch them do the work."

Some time on when it was pointed out to him that he was getting less then his share of star action, he was cheerfully unconcerned.

"I'm not paid to act. I'm paid to turn up."

With the success of *Wild Geese* confidently anticipated, Rich looked forward to a postbag full of offers. It came, but it was not quite what he had hoped for. Instead of big studio projects with the promise of worldwide sales, he was faced with a selection of modestly financed movies which could turn out to be worthy or worthless. It took him two years to find out. They were worthless.

Three of the four films he made in this period were so far departed from popular appeal, the producers had difficulty in finding distributors. *Absolution*, completed in early 1978, did not actually appear until 1981. Rich played yet another priest who hears the confession of a boy murderer. One of the few critics to give it space dismissed it as "pretentious melodrama". A war film called *Breakthrough* (*Sergeant Steiner* in the States) covered its costs but little else (despite the ministrations of Andrew McLaglen).

Then came the extraordinary *Tristan and Isolde*, a costume drama made in Ireland. Rich picked it out as a certain winner. He was wrong. It was one of the dreariest pieces of nonsense in the Burton canon. Rich lost both ways, professionally and financially. He agreed to work exclusively on a percentage which, not surprisingly, failed to materialise.

The run of bad luck came to a merciful end with *Circle for Two* in which the visibly ageing Burton in the guise of a college lecturer was called upon to have an affair with a teenage student (Tatum O'Neal). "At my age," he grumbled, "they should have paid me danger money."

On and off drink and feeling thoroughly sorry for himself, Rich found consolation at Puerto Vallarta, his favourite home. But memories of Elizabeth intruded — there was even a street named after her — and Susan was not best pleased to be offered up to the locals as a comparison to her predecessor. Susan was younger and, arguably, just as attractive but she was not the star turn. She was, well, just Richard Burton's wife. Casting his mind back to the days of *Cleopatra*, Rich may have felt a hint of what it was like for her.

To further the distance from his past, Rich commissioned a new home at Puerto Vallarta, at a spot higher up the mountain. Susan was told she had a free hand on the design. Getting it just right became something of an obsession with her. Friends were called in to help and advise. One who was particularly solicitous was a near neighbour, Jack Hayward.

At a loss as to what to do next Rich talked wildly of this or that long cherished ambition. *Lear* resurfaced briefly and Rich was to be seen going out to dinner with a copy of the play tucked in his pocket. But he knew he was indulging in a pipe dream. He even thought of retiring.

"But the boredom, Gray. Can you imagine the boredom? It would be a living death."

I reminded him he had his books — to read and to write.

"Hobbies, just hobbies," he sighed. "They're not what I call real work."

I could not bear to tell him that twenty years earlier it might have been a different story. Watching the occasional glass become the occasional bottle and knowing that he was suffering excruciating bouts of pain with his back and shoulder, I felt a sad premonition that I was witnessing the last chapter in the career of Richard Burton.

Then, out of the blue, there was a call from Alan Jay Lerner. Could Rich still remember the songs from *Camelot*, he asked? Rich thought so. But, why? It was just that producer Mike Merwick was interested in staging a revival. The engagement was for one year with a fortune at the end of it. Was Rich interested? Wasn't he just.

To return to the stage in a role he created twenty years earlier and which he knew backwards was not perhaps the most adventurous move. But it got him off the treadmill of bad to mediocre films, the money was good and Susan approved.

346

All this he cheerfully conceded. What he was less happy to admit because deep down it suggested a weakness he tried to deny — was that he had a need for a public show of approval, the standing ovations which had sustained him in his last crisis.

So it happened that producer Mike Merwick was received enthusiastically when he came to Geneva to talk with Rich about his *Camelot* plans. Somewhat to his surprise he left with a firm commitment from Rich to reassume King Arthur's crown.

The show opened in Toronto in June 1980. Rehearsals started a month earlier. Recalling the horrendous problems of the first *Camelot*, the latest team had an easy ride. But it was not entirely without incident. The director, Frank Dunlop, came with a distinguished list of credits which missed out on any experience with musicals. The omission soon became apparent. Called in to advise, Alan Jay Lerner started by urging an immediate replacement of the leading lady. This done he raided his memory for the best fruits of his collaboration with Moss Hart, that complete man of the theatre who had died in 1961.

By the first night, something of the old magic had been recaptured. Though Rich still needed time to work his way back into the role it was noticeable that he brought to King Arthur the older dignity Lerner had always wanted but which had been inevitably missing from the 1960 productions. The sheer poetry of the lyrics, the best element in what was acknowledged as a slight and sentimental story, were perfectly suited to the timbery voice of the mature Burton. He had them crying in the aisles.

The buzz was heard in New York; this is a show to

see. Even before opening at the Lincoln Center's State Theater it was a virtual sell-out with advance bookings of over two-and-a-half million dollars, the biggest in Broadway history. The touts did fine business selling tickets at over a hundred dollars a time.

Still, with a nationwide tour to come, the reviews were awaited with the usual trepidation. The opinion of the *New York Times* and the *New York Post* pulled weight throughout the country. Uncharacteristically, Rich stayed late at the first night party to hear the verdict. Only when the murmur of polite conversation turned to a roar of approval, signifying word had come through of high praise from one of the big name critics, did he feel it was time for bed. He went with the superlatives of Frank Rich to comfort him. "He remains every inch the King Arthur of our most majestic storybook dreams," declared the critic whose view from the stalls was rarely expressed with such romantic fervour. He added, "This actor doesn't merely command the stage, he seems to own it by divine right."

It was not until the next morning that another, less flattering view emerged. Clive Barnes had evidently left the theatre in unhappy mood. It was, he said, "a knight to forget". There was a lot more of this before the full force of his invective was released on the leading actor. Burton, he declared, "is little more than a burnt-out dummy. His face leathery and unanimated, arms to his sides and his hands are flaccid".

Hurtful it may have been but Clive Barnes touched on a truth which we all secretly affirmed. Rich was tired; more, he was desperately sick. As early as Toronto he was having trouble with his shoulder and right arm. Called upon to raise a battle sword above his head, he needed a painkiller and the adrenalin of a live performance to show conviction. Knowing what he was going through, Frank Dunlop rechoreographed the duel scenes and gave Rich a light alloy sword to wield about him. Even so, the strain was apparent.

Rich asked Alex Cohen if he had any advice. "Stay sober," said Alex. But that is just what Rich did not do. Two weeks in to the New York run he met up with Peter O'Toole. It was early evening two hours before a performance. They had a few drinks. Not many; just enough. When he made it to the theatre, strictly an hour before curtain up, he took some booster painkillers. The mix was lethal. As he went on to the usual tumultuous applause he felt his eyes misting over. He spoke his first words. The sound of his own voice came back to him like a distant echo. He stumbled, recovered and stumbled again. A whisper went round the audience: "He's drunk." Halfway through the first act the curtain was brought down. When it went up again Rich's understudy stood in his place.

Next day the story was front page news across the world. In a more reflective mood, Rich might have told himself that if he could attract that sort of publicity, he must still be worth something. Instead, he let loose a torrent of anger which, to those who knew him, meant that he was very frightened indeed. To anyone who was prepared to listen, he protested his innocence: "I was *not* drunk." And technically he was right. But there was no escaping the fact that he was living dangerously with a constitution which could no longer be relied upon to sustain his excesses.

After New York, *Camelot* played four weeks in Chicago, three weeks in Dallas, four weeks in Miami

Beach, three weeks in New Orleans and twelve weeks in San Francisco. Rich did not miss a single performance. But on the last stretch, in Los Angeles, where the show was booked for a three-month run, he had to admit defeat. He dropped out of the show and into St John's Hospital where he was told he needed major surgery on his spine. He was warned the operation was risky. If it failed he could be paralysed for life. In fact, it was only when the operation was underway that the surgeons fully realised what a bad state he was in. They had virtually to rebuild his vertebrae. One of his doctors told me he could not begin to understand how Rich had managed to hold an audience night after night.

The operation was successful, but not successful enough. After six months in hospital Rich was told that he would find it easier to move about but would have to go carefully. A release from his dependence on painkillers could not be promised.

To convalesce, he retired to Celigny where he was restless and bored in equal measure. When Susan flew off to Puerto Vallarta it was as much to get a break from nursing a temperamental invalid as to check how the new house was coming along. On the phone to me, Rich asked me, "Is there anything you can think of for me to do? Now I've got time to read, I can't concentrate. I need to be taken out of myself."

As a matter of fact, there was something I could suggest. I put the idea to my masters at BBC Radio. Coming up was the royal wedding between Prince Charles and Lady Diana Spencer. Brian Tremble, a senior producer, said, "How would it be if you asked Rich to be the link man for the radio commentary on the ceremony in Westminster Abbey, the procession and the public celebrations?" The response was enthusiastic. It would be quite a coup for outside broadcasting to attract one of the best-known voices in the English language. But would he do it? The effort required in sustaining six hours of live radio was out of all proportion to the modest fee.

I rang to explain all this to Rich. Was he interested?

"Why not come over and talk about it," he said. "It can't do any harm."

I and a BBC colleague flew over to Geneva in mid-June. Rich met us at the airport. I did not expect him to be in top form but the strength of his voice on the telephone had suggested a part-way return to his old vigour. Instead, it seemed to me that he had slipped back. He walked with a slight stoop which was to stay with him for the rest of his life, and he moved slowly. One arm was held tight by his side and there were frequent nervous twists of his head as if he was being slapped by an invisible hand.

Not wanting to sell him the job as an easy option I explained carefully that he would be on air from morning to evening without much chance of a break. "Not even for a pee."

"Well, I think we might manage that."

We were sitting at lunch. Rich ordered wine and poured himself a large glass. Then without touching his drink he seemed to relax a little, leaning back to his chair as if to say, "There, I can still keep off it, if I want to."

We talked more about the programme, how much of it would be scripted and how much he would be expected to ad lib.

"Can I say what I like?"

"Within reason," I said, remembering some of his oratorial heights and depths.

Rich appeared satisfied.

"Right then," he boomed. "It's just a question of money."

My colleague tightened his lips.

"I know the fee is modest," he apologised. "But, as I've explained, it's contractually impossible for the BBC to exceed its pay guidelines . . ."

My brother raised a hand. "I'm not arguing about the sum. It's just the way it's paid. I want it all to go to charity. If I give the details, can you arrange it?"

We both thought the BBC could rise to the challenge. The conversation turned to other matters and when we finished lunch, Rich was well away on stories of past triumphs. As we got up to go I noticed his glass was empty.

For a first time reporter, Rich did a wonderful job on the wedding. When he ran out of script, he extemporised with poetry and prose on regal topics, much of it acquired for a dramatised history of monarchy he had narrated for the BBC four years earlier.

He made only one minor error. Handing over to Wynford Vaughan-Thomas on the processional route, he told listeners they were off to Clarence House when in fact that distinguished commentator was speaking from Buckingham Palace. Those who were closely following their route maps must have wondered what was going on but otherwise the slip passed unnoticed.

When it was all over I joined Rich and Susan for a celebratory dinner at the Dorchester. Both were in cheerful mood though Rich complained volubly at having to rely indefinitely on painkillers to keep him active. He could not imagine how it would be possible ever to appear again on stage in any role that was worthy of him. But there was one exciting screen possibility, a mammoth internationally backed television series on the life of Richard Wagner.

A little to my surprise, Rich had no trouble in identifying with the great German composer. "I am close to Wagner. I could be Wagner."

The association escaped me until, at home, I checked out a dictionary of biography. Wagner, I read, "was apt to arouse either blind adulation or violent antipathy, but seldom indifference. Supremely egotistical and unable to sense when he was wrong, he was capable of somersaults of opinion and conduct which mystified and sometimes antagonised his friends."

I could see then what Rich meant.

The next day I had a call from Susan. She sounded nervous and distressed.

"Can you come over to the Dorchester? I need some help. Rich is in a bad way."

Driving from the other side of London I made it in less than an hour. When I went into their suite it was to find Rich slouched in a chair, half dressed, his shirt open. Only his eyes moved. Then he saw me.

"Gray, my brother, Gray. A friend, indeed. Get me a drink, dear brother, will you? Get me a drink, my dear chap."

I looked at Susan who was pacing up and down, her clenched fists held against her mouth.

"He's been like this all morning," she babbled. "He must have started hours ago. We've got a plane to catch today. I'll never get him to the airport like this."

Rich stirred himself. His voice was a slurred shout.

"Will someone get me a fucking drink?"

I said something banal like, "Don't you think you've had enough?" which set off a torrent of anger.

"All right," I said, "hang on."

I took a litre bottle of vodka from the drinks tray, went into the bathroom and tipped three fifths of the vodka into the washbasin. Then I refilled the bottle with water. The much diluted Bloody Mary I handed to Rich was enough to keep him quiet.

"It'll take more than the two of us to sober him up," I told Susan. "We need someone he'll listen to."

I rang the first and most obvious candidate to come to mind. Cliff Morgan was BBC's Head of Outside Broadcast on Television but to Rich was better known as "the finest fly half Wales has ever seen". Though not close friends in the ordinary sense, they met whenever the opportunity presented. The conversations were always about rugby. Five years earlier when Cliff had gone into hospital with a heart attack, Rich had insisted on the best treatment.

When Cliff arrived we both talked to Rich, gave him coffee, walked him up and down.

With my arm around him I said in Welsh, "You know don't you, you're killing yourself?" He replied in English, "So be it."

By early afternoon he was just about fit to be taken to the airport. We went in Cliff's car with Susan and Rich in the back. Not much was said on the drive but when we saw them off from the VIP lounge both tried to put on a show of conviviality.

Back in London, Cliff observed gloomily, "If he goes on like that he won't last very long."

I said, "If he goes on like that the marriage won't last another month."

No sooner was Rich back in the States than he fell ill again, this time with a stomach ulcer. In St John's Hospital the doctors warned him that his liver and kidneys were on the danger list. He was told bluntly to cut down on painkillers and to cut out the drink, otherwise his life was forfeit. Rich said he would try and no doubt he did but his resolution was hampered by Susan's absence in Puerto Vallarta and the knowledge that she was attracted there by more than a zest for property development.

Incredibly, the backers for *Wagner* were prepared to take a risk on him. Seven months was a long haul in the life of a middle aged actor with a poor medical record. More, there was the strain of a punishing schedule — filming in twenty-seven locations in six countries, across Europe and back again.

But against the risk of contracting Burton had to be set the conviction that few actors could give the role the authority it demanded. And unlike some of his possible rivals, Rich came at a reasonable price. One million dollars was not chicken feed but inflation had robbed the figure of its mysticism. For younger Hollywood stars it had more significance as a starting price. For Richard Burton, who had commanded a million-dollar fee twenty years earlier, it was enough to take him to the finishing post. My guess is that, if pushed, he would have accepted a lower offer.

To be Wagner was his compensation for his failure to be Lear. And there was a bonus, the chance to work in such august company. The three white knights of the theatre — Olivier, Gielgud and Richardson — were enticed into playing cameo roles. To overcome delicate questions of precedence, a neat compromise was achieved whereby the three eminent guests appeared together but not with Wagner, thus overcoming any suggestion that they might be playing second fiddle to Richard Burton.

It gave Rich pause for thought when he found that while Olivier was an obviously sick man, Gielgud and Richardson were hale and hearty septuagenarians.

"Do you think I'll last that long?" he asked rhetorically.

The celebrated trio treated him with respect but not, he thought, with affection. He detected a certain condescension. When in reminiscent mood Olivier was heard to murmur, "We were the best," he was looking away from Rich.

As *Wagner* got underway in January 1982, Rich was on his own. When the time for Susan to join him in Vienna came and went without word, he knew his marriage was in bad trouble. He sought consolation in the company of other women and of old friends like Ron Berkeley who was in charge of make-up and of Bob Wilson and Brook Williams, his convivial gofers.

But whoever his companions, they had one thing in common — a tolerance for fond stories about Elizabeth Taylor.

For five eventful years Rich and Elizabeth had seen little of each other. Elizabeth had married again (husband number six was Senator John Warner) and divorced again. Her liking for hard liquor had taken a leap. If not quite up to the Burton scale it was enough for her to put on thirty pounds in weight and to qualify for the front cover of Kenneth Anger's *Hollywood Babylon II* — a living symbol of Tinsel Town excess.

But at forty-nine the star still sparkled. Even without the big film roles she could still pull in the crowds. This was made evident by the commercial success of the otherwise undistinguished touring production of *The Little Foxes*. As the villainous Regina she competed valiantly but unsuccessfully against the memory of Bette Davis's film portrayal. No matter, the audiences loved her.

In February, Elizabeth was in London to prepare for her West End debut in *Little Foxes*. Coincidentally, Rich also had a London date, to lead a St David's Day retrospective of Dylan Thomas at the Duke of York's theatre. Elizabeth cabled him an invitation to her fiftieth birthday party. The acceptance came by return.

Before departing Vienna for his long weekend break from filming, Rich was made aware of a thirty-four-year-old production assistant, Sally Hay. She was not the type to stand out in a crowd. She had neither the salary nor the style to make the best of herself. But she was conscientious at her job which required an attention to details and a willingness to rush in to help solve any problem which threatened to interrupt filming. Rich liked to have her around but, off the set, was unable to put a name to her.

Until, that is, one evening in a restaurant with Ron Berkeley, he spotted Sally Hay, alone, at another table. After a few puzzled glances in her direction, he asked Ron, "Who is that girl?" Ron told him. Whereupon he shouted across the room, "Hey, Sally, come over here. Help to bring a little joy into a dull life."

Rich and Sally spent some time together that night. And on subsequent nights.

In London, it was just like old times, in the best and the worst sense. Elizabeth's party, not for once at the Dorchester, was nonetheless a splendid affair. Pictures of Elizabeth alternating between a *Time Magazine* cover and a publicity still of her in a bubble bath, covered every inch of wallspace. As the guest of honour, Rich was suitably attentive to his hostess, hardly leaving her side. To those who asked the inevitable question, he was charmingly enigmatic.

"Elizabeth and I are like a pair of bookends. Other people may come between us but in the end the two of us are still there, opposite each other."

That was said before Rich got drunk. By midnight he was incapable of much more than incoherent ramblings. The photographers gathered to record the depressing spectacle of Rich being lifted into his car like a helpless invalid.

On Monday evening, he had sufficiently recovered his professional poise to appear at the Duke of York's theatre for the Dylan Thomas reading. Early on in his performance as he waited for the silence after the applause, he was distracted and then thrown by the extraordinary sight of Elizabeth, unannounced, appearing on stage. In front of six hundred witnesses she spoke to him in faultless Welsh, "*Rwyn dy garu di mwy na un arall yn yr holl fyd*" — "I love you more than anyone in the world." Rich stared amazed for a moment then gave her a great hug and said, "Would you mind repeating that?" She did so and made her exit to rapturous applause from the largely Welsh audience. Rich was left rummaging through his script for a way back into the programme while apologising for his confusion.

"You must forgive me. Elizabeth always has this effect on me."

Elizabeth joined him on stage for the curtain call and backstage for a party. When I saw them off to dinner they were holding hands.

The idyll was brief. Early on Wednesday morning, Elizabeth rang me at home. She skipped the preliminaries.

"I could kill your brother."

I was half awake.

"Why, what's he done?"

"Don't you read the papers?"

"Elizabeth," I pleaded, "I'm not even out of bed yet. I'm not so desperate to catch the headlines."

"Well, here's one that should interest you. 'It Looks Like Love Again' over a picture of me and Richard."

"Well, what's wrong with that?"

"Nothing, it's what comes afterwards. He's shouted his mouth off about making love to me on the night of my birthday."

"Oh no."

"Oh, yes."

There was not much I could do but sympathise. I urged her not to demand a retraction; it would just fuel the interest of the gossip writers. "Especially," I added incautiously, "if what he says is true."

"True?" she shouted. "Did you say true? Of course it's not true. He was too drunk to find his way down the street, let alone into my bedroom."

The best I could do was to warn Rich of the impending storm. I tracked him down at the Gritti Palace in Venice,

359

the latest stopover in this peripatetic production. But first I got through to Ron Berkeley. I asked, "What state is he in?" Ron sounded as if he did not want anyone to overhear.

"He must have put away a load of drink. He's spent all day in bed. That means we've lost a day's shooting. Not good news."

When Rich came on and heard that Elizabeth was gunning for him, I could almost feel the weight of his hangover bearing down yet more heavily.

"Oh God, did I say that? I must have been talking metaphorically."

"Okay,"I said, "but don't be surprised when Elizabeth breaks a metaphorical vase over your head."

Rich did not miss out on any more shooting. For the rest of the film he was a model of punctuality if not, sadly, of sobriety. He relied increasingly on Sally to organise his life. She was only too happy to oblige. When Rich felt pain in his shoulder, she was his masseuse. When he forgot a line, she was there to feed it to him. When he needed someone to tell him he was still in the game, she was ready to comfort and reassure. But Sally had her demands. Her jealousy of Elizabeth was obsessive and she made no attempt to disguise it from Rich. Twice, plans for Rich to fly in to see *The Little Foxes* had to be cancelled at the last moment. The pressure of a tight schedule was the formal excuse but, on location, it was known that Sally pulled every trick she could think of to stop him from coming. At the second disappointment (a cancellation that came so late there was a £600 bill for time the hired Rolls-Royce had to wait at Heathrow), I stood in for Rich by taking Elizabeth to dinner after the show. It was an evening of reminiscences with my guest clearly finding me a poor substitute for the man she really wanted to see. I hesitated to ask the obvious question.

"Go on, say it," Elizabeth demanded and then, before I could open my mouth, "You want to know if we'll ever marry again."

I confessed, the thought had crossed my mind. She was silent for a moment. "Do you know what he calls me?"

I said I had no idea.

"Instant nostalgia. He says it's because every time he sees me, I bring out in him a longing for home."

"What does that mean?"

"It means, I don't know if we'll ever marry again. But what I do know is that in the end, every man comes home."

As they entered the last stretch of Wagner's life story, Sally devoted herself exclusively to Rich. Though still on the production payroll she was no longer a humble PA. Now, she was assistant to Mr Burton. Her rise in the pecking order was clearly noticeable to Cheryl Campbell who had befriended Sally when they first met on location.

"We saw a lot of each other early on and I heard all about her affair with Richard. But after a while she became a different person. She bought herself a fur coat, lost some weight and looked much more glamorous. After that, there was no time for lunches or shopping trips. She stayed close to Richard and held aloof from the rest of us."

Emotionally washed out and physically in poor shape, Rich allowed himself to be carried along by events. There were few humdinger rows. The pleasure of verbal combat had long since faded. When he felt that Sally was intruding too closely on his life he simply wandered away to spend time with friends or with an accommodating lady.

That he was not too choosy about some of his partners became obvious when the *National Enquirer* in the States and the *News of the World* in the UK gave a prominent splash to the kiss-and-tell story of Judith Chisholm, a pliable young journalist who occupied Rich for a week in Venice. The articles — scrambled reflections on sex and booze — made sad reading. But thankfully they were cut short by the intervention of Ron Berkeley and Bob Wilson. Realising what was happening they confronted Rich, told the girl precisely what they thought of her and then threw her out of the hotel. It was one of the rare occasions when I felt that Sally was entitled to all our sympathy.

Where Sally deserved great credit was in bringing some semblance of order to Rich's life, reviving his confidence and in keeping him away from hard spirits. Wine was another matter. Cheryl Campbell remembers whiling away a rainy morning with Rich when he got through three bottles. Still, when on the completion of *Wagner* he came to London with Sally, he appeared in reasonable shape. Elizabeth was there too, completing her run in *The Little Foxes*. Since there were no further excuses for not seeing the play Rich took Sally to the theatre and afterwards talked with Elizabeth. She asked Rich what he planned to do next. He had no idea. Though he expected *Wagner* to put up his value, the editing of that production was such a mammoth task neither the four-hour cinema version nor the nine-hour television serial could be expected to appear in less than a year. Meanwhile . . .

"Meanwhile," said Elizabeth, "what do you say to having some fun and making a pile of money on Broadway?"

The idea was to revive *Private Lives*, a 1930 comedy by Noel Coward at his most acidic. To recall the plot was to see immediately how it appealed to Elizabeth and her backers. A divorced couple who love each other venomously book into adjoining honeymoon suites with their new partners. The dialogue read like a case study of the Burton-Taylor partnership. It was like saying to the public, you've read the story in the gossip columns, now see it live on stage.

There were loud voices urging caution. That the stars were at least twenty years too old for their parts was the least of their problems. Neither was strong on acerbic quick fire comedy and without this talent there was a terrible danger of getting all the laughs in the wrong places. It would be so easy for good clean fun to descend into excruciatingly bad taste. Among those who warned of disaster was Robby Lantz, now Elizabeth's agent, who flatly refused to have anything to do with the venture.

But Rich was hooked. As his friend Richard Harris said of him, he could never turn away from a gamble. The more outrageous the risk, the less likely it was that he would take good advice. The time for cool, rational thought — and the regrets — came later.

Early signs were that Elizabeth had made a sound commercial judgement. With bookings solid from Boston to New York the two stars would look forward to a clear $60,000 a week — each.

But what they had to do to earn the money was humiliating beyond belief.

The Boston critics led the assault on what was popularly known as the Dick and Liz show or The Private Lives of Burton and Taylor. The production was said to be shabby, self indulgent and a shrieking self parody. As for the principals, Elizabeth was described as "a dumpy middle-aged woman with . . . legs too short for her size", and Rich as a "sick, burned-out dissolute man". But the audience kept coming to roar their approval at unintentional double entendres. The biggest cheer of the evening went to Elizabeth for her declaration via her character Amanda Prynne that "Marriage scares me really."

In New York, the pre-opening publicity was phenomenal and while the reviews were damning there was no let up at the box office. Such was the enthusiasm of the punters to see the two celebrities slug it out in public that a lively trade developed at the interval with those on the way out finding ready buyers for tickets for the second half. A television station asked viewers to phone in and vote whether Liz and Dick should marry again. Out of 3500 votes, seventy-three per cent were in favour of a third try.

Whatever else was said of *Private Lives*, no one could deny it was the show business event of the season.

But on a personal level the old stresses were beginning to reappear. Ex-husband and ex-wife took an almost sadistic — or was it masochistic? — pleasure in provoking jealousy. Rich did nothing to discourage Sally from talking about marriage. With the divorce from Susan now finalised, a reattachment was feasible, but to the extent that Rich was thinking of it as a serious possibility, he might sensibly have dampened the speculation until the end of the run. For her part, Elizabeth made a great show of her consort, the Mexican businessman, Victor Luna, a kindly and unpretentious character who gave every indication of wanting to be elsewhere.

A month after the New York opening, Rich came up against an agonising conflict of interest. He was offered the lead in a film adaptation of Malcolm Lowry's *Under the Volcano*. But John Huston, who was to direct, had to start work in August. This meant Rich backing off *Private Lives* well before the end of the tour. He put the case to Elizabeth. The Lowry role was, he insisted, one that he badly wanted to do. By comparison, *Private Lives* was mere frivolity. But that was not the way Elizabeth saw it. This was her creation Rich was trying to break up. She had not even read *Under the Volcano*. No way was she going to lose her percentage for the sake of an arty film.

Rich agreed to stick to his contract but his anguish at losing the opportunity of working again with John Huston (the part eventually went to Albert Finney) was increased by the embarrassment of the nightly fiasco on stage. He realised now what he had previously ignored, that for Elizabeth the theatre was the sideline to her career whereas for Rich, it was the centre of his existence.

Every entrance he made at the Lunt-Fontanne reminded him of the days at that theatre when he had played Hamlet and later, Arthur in *Camelot*. He was still winning the applause but now he felt like a monarch who was wantonly abdicating his kingdom.

"How can I redeem myself?"

The question was asked of Richard Harris who urged his friend to think again about a Broadway production of *King Lear*. But that chance had gone for ever. On the other hand, there was a realistic prospect of returning to Shakespeare in a less demanding role. The previous autumn Rich had been contacted by Anthony Quayle, the actor and director who had given him his great chance at Stratford back in the fifties. Ever restless and eager to try new schemes, Tony Quayle was putting together a touring company, to be known as Compass, to present mainly classical work. A probable London venue for his first production was the Old Vic, recently bought and restored to its former splendour by a Canadian businessman, Ed Mirvish. It seemed only appropriate that the Old Vic should reopen with Shakespeare, that the play should be *The Tempest* which holds the substance of all that Shakespeare believed about the theatre and that the world-weary Prospero should be played by Richard Burton.

The idea was first talked over in any detail at Celigny just before Rich embarked on *Private Lives*. Tony Quayle and Andrew Leigh, the administrator at the Old Vic, flew to Geneva. They were met by a relaxed and confident host who, resplendent in a long scarlet coat, outdressed everyone else at the airport. The business was cleared with hassle. Rich agreed in principle to a touring schedule for the first quarter of 1984, which took him to Leicester, Manchester and London. The possibility was held open of a West End transfer followed by visits to European cities and to New York. Rich did not balk at the niggardly fee (£250 a week in rehearsals rising to £650 a week playing salary in the UK) but asked for thought to be given to a video spinoff. Memories of Nevill Coghill's audacious plan for filming *The Tempest* were vividly revived when Tony Quayle suggested this should be done on location — "either in the Caribbean or on one of the Greek islands".

Dinner that night at the Café de la Gare was devoted to reminiscences of great days at Stratford. Rich and Tony Quayle shared the talking. Andrew Leigh and Sally did all the listening.

Just before departing for the States, Rich sent a note to Tony Quayle.

"I am more than merely excited at the thought of coming back home to play my favourite theatre in the world and equally delighted that you will be in charge."

What happened in New York to make him change his mind? Well, *Private Lives* happened but, on earlier reasoning this should have strengthened his resolve. Sadly, it was not that simple. Losing the gamble on *Private Lives* robbed him of his self-assurance. He no longer believed he could do anything more on stage that was worthwhile. By their inability to give the right advice those close to him reinforced his insecurity and his tendency towards depression. When *The Tempest* and the Old Vic came up in conversation the only reaction from the people who were supposed to represent his interests was incredulity. How could he possibly think of working for peanuts?

Friends and colleagues who understood his problem were not around long enough to give proper weight to their countervailing view. Among those who did try, Richard Harris expressed himself most forcefully, and not just on the way Rich was damaging his career. At the end of what purported to be an alcohol-free dinner at Sardi's, Rich had difficulty in moving.

"Are you ill?" asked Harris.

"No, no. Don't worry. It's just that, for the moment, I can't get up."

Suspecting more than fatigue, Harris took the head waiter aside.

"What's going on?" he wanted to know.

"It's the coffee," he was told. "Every cup he has is laced with brandy."

Harris stormed back to the table. Sitting opposite Rich was one of his party. Harris tapped him on the shoulder.

"Come outside for a moment, will you? I want a word."

Their exchange was conducted in a fierce whisper.

"What do you think you're doing to him?" asked Harris. The response was characteristically bland.

"Just giving him a good time."

"Oh yes," said Harris. "You're certainly doing that. And you're doing something else. You bastard. You're killing him."

When, after several weeks of not hearing from Rich or his agent, Tony Quayle flew to New York for another meeting, he still assumed that an agreement on *The Tempest* could be worked out. But it did not take long for him to discover otherwise. After seeing *Private Lives*, he and Rich went off to a restaurant, one of the busiest and noisiest off Broadway. The suspicion grew that Rich had chosen the place deliberately to forestall questions. The suspicion became a certainty when, on the way back to the hotel, Rich admitted strong opposition in his camp to any thought of going to London. "But don't worry," he added quickly. "Let's talk about it tomorrow."

At the meeting next day, Tony Quayle was confronted by Valerie Douglas and a sharp young lady who described herself as an agent. They accused him of going behind their backs to get a deal on the cheap. The way they saw it, he had taken unfair advantage of Rich's good nature. Rich sat listening, not saying a word. Tony Quayle waited for the attack to end. When he was allowed to speak, he observed calmly,

"Then we do not have an agreement."

"That's about it," said the girl.

"In that case," said Quayle, "I see no point in continuing."

It was Rich's last chance to play Shakespeare. And he blew it.

Working together in an unsuitable play brought out the worst in Rich and Elizabeth. He resented being made to do what he did not want to do and let his resentment show. His partner found this hard to take. She held doggedly to the view that she deserved something better — like a vote of thanks for earning them both a lot of money. They continued to flirt outrageously on and off stage but their exchanges had a steely edge.

When in late June Elizabeth fell ill and had to drop out of four performances, Rich was not sympathetic. His irritation mounted when Elizabeth announced she had to go away for a few days to recuperate and proposed taking Victor Luna with her. In a mood of angry depression he summoned Ron Berkeley and Bob Wilson to his suite at the Laurent Hotel. He had important news, he told them. He was intending to marry again, immediately. Ron Berkeley urged caution.

"You're only doing this to spite Elizabeth," he warned.

"Maybe you're right," said Rich, "but it doesn't make any difference."

Shortly afterwards Rich and Sally departed for Las Vegas. They were married on Sunday, 3 July.

He rang me that night and I, not realising the information was in any way confidential, passed on the story to my colleagues at the BBC.

Featuring prominently in the early morning bulletins, news of the marriage was quickly picked up by the rest of the media at home and abroad. Rich came back on to the phone. "What are you trying to do to me?" he shouted. "Why couldn't you have kept quiet for a few hours? I wanted a chance to tell Elizabeth. She should have been the first to know."

Marriage to Sally spelt the end of *Private Lives*. To that extent, at least, Rich got what he wanted. After Washington and Chicago the show ground to a halt in Los Angeles were poor health forced Elizabeth to miss more performances. The Burtons then went off to Haiti where Rich had just bought a new house. They stayed there for two months, taking them through until the end of 1983.

By then *Wagner* had been seen by the critics though it was still waiting for its television premiere. First reactions were generally favourable to Rich though inevitably he was thought to be best in the later episodes when he could act "with all the appropriate dignity, stature, contradiction and arrogance" of the older Wagner. The problem with this mammoth production was that nobody could think what to do with it. Though visually splendid and with some fine performances, *Wagner* was too weighty and ponderous to justify peak viewing in television or, in its shorter version, a movie distribution beyond the art houses. When the public did eventually get the chance to see what must be counted as one of the outstanding Burton portrayals, the initial excitement had worn off and the response was disappointingly muted.

There was just one film to go. It was produced by Virgin, a new British company founded on the commercial genius of Richard Branson and profits of the pop music industry.

Given the year, a remake of the George Orwell classic, *1984*, seemed entirely appropriate. It had a young director, Michael Radford, and a notable acting talent in John Hurt who was cast as the much persecuted Winston Smith. Now all that was needed was a bankable name to occupy the role of O'Brien, the evilly self-righteous interrogator.

Rich was not first choice. Paul Scofield was asked, so too was Jason Robards. When, among the late starters, Richard Burton was mentioned as a possibility, worried questions were exchanged as to his fitness and his capacity for staying sober. The film had to be finished by mid-year. There was no margin for changing an actor halfway.

But the testimony of *Wagner* was hard to fault. Evidently, Rich could sustain an exacting performance and still win plaudits. And there was the voice, with its hypnotic intonation, so right for the seductive persecutor that Orwell envisaged.

His contract ran from May to July. For most of that time he and Sally stayed at the Dorchester.

"Home again," he greeted Marjorie Lee.

But it was not at all like old times. Rich looked tired and much older than his fifty-eight years. The pain in his neck and back dogged him all his waking hours and he had trouble lifting either arm above shoulder level. On set for rehearsals he wore a neck brace.

He was still a great raconteur. Some of the stories had worn thin with repetition but the younger people in the production — and nearly all were younger — may not have heard them before. At any rate, they gave every indication of enjoying his company and Rich, for his part, was happy to relax as the convivial elder.

I saw Rich for the last time three weeks before he died. We had dinner, just the two of us. When I arrived at the Dorchester I was waylaid by Brook Williams. "He's not at his best," he said. "You won't overstay your welcome, will you love?"

Rich was in the mood for a heart to heart. We had barely sat down before he was cogitating on the way his life had turned out. Every time he opened a paper he dreaded yet another lament on Richard Burton, the actor who had sacrificed his great talents to booze and the fast life.

"Do you think it's all been a waste?" he asked me.

I reeled off a dozen of his performances which I reckoned were as good as any of his time. "You've given pleasure to millions of people. How can that be a waste?"

He ignored the question, choosing instead to follow his own thoughts.

"Olivier and Gielgud, they've acted in rubbish. We can't be good for all of the time."

"But there is a difference," I reminded him. "You've spent most of your life on a film set. Olivier and Gielgud have given more to the theatre."

He laughed.

"You mean, if the rubbish is on film people remember it for longer."

"Something like that."

He went serious again.

"Do you know what I heard the other day? That I've never found a part as good as playing the husband of Elizabeth Taylor."

I skirted that one. "Do you miss Elizabeth?"

"Of course," he said. "All the time. But Elizabeth can't look after me. I need Sally. She takes care of an old man."

We talked on about Elizabeth. It was his greatest pleasure. At the end of the evening he said to me, "We've never really split up. And we never will. We're always there when we need each other."

Leaving the hotel I remembered a visit to Elizabeth's home in Los Angeles. In every room and every corridor there were pictures of Rich. Sometimes whole rows of them.

"He's where I can keep an eye on him," joked Elizabeth. "And he'd better believe it."

If they could not live together in harmony, the bond between them defied all efforts, including their own, to make a clean break. If Rich had lived, I don't doubt they would have tried again to work it out between themselves. Who knows, it might have been a case of third time lucky.

1984 was the last film but Rich did make one other appearance on screen — a cameo role in *Ellis Island*, a made-for-television film about the European immigrants who poured into America at the turn of the century. It was not the sort of production he would normally have taken on but he had a special reason for making this an exception. His daughter Kate played one of the lead roles. Rich had tried to persuade her, as he said, "to do something sensible for a living" but when she showed her determination to be an actress, he insisted only that she should go to a decent drama school. After three years at Yale her first big break was a revival of *Present Laughter* in which she made her Broadway debut. Rich was there on the first night to show his pride. With *Ellis Island*, there were not the same opportunities for Kate to prove her talent but she made the best of modest material.

"A chip off the old block," said Rich with feeling.

The reviews for *1984* came out a month after Rich died. Greeted as "one of his best appearances on film", the premiere gave the critics their opportunity to pay tribute to one of the great screen personalities. In the best tradition of the movie business, Rich went out in fine style.

CHAPTER
EIGHTEEN

Elizabeth did not come to the memorial service in Wales. There was, I know, pressure from Sally to keep her away but by Sally's own testimony she relented at the last moment, ringing Elizabeth in Los Angeles to say that, after all, the Pontrhydyfen service was open to ex-wives. She made a great show of telling me of her munificent gesture.

"But that gave her much less than twenty-four hours," I pointed out. "There was no way she could get to Pontrhydyfen in time."

"No," mused Sally, "I suppose not."

The Bethel Chapel, solid grey stone set into the hill, was not built for crowds or grand occasions. Normally, a congregation of more than twenty signalled an event of special interest. On Saturday 11 August 1984 over four hundred friends of Richard Burton squeezed inside the building while outside twice that number listened to the service as it echoed over the tannoy and joined in the hymns. It was an unfussy goodbye made all the more effective because of that. No one who was in the chapel is ever likely to forget the simple display of red carnations resting on a Welsh flag beneath the pulpit.

The Minister, Eric Williams, spoke of Rich's love for his homeland.

"He never forgot his roots. He never forgot the rock from which he was hewn." He went on, "Richard

Burton was a man of genius, a man of generosity; he gave, he shared, he showed tremendous kindness."

Among hundreds of letters which bore testimony to my brother's capacity for giving was one from a Biafran family who thanked Rich for saving them and many of their tribe from starvation. It would be tedious to list the charities which, at one time or another, were helped by Rich or by Rich and Elizabeth together. But no one has ever quarrelled with the estimate of an annual handout in the region of one million dollars. I cannot help adding, for the sake of all those journalists who maintained the Burtons would do anything for publicity, that neither ever sought an atom of recognition for their generosity.

After the service, the crowds gathered at the Miners Arms and at the rugby club. We sang "Calon Ian", "Sospan Fach" and "Guide Me O'er Thou Great Redeemer". Eddie Thomas, a celebrated Welsh boxer, gave a solo of "Bless This House". The first time I heard him sing it, we were all thirty years younger. Eddie had just won the British Welterweight championship. He went to the ringside radio microphone to prove his voice was as powerful as his punches. Then, as now, there was not a dry eye in the house.

Sally did not stay with the family but she did spend time with us at Hilda and Dai's house. When she left, there was a gathering outside to see her off. On a sudden impulse I led into a chorus of "Sospan Fach", waving to the onlookers to join in. Sally smiled and held my arm. It was the closest I ever got to her. When the family were talking together that evening, Verdun said, "It's not right, Rich being buried in Switzerland. This is where he should rest. The plot was all picked out and paid for."

I went over to him.

"Don't let it trouble you," I said. "It doesn't matter where he's buried. His spirit is right here in Wales."

Ten days after Rich's funeral and eight days after the Welsh memorial service, Elizabeth came to Pontrhydyfen. I picked her up from Swansea airport in a hired car. She was late. A crowd of about a hundred waited patiently and gave her a big cheer when, dressed all in pink, she stepped down from her executive jet. Her only jewellery was a large diamond ring, a gift from Rich.

The plan was for Elizabeth to stay overnight with Hilda and Dai. Inevitably, there was a large reception committee out in the street. As we pulled up at the front door they raised their voices for that best loved of all Welsh songs, "We'll keep a welcome in the hillside". Elizabeth smiled her thanks. "I feel as if I'm home," she told them.

At dinner that evening with the Jenkins clan, I heard about Elizabeth's belated visit to Celigny, two days earlier.

A hardy group of photographers who had stayed on in expectation of her arrival followed her to the cemetery. When they refused to leave her she went back to her hotel, but returned early the following morning.

"I couldn't help thinking," she said, almost wistfully, "it was one of the few occasions ever that Richard and I were alone."

Elizabeth was naturally sad to have missed the funeral; sad too that apparently there was nothing she could do to convince Sally of her goodwill.

"If we had been at Celigny together," said Elizabeth,

"I would have been happy to have walked with her hand in hand."

We all stayed up late going through the vast number of cards and letters which had made our local post office look like Cardiff central. Much of the correspondence was addressed simply to Elizabeth Taylor c/o The Burton Family.

When our guest left the next morning she took with her a painting by Verdun of the house where Rich was born. Today, it has a place of honour in her Los Angeles home.

Three more memorial services were held in the last week of August. The first, at the Wilshire Theater in Beverly Hills, had Richard Harris leading the tributes. In the middle of his address he broke down and had to leave the stage. When he came back he confessed, "If Rich had seen me a moment ago he would have howled with laughter."

Of all the tributes to Rich, one of the most touching came from his co-star in *Who's Afraid of Virginia Woolf?*

"There is nothing in my life that comes close to the experience of working with Richard Burton," declared George Segal. "We have always known, those of us who act, that he was the best one. He makes us all proud to be actors."

George Segal cancelled two days' filming to be at the service. Some other big names who had worked closely with Rich were not prepared to take the same trouble. Noting their absences and their reasons (one lady of the screen backed off when she heard that television cameras were not expected) John Huston growled, "So what's new? We just have a few more candidates for the shit list."

378

In New York as in Los Angeles the service ended with Rich singing the title song from *Camelot*, his own sweet dedication to "one, brief, shining moment". Pamela Mason had the best line: "We should feel bad that he has gone, good that he was here."

Over the Atlantic, invitations went out to some fourteen hundred friends and colleagues of Rich to attend the Church of St Martin-in-the-Fields, just off Trafalgar Square on 30 August. As master of ceremonies, Tim Hardy had first thought of the actors' church in Covent Garden as the obvious choice but changed his mind after talking to Emlyn Williams.

"It'll never do," said Emlyn. "Far too small."

Tim was slightly taken aback.

"Where would you suggest, Emlyn? Westminster Abbey?"

"Don't be flippant," said Emlyn sternly.

Come the day, the press photographers focused their lenses for three women. Elizabeth in black silk came first, arm in arm with Cis. Susan followed, a cockade of red and black flowers at her shoulder. Then Sally, belying her unglamorous image with a close-fitting black dress with a dash of red. She alone of the three wore a veil. Sybil was not there. For her, I guess, it was all too long ago.

The orchestration was impeccable. The only hiccup was the late arrival of John Gielgud who had gone to the wrong church. Flustered and evidently distressed at his failure to be on time, he quickly transformed into a model of composure to read John Donne's *Death Be Not Proud*. A favourite of Rich, he would have loved to have heard that sweet voice ("like an A-string on a violin," said Tim Hardy).

Hopes of an easier relationship with Sally were disappointed. She objected strongly to Elizabeth sitting with the family in church, a sin of commission for which she blamed Marjorie Lee who had taken on the administration. Having given her time freely and generously Marjorie was upbraided by Sally as if she was a naughty schoolgirl. For thanks, Marjorie had to look elsewhere.

There was more trouble from Sally over the tribute from Emlyn Williams. Why so many references to Elizabeth and none at all for Sally? Well, as a matter of tact, it might have been wise to shift the balance slightly. But if Emlyn was seeking truth in his portrayal of Richard Burton, he got it just about right.

My brother was a star. Many have tried to dissect and analyse that word. But it is enough to say that you know a star when you meet one. He compels attention. Rich did it as a small boy. He went on doing it throughout his life.

Richard Harris said of him, "If there were twelve elephants on a stage and Rich was there too, you would look at Rich."

When the script was on his side he could raise it to greatness; when the script was against him he would still give it a touch of distinction.

A wasted life? Only by his own estimation. He was a confused man, often carried along by events because he could not think of any better way of arranging matters. His gifts were a mystery to him; his power, such as it was, frightened him. He made many mistakes but at least he recognised his failures and, to his credit, agonised over them.

There are those who believe Rich should have persevered with his stage career. Perhaps he would have reached the heights. But there was no certainty, as others found to their cost. John Neville, who shared with Rich the glory of the Old Vic, stayed slavishly loyal to the theatre. Whatever happened to him?

Anyway, as Warren Mitchell, a friend of Rich from RAF days, reminded me, "It's the same old story. We want people to be what we want them to be which is not necessarily what they want for themselves."

If there was some way of calling him back to judge his own life, I believe that Rich would say that he took his chances and stood by the consequences. He always kept his pride. He was his father's son. He was Richard Jenkins.

As my father would ask outside the Miners Arms on a summer Saturday evening, in the massive stupor of his cups, fixing his stoned eyes on his assembled miner cronies as he drank a toast to the setting sun as it slipped down the wall of the world just beyond Swansea and Mumbles Head:

"*Pwy sydd fel nyni?*"
"*Neb,*" they would answer.
"*Pwy sydd fel fi?*"
"*Neb.*"

"Who is like us?"
"Nobody."
"Who is like me?"
"Nobody."

Cu oedd gennym

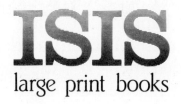

ISIS

large print books

We hope that you have enjoyed this book and will want to read more.

We list some other titles on the next few pages. All our books may be purchased from ISIS at either of the addresses below.

If you are not already a customer, or on our mailing list, please write and ask to be put on the mailing list for regular information about new ISIS titles.

We would also be pleased to receive your suggestions for titles that you would like us to publish in large print. We will look into any suggestions that you send to us.

Happy reading.

ISIS, 55 St Thomas' Street, Oxford OX1 1JG, ENGLAND, tel (0865) 250333

BIOGRAPHY AND AUTOBIOGRAPHY

Bill Adler	**Fred Astaire**
Charles Allen	**Plain Tales from the Raj**
Chuck Ashman & Pamela Trescott	**Cary Grant**
Hilary Bailey	**Vera Brittain**
Trevor Barnes	**Terry Waite**
Winifred Beechey	**The Rich Mrs Robinson**
Cilla Black	**Step Inside**
Sydney Biddle Barrows	**Mayflower Madam**
Peter Harry Brown	**Such Devoted Sisters: Those Fabulous Gabors**
Patrick Campbell	**Selections from 35 Years on the Job**
Joe Collins	**A Touch of Collins**
Bill Cosby	**Time Flies**
George Courtauld	**Odd Noises from the Barn**
Mary Craig	**The Crystal Spirit: Lech Walesa and his Poland**
Peter Cushing	**An Autobiography**
Peter Cushing	**'Past Forgetting'**
Roald Dahl	**Going Solo**
Betty Davis	**This 'n' That**

BIOGRAPHY AND AUTOBIOGRAPHY

Peter Evans	**Ari: The Life and Times of Aristotle Socrates Onassis**
Diana Farr	**Five at 10: Prime Ministers' Consorts Since 1957**
David Fingleton	**Kiri**
Angela Fox	**Slightly Foxed**
Michael Freeland	**A Salute to Irving Berlin**
Joyce Fussey	**Cats in the Coffee**
Joyce Fussey	**'Milk My Ewes and Weep'**
Eve Garnett	**First Affections**
Jon Godden & Rumer Godden	**Two under the Indian Sun**
Unity Hall	**Philip**
Helen Hayes	**Loving Life**
Bob Hope	**Confessions of a Hooker**
Graham Jenkins	**Richard Burton, My Brother**
Penny Junor	**Charles**
Roger Kahn	**Joe and Marilyn**
Vincent V Loomis	**Amelia Earhart**
Suzanne Lowry	**Cult of Diana**
Ralph G Martin	**Charles & Diana**
John McCabe	**Mr Laurel and Mr Hardy**

BIOGRAPHY AND AUTOBIOGRAPHY

Jeanine McMullen	**Wind in the Ash Tree**
Spike Milligan	**Adolf Hitler: My Part in His Downfall**
Eugene McCarthy	**Up 'Till Now**
Joe Morella & Edward Z Epstein	**Forever Lucy**
Joe Morella & Edward Z Epstein	**Loretta Young**
Eric Newby	**Something Wholesale**
Christopher Nolan	**Under the Eye of the Clock**
Barry Norman	**The Hollywood Greats**
Spero Pastos	**Pin-Up**
Carol Lynn Pearson	**Good-bye, I Love You**
Dolly Shepherd	**When the 'Chute Went up**
Isaac Bashevis Singer	**Love and Exile**
Daniel Snowman	**The World of Placido Domingo**
Roger Vadim	**Bardot, Deneuve and Fonda**
John Van der Kiste	**Queen Victoria's Children**
Alexander Walker	**Vivien**
Terry Wogan	**Wogan on Wogan**
Ian Woodward	**Glenda Jackson**

FICTION

Douglas Adams	**The Hitch Hiker's Guide to the Galaxy**
Harold Adams	**When Rich Men Die**
Kingsley Amis	**One Fat Englishman**
Jack Barnao	**Hammerlocke**
Stan Barstow	**Joby**
Simon Brett	**A Box of Tricks**
Simon Brett	**A Nice Class of Corpse**
Vera Brittain	**Account Rendered**
Vera Brittain	**Born 1925**
John Buchan	**Huntingtower**
Anthony Burgess	**The Pianoplayers**
J L Carr	**A Month in the Country**
Truman Capote	**Breakfast at Tiffany's**
Angela Carter	**Fireworks**
Susan Cheever	**Doctors and Women**
Colette	**Gigi and The Cat**
Joseph Conrad	**The Secret Agent**
Margaret Drabble	**The Waterfall**
William Faulkner	**The Sound and the Fury**
Timothy Findley	**Famous Last Words**
Paul Gallico	**Thomasina**
John Gardner	**Icebreaker**
John Gardner	**No Deals Mr Bond**
Leon Garfield	**Shakespeare Stories**

FICTION

Stella Gibbons	**Cold Comfort Farm**
Nadine Gordimer	**A Sport of Nature**
Graham Greene	**The Tenth Man**
Doris Grumbach	**The Magician's Girl**
Giovanni Guareschi	**Dom Camillo and the Devil**
Jeremiah Healy	**The Staked Goat**
Patricia Highsmith	**The Talented Mr Ripley**
Anthony Hope	**The Prisoner of Zenda**
Geoffrey Household	**Watcher in the Shadows**
Elspeth Huxley	**The African Poison Murders**
Christopher Isherwood	**Goodbye to Berlin**
M R James	**A Warning to the Curious**
Haynes Johnson & Howard Simons	**The Landing**
H R F Keating	**The Body in the Billiard Room**
H R F Keating	**Under a Monsoon Cloud**
Margaret Kennedy	**The Constant Nymph**
Rudyard Kipling	**The Light that Failed**
Gaston Leroux	**The Phantom of the Opera**
Doris Lessing	**The Grass is Singing**
Doris Lessing	**The Fifth Child**
Jack London	**The Call of the Wild**
Peter Lovesey	**Rough Cider**
Peter Lovesey	**Bertie and the Tinman**
Bernard Malamud	**The Fixer**

FICTION

David Malouf	**Harland's Half Acre**
W Somerset Maugham	**The Moon and Sixpence**
A E Maxwell	**Gatsby's Vineyard**
Carson McCullers	**The Heart is a Lonely Hunter**
Ralph McInerny	**Cause and Effect**
Brian Moore	**The Colour of Blood**
Katherine Moore	**Moving House**
Edna O'Brien	**Girls in their Married Bliss**
Edna O'Brien	**The Lonely Girl**
Edna O'Brien	**A Pagan Place**
Jerry Oster	**Nowhere Man**
Alan Paton	**Cry, The Beloved Country**
Anthony Powell	**The Fisher King**
Mary Renault	**The King Must Die**
Mary Renault	**The Bull from the Sea**
Mary Shelley	**Frankenstein**
Alan Sillitoe	**Out of the Whirlpool**
Muriel Spark	**The Girls of Slender Means**
John Steinbeck	**Cannery Row**
Patrick Süskind	**Perfume**
Alice Walker	**Meridian**
Rebecca West	**Sunflower**
Tenessee Williams	**The Roman Spring of Mrs Stone**
Dornford Yates	**Blood Royal**
Dornford Yates	**She Fell among Thieves**

THRILLERS, CRIME AND ADVENTURE

Simon Brett	**A Nice Class of Corpse**
John Buchan	**Huntingtower**
Joseph Conrad	**The Secret Agent**
Peter Dickinson	**Perfect Gallows**
John Gardner	**Icebreaker**
John Gardner	**No Deals Mr Bond**
Patricia Highsmith	**The Talented Mr Ripley**
Elspeth Huxley	**Murder on Safari**
M R James	**A Warning to the Curious**
H R F Keating	**The Body in the Billiard Room**
H R F Keating	**Under a Monsoon Cloud**
Peter Lovesey	**Rough Cider**
Peter Lovesey	**Bertie and the Tinman**
A E Maxwell	**Gatsby's Vineyard**
Ralph McInerny	**Cause and Effect**
Brian Moore	**The Colour of Blood**
Mary Shelley	**Frankenstein**
Patrick Süskind	**Perfume**
Dornford Yates	**Blood Royal**
Dornford Yates	**She Fell among Thieves**

SHORT STORIES

Echoes of Laughter

Angela Carter	**Fireworks**
Roald Dahl	**Roald Dahl's Book of Ghost Stories**
Leon Garfield	**Shakespeare Stories**
Thomas Hardy	**Wessex Tales**
M R James	**A Warning to the Curious**
Barry Pain	**The Eliza Stories**
Saki	**Beasts and Superbeasts**
E OE Somerville & Martin Ross	**Further Experiences of an Irish RM, Volume 2**
E OE Somerville & Martin Ross	**In Mr Knox's Country: An Irish RM, Volume 3**

POETRY AND DRAMA

Lord Birkenhead (Editor)	**John Betjeman's Early Poems**
Joan Duce	**I Remember, I Remember...**
Joan Duce	**Remember, If you will...**
Robert Louis Stevenson	**A Child's Garden of Verses**
Leon Garfield	**Shakespeare Stories**
Dan Sutherland	**Six Miniatures**

HUMOUR

Echoes of Laughter

Mary Dunn — **Lady Addle Remembers**

George & Weedon Grossmith — **The Diary of a Nobody**

Barry Pain — **The Eliza Stories**

Walter Carruthers Sellar & Robert Julian Yeatman — **1066 and All That**

Spike Milligan — **Adolf Hitler: My Part in His Downfall**

Tom Sharpe — **Blott on the Landscape**

Tom Sharpe — **Wilt**

Tom Sharpe — **Wilt on High**

Tom Sharpe — **Vintage Stuff**

E OE Somerville & Martin Ross — **Further Experiences of an Irish RM, Volume 2**

E OE Somerville & Martin Ross — **In Mr Knox's Country: An Irish RM, Volume 3**

ALSO AVAILABLE IN LARGE PRINT